CHRISTOS TSIOLKAS:
THE UNTOLD STORY

ALSO BY JOHN VASILAKAKOS

FICTION

Adumbrations of the World
The Shipwreck of the SOS
According to St. John: Memoirs of a Greek Pupil
The Shipwreck of the SOS – Profile of Tyranny*
The Set-Up*
In Chloe's Secret Parts and Other Portents and Monsters**

PLAYS

The Identity**
Attention: Fragile!**
Honeymoon in "One Thousand and One Nights"**

POETRY

Memoirs of an Embryo**

BIOGRAPHIES

Costas Taktsis: The Dark Side of the Moon

APHORISMS

A Psychological Portrait of a Greek Migrant

ESSAYS

Studies in Modern Greek Literature
Modern Greek Literature of the Diaspora: Australia
The Greek Civil War in Post-War Fiction:1946-1958

ANTHOLOGIES

Reflections: Selected Works from Greek-Australian Literature*
(Bilingual edition English-Greek)

(*Published in English. **Available in English soon.
All other works are published in Greek)

Christos Tsiolkas

The Untold Story

His Life & Work

JOHN VASILAKAKOS

Published in 2013 by Connor Court Publishing Pty Ltd

Copyright © John Vasilakakos 2013

ALL RIGHTS RESERVED. This book contains material protected under International and Federal Copyright Laws and Treaties. Any unauthorised reprint or use of this material is prohibited. No part of this book may be reproduced or transmitted in any form or by any means, electronic or mechanical, including photocopying, recording, or by any information storage and retrieval system without express written permission from the publisher.

Connor Court Publishing Pty Ltd.
PO Box 1
Ballan VIC 3342
sales@connorcourt.com
www.connorcourt.com

ISBN: 978-1-922168-59-7 (pbk.)

Cover design by Ian James

Front cover photo: Zoe Ali, used with permission

Printed in Australia

CONTENTS

Introduction	v

LIFE

1. Childhood	3
2. Adolescence	19
3. Adulthood	37
4. Literature and Criticism	45
5. Identity	63
6. The State of Humanity	69
7. Religion and Death	77
8. *Loaded*	83
9. *The Jesus man*	89
10. *Dead Europe*	95
11. *The Slap*	103

WORK

1. *Loaded*: To walk the tight rope over chaos	113
2. *The Jesus Man*: The curse of the (in)human condition	165
3. *Dead Europe*: A road map to self-knowledge through Hell*us*	223
4. *The Slap*: The bitter apple of (Greek-Australian) discord	259
Epilogue	293

INTRODUCTION

I can't remember exactly when I first read Christos Tsiolkas' first novel *Loaded* – whether it was immediately upon publication, later on, or after the uproar caused by Ana Kokkinos' film *Head On* which was based on this novel. But having read *Loaded*, I began to understand the persistence of various friends in asking me about this book. It was not just the fact that we were dealing with a writer of Greek background who had written a provocative and controversial book but mainly, I think, the fact that I had trouble decoding it – something which, I suspect, happened with my friends and perhaps with other readers too. Because much as it may have seemed black and white in the face of it – that is, a book which you either hated or loved instantly – the truth is that the book consisted of an element of "mystery" which the careful and demanding reader was called upon to decode. Because, to put it simply – in my case at least – I both liked and disliked the book. Which means that it was not what it seemed, and its secret was likely to be found precisely in this elusiveness and ambivalence.

On the one hand, I was annoyed by its diverse extremities – vulgar language, inflammatory views, provocative lifestyle, abuse of drugs and sex, etc – because I was obviously unable to understand the deeper meaning and narrative function of all those excesses. On the other hand, I could distinguish that there was a vitality and freshness about the book, not very common for a beginner novelist. Furthermore, many of its ascertainments – in relation to the hypocrisy of society, multiculturalism and especially the Greek Community and the Greeks of Australia, and not just that – were incredibly discerning, timely and spot-on, for someone without blinkers. I therefore had come to the conclusion that this book was of a strangely fascinating interest and a peculiar originality which, nevertheless, I could not locate precisely. This by no means meant that my various question marks about the writer Tsiolkas had ceased to exist. That is why, I remember, I had promised myself to come back at some point in the future and pore over the work of this bizarre new writer, for the simple reason that I sensed a "hidden treasure." In the meantime, until I had this opportunity, I contented myself in following, occasionally, Tsilokas' writing progress mainly through the various journals that were reporting on his writing endeavours, but without ever forgetting my promise to myself.

However, what is odd in this case is that the second novel by Tsiolkas (*The Jesus Man*) passed rather unnoticed, not only by the majority of readers and critics but also by myself. Because not only did I disdain to read it, but I never read anything that was written about it either. I find it difficult to say with certainty whether this was done deliberately or accidentally. I do not exclude the possibility that my indifference was encouraged by the deceptive title of the book which led me to assume, wrongly, that it was about another blasphemous libel which aimed at scandalizing and causing noise. My psychological state at that time, I have to admit, was not the ideal one to secure a sober and objective glance on things. Which easily explains why, without knowing anything about this book, I light-heartedly concluded, from its deceptive title alone, that this time the writer had indeed gone too far! But what astonishes me even today, after so many years, is that – regardless of how absurd all this may sound – my gut feeling was not entirely wrong, judging from the indifference so many others like me had shown about this particular book.

My interest in Tsiolkas' writing started to get reignited with the publication of his third novel (*Dead Europe*). But, again, I had not read the novel and whatever I knew about it came from secondary sources – reviews, press reports, interviews etc. Despite all this, however, the fact is that my attitude towards Tsiolkas had started to change dramatically as I could "smell" that something really was under way with this writer.

In 2008 Tsiolkas' fourth and most talked about and commercially successful novel (*The Slap*) was released. Again, with this book, it waited patiently for a long time on my book-shelves to be read, but this did not eventuate until two years later and indeed by crooked means – specifically when the Greek edition of the novel was published in Athens in 2010! However, reading this novel was a catalyst for me, as I realized now that, despite my previous vacillations regarding Tsiolkas' writing, my very initial instinct about his literary talent had not proven to be wrong. Because, eventually, there was indeed a "treasure" hidden inside this peculiar Greek-Australian writer.

After this exhilarating ascertainment, it did not take me long to realize how hopelessly little I knew both about the writer and his work as well as about the individual Christos Tsiolkas. But my disappointment was even greater when, after a quick search, I also realized in astonishment how very little information existed which could shed even some dim light on the "Christos Tsiolkas phenomenon." It was then that the idea first entered my mind – to perhaps undertake a project on this enigmatic writer. But in order to do that I had to approach him first and see how he would react.

The first step was taken when I sent him a laconic email in which I introduced myself and explained to him my intention, and if we could meet to discuss the matter further... He answered with a polite message that he was quite happy to meet me. Our appointment was made for a Wednesday morning in late 2011 in a Brunswick Café near his studio. Strangely enough, as the day of our meeting was approaching, I felt increasingly nervous, with the persistent preoccupying question "Would we be on the same wave length?" Perhaps because, from the reading of his books, I had formed a particular picture of Tsiolkas the writer, which I wrongly identified with Tsiolkas the man, and I had assumed that this picture might perhaps be in opposition with my temperament and personality...

I first sought him in his nearby studio. We met on the stairs and he welcomed me cordially with a wide bright smile and warm handshake and the urge, "Come and have a look at my workplace..." showing me around his studio, which was anything but a quiet, private place... It was a vast, impersonal floor, shared by many people or groups of people who were doing different jobs and there was even more noise, or at least that is the impression I got, due to the echoes from the unusual spaciousness of the place. The writer's studio was situated in the right hand corner, straight after the entrance to the first floor building and was quite small. There was a little desk with a computer, a small bookshelf, and the partition was struggling in vain to keep out the commotion. I frankly wondered to myself how on earth Christos managed to concentrate and work in such a noisy environment... But the next minute I comforted myself with the thought that there were far worse places, remembering the case of Sartre, who used to write surrounded by the pandemonium of the Café de Flore in Paris – which I had visited in January 2009 with my Greek writer friend Vassilis Vassilikos, who was at that time Greek Ambassador at UNESCO.

We were soon down in the nearby Café sipping coffees and hot chocolates and chatting in full swing. My first impression was of the cordiality and familiarity which my interlocutor was showing me. As if we were old friends, reunited after so many years, both anxious to catch up with things. Because, all of a sudden, we found ourselves to have common friends, mainly from the literary world, common migrant experiences, common artistic interests, as well as issues that were "burning" us both. I was equally impressed with the diversity of his interests, as he never stopped bombarding me with a plethora of questions. These ranged from Modern Greek and Greek-Australian literatures (Kazantzakis, Cavafy, Taktsis, Tsaloumas, Papaellinas and numerous others), the Greek and European economic crisis, modern Greek Cinema, literary translation, to Taktsis life in Australia (which I had explored in my recent biography of him) and the opinion the Greek Community had of Tsiolkas and his work. His persistent curiosity to be informed about almost anything and everything that was happening in Greece and the Greek Community in Australia, as well as his tendency to talk to me often in Greek, or to use Greek words and phrases in the flow of our English conversation, astonished me.

But what impressed me the most with Christos were two things: Firstly, his incredible spontaneity and the frankness of his words and feelings, condensed in a bursting vivacity of energy, channelled through a vibrating body language and penetrating glance and, secondly, his instinctive, unassuming modesty. There was not a single trace of conceit or haughtiness, despite the huge success of his work and his international acclaim. The most irrefutable evidence of this is that, if there is one thing that was indelibly marked in my mind since day one of our meeting until today, it is the number of times he has repeated to me the same unchanging phrase: "What is most important to me in life is to try, every day, to become a better writer and a better person."

When, at last, I managed to raise the issue of my intention to write a book on him and the reasons why I thought such a task was due, he remained silent for a moment, as if I took him by surprise and he did not know what to say and how to react. As he subsequently told me, almost embarrassingly, he never expected that a scholar and indeed a Greek one for that matter would ever be interested in his work! That is why, he added seemingly touched, he thought that my proposal was a great honour for him and that he was extremely appreciative of my idea. He reassured me that he agreed with the way I had planned the book in my mind and that he would collaborate happily with the part of the book which dealt with his life. A warm handshake sealed our agreement. On departing, he embraced me and thanked me once again, moved by this unexpected initiative of mine.

As I was returning home, elated by the successful outcome of our meeting, I realized that any encounter with Tsiolkas – whether literary or individual – constitutes an apocalyptic experience – overturning things taken for granted, assumptions, stereotypes etc. A year later, having completed my project on him, my initial belief that the latter is perhaps one of the most bizarre but also misunderstood and misread writers of Australian literature remains as unshakeable as ever. Hence the need for a book such as the present one, which aims at, aspires and hopes to dissolve some of the myths, deceptions and prejudices, by clearing up the landscape in relation to the "Tsiolkas phenomenon."

PS: (i) The reason I chose this type of "autobiographical self-confession" in interview mode (Part A) is due to the fact that the fullness of time has not yet come that would justify the writing of a classic biography of Tsiolkas, given that the writer, both as far as his age and writing career are concerned, is still on his course. Any other approach that would illuminate satisfactorily his personality was likely to be dubious and do injustice to him.

(ii) Part B examines Tsiolkas' novels to date, individually and somewhat comparatively. It is implied that this is not an exhaustive study of his novels but only an examination of various aspects of those works which, because of their importance, present a particular interest to the reader and perhaps the future scholar of Tsiolkas. Except for rare occasions where this was absolutely necessary, I consciously avoided the use of footnotes, references and bibliography here, simply because I did not want this book to take on an academic character as it aims for a wider readership. Such elements could possibly detract from my main aim – to illuminate spherically the novels of the writer in the simplest and most comprehensible manner possible.

(iii) The juxtaposition of the life (Part A) and work (Part B) of Tsiolkas facilitates, I think, the reader in a smooth approach to understanding and evaluating his work.

(iv) The book at hand is not in any way a definitive work, since the writer's creative work is still in progress. On the contrary, it should be seen as a first attempt to explore the whole spectrum of life and work of this controversial, much discussed and popular writer. In conclusion, this book is nothing more or less than an introduction to the "Tsiolkas phenomenon."

LIFE

North Richmond Primary School, 1974. (Christos top row, centre)

1
CHILDHOOD

How well do you remember your childhood and which images are indelibly etched in your memory?

I've been thinking a lot about this. There is a part of me that thinks I had a really charmed childhood, in comparison to my adolescence, which was a very difficult period. What I remember most about my childhood, the images that are indelible really are the number of people in my life. I was born and grew up in Richmond until I was thirteen. I was about six or seven, I shared the one room with my mum and dad, and then my younger brother who was two years younger than me. There was another family who lived in the house as well. In one of the rooms there was also a guy, Stavros, who worked with my father. I remember that the house was always full of people. And the whole street was Greek. There were also some Italians. Right at the end of the street there was some old working class Australian.

Which street was that?

Lincoln Street, which is off Church Street. The other thing which is very strong in my memory is the alleys where we would play with the neighbourhood kids. There is a part in *Loaded* that participates in that world. What is also coming to my memory is that I used to spend hours in the garden and I would create stories out of different universes and different worlds and almost sometimes out of different planets. I just used to love hiding amongst the tomatoes and the zucchini, which was a place of quiet safety. Other things I remember: My dad and mum were migrants here in Australia. Dad came in 1955, mum came in 1963. Sunday would be the day that dad would spend with us. He was also a gambler. So unless there was a party, I would rarely see mum Friday or Saturday night, but on Sundays dad could always make it. He would grab my brother and me and we would walk to the City. I loved going off the road over the Punt Road, looking down to the parks, because as soon as we crossed Punt Road we were left off the leash and went running. That was quite magical actually, that sense of owning the parks, climbing the City! Melbourne back then, I remember, was such a cold, lifeless place, in comparison to Bridge Road. So, for me, Richmond and Collingwood were places of importance and all my friends were within a couple of blocks where I grew up. My cousins were within a couple of blocks where I grew up too. There was life, there was always in and out of each other's house. We possessed the alleys as when we were playing games. We would play soccer, cricket, hide and seek, we would run. Whereas the City was this really cold creepy place. There was no life at all. I remember my mum crying when she said in Greek "*gamoto, oute ena kafe den mporo na pio...*" (that is, "shit, I can't even have a coffee...").

What year are you talking about?

I was born in 1965, so we are talking late sixties or early seventies. The other vivid memory I have – and I'm not trying to be at all provocative here – is this: I must have been two and a half or three, and because we shared the same room, I still remember the cot and my mum and dad in their bed and – it's still so vivid in my memory – for some reason I thought my dad was thrusting a turd into my mum's vagina and I started screaming! So dad got up to console me and, at that point, I must have realised that that turd was really his penis! That was one of my early memories.

In the fifties and sixties in Greece, when things were very tough, parents and children had to share the same room. So it was natural for kids to witness such scenes.

As I said, we were in a house where I was sleeping with my parents, they were very young people then, so you did see things. I also remember

Irini and Giorgo, a couple with no kids at the time when they first started living in the same house with my parents, so I used to peep through the keyhole to see what they were doing... But I do think that, in terms of memories, it's in that sense of why I think it was a charmed childhood. That sense of all the world being open to me at that time, in retrospect. You view a memory of nostalgia, it's inevitable, but I do think it was a good way to grow up.

A kind of lost paradise?

Yes. You would have had this experience going to the Greek theatre on Bridge Road Richmond.

Tell me a few things about your family's background. When and where were your parents born and when and why did they come to Australia?

My father was born in 1929 in a village called Argiro Pigadi, which is outside of Agrinio. I guess Thermo is the newest town. Even now to get there is quite a trip because the road is still not asphalted, very high up in the mountains. My grandmother had fourteen births and eleven of them survived past childhood. He was the third brother. It was a very hard, harsh life. I remember, just very recently, my brother got some documents from the Department of Immigration for my parents' papers when they both migrated. I looked at the photos of my father and mother and they look so thin you could see the poverty on their face. You've got to think about this: In 1929 my father was a teenager in World War II, experiencing the Civil War. Mum was born in 1939 and was a triplet. There were eight children in her family, four girls and four boys. One of the boys died very soon after birth. They were the youngest. I think my mother is someone who should never have migrated from Greece. She really wears her migration as exile and I think that's been really important for my whole understanding of migration as a theme in my work. She was from a village called Dorvitsa, which is a half hour north of Nafpaktos, just above the strait. At fifteen she actually left the village to work in a textile factory as a seamstress in Athens.

Why did your mother migrate?

My mother always says, "*ego efyga ap' tin Ellada giati den eixame lefta*" (meaning, "I left Greece because we had no money").

Where did your parents meet?

They met here in Australia. Dad came in 1955 and went to Bonegilla, Tasmania, Queensland, and then came to Melbourne where the work was. My mum came in 1963. She only had a relative here, my uncle Thanassi, her first cousin, and he introduced her to my father. They got married in 1964 and I was born literally ten months after.

How did your parents get married?

It was an arranged marriage. You've got to understand their politics were different too. Mum still says the happiest days of her life were the three years she had in Athens before she migrated. Dad wants the garden and the village. They are such dissimilar people, very different characters, and if there was anything difficult in that early part of my life, it was exactly that awareness.

Were there quarrels in the family?

God yes! My mum walked out twice on my dad and that had to do with gambling. An unhappy partnership has its energy. You feel it, you understand it, and it's coloured the way I grew up. It coloured my attitude to the Greeks, I think, from very early on.

In what way?

Not as much as gambling is concerned but as in the idea of marriage. You've got to understand that, for me, all I saw was my mum's anger that money has gone when dad was losing. But when dad won it was paradise for me and my brother John. He would come with hands full of gifts, we would be very happy. So that caused even more anger for my mother.

Was your father a gambler from Greece or did he become one in Australia?

It must have been here in Australia, because he was such a young man in Greece. From what I understand – I found this out again when I was a young man going to Greece – dad's intention was to come here, as everyone's intention was, and he gave money to put uncle Dimitri through high school. Uncle Dimitri was the only one from my family who went to high school, thanks to my dad's money, which he never regretted. Because if they didn't have at least one brother graduating from high school, the whole family would be fucked, excuse my language, but that's how my dad talks about it, and this is the reason why he thinks Greece stinks. But he also sent some more money to start a business and unfortunately that money was squandered. So from what I understand, from what my aunt and mum have told me – because dad finds it very difficult to talk about – that's when he started gambling and drinking quite heavily, after that incident. I first heard these stories when I first went to Greece as a young man, and dad got really angry that his brothers and sisters had told me all this. But it does make sense of why my father's attitude has always been so consistently negative, I think. Anyway, in terms of that second time my mother walked out, I remember this horrific fight and her packing her bags and getting to the end of Lincoln Street where the tram is, and then jumping on the 72 tram heading towards Chapel Street and crying and asking herself, what the hell am I doing? But after that, my father promised to stop gambling, because she was very firm on leaving.

How old were you then?

I was still in primary school, nine or ten. So dad promised he would never gamble again and has kept his word. You've got to remember though that, again, all that was exciting for me as there were always men in the house gambling...

Gambling in your house?

Sometimes in our house, sometimes in Bridge Road, sometimes elsewhere. My mum would send me out to fetch dad for dinner and I'd go up Victoria Street, to the *kafeneio*... I thought it was really exciting. But, fortunately, I've never become a gambler. That was one promise she had asked of me when I was about thirteen.

Many parents do not want to talk about various things with their young children when they are little. In your case, what subjects did they love talking about with you and what subjects did they avoid? Were there any taboos?

That's exactly right. With dad there were certainly taboos. He was uncomfortable talking about anything to do with sex, sexuality, the body. Having said that, one thing that I did enjoy about my parents is that sense of humour – I guess a lot of Greeks would have been like this – because they loved sex comedies. Dad is quite a ribald character, he loves dirty jokes in a very innocent way. My parents used to love the TV series *Number 96* and we would all watch that together. Even though it was unsuitable for children my parents wouldn't mind if we watched a little bit of a vagina. Later on I was reading a lot and I was starting to ask a lot of questions. I think my mum was just hungry for conversation, so she was the one I had most fights with and also most of my conversations with, regardless of whether the subject was divorce, religion and so on. It's interesting that there didn't seem to be any subject in and of itself that was taboo. I could start a conversation at the table about anything and my dad may go, *"ti vlakeia!..."* (meaning "how stupid!..."). Conversation about sex I did put, because I remember a conversation about menstruation. As there were no girls in the family, when friends who were girls started whispering, I was thinking, what is this *period...*, so I remember asking my mum about it. She said "I don't want to talk about this, because it's natural." So there were taboos, but I was pushing it from an early age. I would never ever directly talk about these issues. I would make snipper attacks. I wouldn't talk about sexuality per se, but I would talk about divorce or marriage or women's rights.

What kind of subjects did your parents love to talk with you about?

They loved talking about the old days in the village. Dad loved talking about being a boy in the village. He loved talking about gossip from the village. He loved talking about the ghost stories from the village. He is a great spinner of stories and a great story-teller. So in my mind I had this whole smorgasbord of characters that I never met who would come from my dad's narratives. So would Father Nikos and the affairs he would have and Saki who was a *vrikolakas* (a vampire). For me these characters feel sometimes as real as my relatives. My parents would also talk about politics.

Talking about politics, you've told me that when your dad went to Greece during the junta period, he felt uncomfortable. How is that justified, given that he was right-wing?

Dad had never said "I'm right wing", never. He has said "I'm an anti-Communist."

Isn't it the same thing?

For a long time I thought it was. Dad was not passionate about his politics, mum was. It wasn't a sense of identity for him. He would say, for example, when he talked to us about the Civil War – remember his brother was killed during the Civil War – so his lesson to me about the Civil War was the behaviour of the English. That was the most important thing for him. He thought that the reason the war was a disaster, was partly due to the British. I've met a lot of virulent right wing Greek men of his generation. He wasn't like that at all. He was against the junta from the beginning.

Why was that?

Because he saw it as a dictatorship. Maybe my mother had an influence on him as well, as she had a brother who was imprisoned by the junta. It's a good question and I'm trying to nail it because it still confuses me. He was a very big supporter of Australia in the sense that he felt a despair and grief about Greece. Maybe he was just comparing the politics of Greece to what he had back on. The pictures we had on our walls were of Whitlam. He wasn't exactly being right-wing or anti-Communist. The understanding that I have as a bourgeois man of politics to some of my parents' responses are so very different. Nothing feels like separating me from their world as much as some of their attitudes. So, for example, dad was really upset with the dissolving of the Soviet Union. However, if you sat down with him now, you would find a lot of contradictory elements in his politics.

Did your father participate in the Resistance Movement in Greece?

This is a key reason for some of the politics that I have. No, my father never did. My mum's family was Communist, my dad's family was right-wing. My father's brother, Christos, was killed in the Civil War – I only found this out much later, because he never talked to me about it – and dad, who was then a young man, was the one to go and collect his body. He was killed by the partisans. I'm not sure what the story was but they were a poor peasant family and were not at all interested in politics. However that event created a very virulent anti-Communism in dad's family. Mum's experiences were the exact opposite. Her older brother, my uncle Mitsos, joined the Resistance at fifteen, and he was a Communist to the end. He was also involved in the Union Movement in Greece. So I grew up in a household where the rage of war had always been there. All this infused me when I was younger. It wasn't until I studied Greek history that I realised that, even though Dad was anti-Communist, he was a very strong supporter of the Trade Union Movement, a very strong supporter of the ALP. So growing up in that context, my family was seen as quite left-wing, both my parents.

I don't have a memory of this. I've always said that my first demonstration was when my father took me and my brother when Whitlam was sacked and we went to the Town Hall with a bag of tomatoes to throw at John Kerr. I was ten and it was a very exciting period. But my mum had said – because I was talking about that particular day – that "it wasn't your first demonstration; the first demonstration we took you to was an anti-junta demonstration, but you were in the pram." Her brother was imprisoned by the colonels. So I think that was a very difficult time for my mother, because of her family's politics. I think she was really terrified about what was happening in Greece, not to mention the fact that she had nobody else here in Australia, brother or sister, all her family were back there. So my parents are of that generation of migrants whose sense was that our children will never experience what we went through. So they didn't keep a lot hidden from me and my brother. But once I became an adult, once I became interested in that history, once I went to Greece as an adult, that's what allowed us to have a much more honest conversation about all this.

How was your life as a child in terms of entertainment? Did you have friends, did you play with other kids or were you a loner?

I would not exactly lock myself away and read – I would just read. There would be opportunities for me to read and I would find them, but also I would be out playing most nights. I had lots of friends in primary school. I was very close, and still am, to two of my cousins who lived down the road in Richmond and we were always in and out of each other's houses. So I wouldn't describe myself as a loner, but I did enjoy finding moments of being alone. I enjoyed being with other kids and doing things. When I was talking before about hiding in the garden, I actually liked to be spending hours there knowing that no one knew where I was or there was no one else there but me. I really enjoyed just getting a book and I used to have a spot in the house where we were living, just near the laundry, where I would put a pillow there and I just wanted to spend that time on my own. But it didn't feel like I was a loner. It was just that I was chasing those moments.

And did you use to daydream?

All the time. And that's part of the pleasure I think of what I enjoyed doing. When I talked about being a loner in the back of the garden, I would just make up stories, aimless stories... Also walking to school would be a constant dream.

What kind of educational resources did you have at home? I mean, did you read any books, did you listen to music or watched television? Did your parents take you to the movies, visits, excursions? Did they read or tell you stories?

There was always Greek music in the house. My mum loves music, so I always grew up with music, *demotic songs* (folksongs), *laika songs* (popular songs) and *rembetika songs* (Greek blues). Mum's favourite singers were Polly Panou and Stelios Kazantzidis. There would also be *kalamatiana, tsamika* and things like that. In terms of books, my parents were of working class, so I didn't grow up with books being part of the house. But as a child, once my parents saw that I was very keen to read, they would just start buying me books.

Starting from what age?

Primary school. I was reading from primary school.

What kind of books were they buying you?

There was a newsagency in Bridge Road Richmond where they had a little stall of books and when dad got paid he would always buy me two books. He would ask the shopkeeper to suggest stuff. So it would be *Treasure Island* or *The Adventures of Tom Sawyer*, the classics and children's books. But I also remember him buying me Henry Miller, Harold Robins, Charles Dickens. It was a very eclectic mix of books and I started reading from a very young age. My mum loves the movies and we would go to the Greek movies a lot, at Westgarth Theatre and the National Theatre, but me and my parents would also go and see a lot of Hollywood cinema. When I was in late primary school I would start going with my friends of course.

So when you were little, did you have a preference for any specific writers?

No, I was a sponge.

As a child, had you ever thought of what you wanted to become later in life?

I used to get these little exercise books and I would design the colours of books I was going to write. I would have those fantasies and would do that. The other thing was, because I was fascinated by film and still am, in these exercise books I would write little scripts and I would imagine those films that I was going to direct. I knew from very early on that what my parents wanted me to be was a professional of some sort, such as doctor or lawyer, but never once did I believe it for myself, I realise in retrospect. I had a gut feeling then that that challenge was coming, because my only fantasy was about creating stuff.

How ambitious were you as a kid? Did you want to achieve things in life?

I didn't know what it would mean to be a director or a writer, but there was that fantastical element...Yes, I wanted to be a writer, I knew that very strongly. As I was emerging into pubescence, yes, I wanted to be creative. That would be certainly true.

How strict were your parents with school? Did they expect you to be diligent and pursue higher studies later in life?

God yes! My parents were very strict about that and very strict about time and behaviour. Both my brother and I were very spoiled by them but, at the same time, they were very strict. I remember Dad asking me to tell my school teachers – because we would go to parent-teacher nights and I had to interpret for him – "tell the teacher that if you play up, he's got every right to hit you. I give him permission now." My brother and I both knew that it was expected from us to study.

In what ways were your parents spoiling you?

They protected us from the ugly aspects of the world. I understand their intentions completely. I think it would be actually better that we would toughen up a little more than we were and that's not being critical of them. It's only in hindsight – as I left home quite young – I realise how fortunate I was to have the family I did. Because when you are under ten, you can't appreciate that strictness, especially when there was enough excitement, enough people, enough friends in my life that it didn't feel like being repressed. I knew my parents were stricter than, say, some of the other parents, but it was only a level, it was a matter of degree rather than kind. It wasn't until I became older and wanted to see more things and do more things that it became a problem.

What methods did your parents apply to discipline you?

They would punish me, they would hit me. Dad has hit me two or three times in my life. Mum a lot more often. But look, the problem in my family wasn't between the adults and the kids really. It was between my parents. They were two people whom circumstances brought together, who were not happy for a very long time. And my brother and I both grew up in an understanding of that unhappiness.

Some things in your books are contradictory too.

I think it's completely human. How can you look back in the history that my parents were part of and not be aware of these contradictions...

Some writers tend to mythologise or demythologise their family or personal story in their works, regardless of how interesting it is. Why do you think they are tempted to do that and which category do you belong to?

My sense is that probably there is an element of mythologising when it comes to family and my family background, that I use my family background to create certain myths around the notion of the family. Yes, I think I mythologise the family, I create certain archetypes, and in particular I create certain notions of gender from the experiences I got growing up in the family that I had.

What is the reason for doing it? Do you see it as a goldmine that provides rich material for the needs of your fiction and your readership?

It's much more selfish than that. I don't know that I'm doing it because it's got to be very interesting to readers. I think I do it because that mine you've mentioned is something that is of interest to me. I think I do it (mythologising) because growing up in a family – where human experience was so vast and so different and then translating these experiences – was for a long time so impossible for me and therefore a very challenging area to talk about human life. Especially how so much of what you experience is true, real, or authentic, with a shift in perspective. I think that is what's fascinating for me and that's where I use my own family background to fuel my writing. I feel that all my life or part of my life has been a struggle to learn how to translate experiences back and forth between family. That still hasn't ended, you know. I'm still trying to find a language to do that.

Sometimes it never ends.

No, I don't think it does.

It has been said that childhood is our lost paradise. To what extent is this true in your case?

It was certainly not hell. I do think it was a charmed life and so, yes, there was an element of the idyllic in my childhood. I wouldn't use the term "paradise" but I would use the term "idyllic."

Do you feel nostalgic about it?

Yes. What I miss, what I feel nostalgic about my childhood, is that it was the only time in my life that I felt that a sense of home was in childhood. That was the only point in my life where I felt that Christos Tsiolkas who was here in my head, and Christos Tsiolkas in the world, were the same person. That doesn't mean that there weren't unhappy and ugly things in my childhood, but that sense of bliss is something that I am nostalgic for.

What do you think was the most important thing that influenced you most as a person in the first six years of your life?

What comes to mind is the smell of men. As I said before, I was part of a world where there were a lot of people in my life, a lot of adults, even in the family home. So the memories that are flashing back are this man, Stelios, in a singlet and me sniffing the smell of him. The physicality of men is what is most vivid. And I think that it's something I'm trying to get back to in my writings: an awareness of the erotic – before I even knew what erotic was – was there from very early on. That is what I remember, what is most vivid in my memory and affected my late life.

When did childhood actually end for you? Was this a pleasant or unpleasant experience?

For me, the moment my world of innocence ended was at a moment in school where someone told a lie that I knew was a lie. I remember being so unhappy and confused about that moment. I think that's the moment I could pinpoint – the moment of the lie. Because my sense of sensuality and the erotic started very early on – even before I knew what an erection was, before wet dreams – it's part of the heritage of Christian and religious culture, to mark the end of innocence by sexuality. As I said, for me, the erotic was in the Garden of Eden, it was part of my childhood.

If you could change something in your childhood, what would that be?

There is nothing I could change there. There are moments I hated, but there is nothing I would like to change.

1984: A year after Christos left home

2
ADOLESCENCE

Adolescence is perhaps the most difficult but also most exciting stage of our lives. How difficult was your adolescence and how did you deal with it? Let's start with secondary school. What were the challenges there?

The big challenge was moving from the City to a new school and a new suburb in Blackburn that was very different to the one I was used to. It was a horrible time. I didn't like myself, I didn't like my body, I didn't like the world I was in, and it was the first time in my life that I felt real loneliness. I felt bereft of where I was in the world and felt I was evil and dirty, because of the sexual fantasies and thoughts I had. It was a very difficult time. Everything became really dirty over that period. It took me a long time to be able to make friends.

So, was your sexuality the most tormenting part of your adolescent life?

Yes, it would be, because I thought that in a religious sense it would damn me and I didn't want it. It was this burden that if I could have done anything to get rid of, I would have. That's how I felt about it. To give a sense of the story, I knew from a much earlier age, from primary school, that I was gay. So when I went to Blackburn High, I was very lonely and got involved with someone who was friendly to me. It was this Australian woman who was part of a Christian fundamentalist Church and, just because I was so hungry to have a friend, I used to go to church with her and started becoming quite religious. That's when I started masturbating and scratching myself afterwards to bleed – it was a way of punishing myself. It was crucial at that time that I had not stopped seeing films, especially when, at the same time, I was going through this troubled period. I was reading Miller and Mailer. I first started reading Roth, together with the Russians. Those sorts of things really saved my life. I had also started reading philosophy and theology and I came to a position where I knew that I no longer had faith, no longer believed in that kind of God, so I became an atheist. I remember thinking, well, if this is not the truth, then anything goes, I can explore anything and everything I needed to explore. So that's when I started having a sexual life. I started going to parks and toilets and started taking drugs. So that period was very confronting for my parents. They didn't know about my sexual life, but they knew they were losing control of me.

What age were you then?

Fifteen.

By becoming an atheist, did you get a sense of freedom to do whatever you liked without feeling guilty?

I never stopped feeling guilty, because I don't think guilt works that way.

Why did you stop believing in God?

The word of faith that had been given to me from my family – my parents were not very religious, but they did believe in God, even though they were anti-clerical – was not an intellectual belief, it was almost cultural. So I got involved with a fundamentalist Protestant sect. What Protestantism offered me was an intellectual attempt to know God. That's how I saw it, in opposition to the Greek Orthodox faith that I knew, and a little bit of Catholicism, because a lot of my friends were Catholic. I had never read the Bible before I got involved with Protestants, so I started reading the Bible. I started reading books about God and I started trying to make sense of the God in the Bible, my experience and the world around me. But I could not reconcile the God of the Bible with the truth. It was as simple as that, I think. This is a very young man's understanding. What was presented to me was a literal truth in this text, but I realised, I had no faith in the literal truth of the Bible, so I stopped believing in God. If you ask me now as an older man, I have a different relationship to questions of faith. But that's what was happening at that stage of my life.

Were you afraid that God would punish you because of your sexual orientation?

Yes.

And wasn't this an attempt on your part to change your belief system in order to suit your lifestyle?

No. Protestantism, as an institution, is very different to Orthodoxy. I'm really glad that I had that experience because that was a horrific time for me. No, I wasn't trying to create a religion that would make what I was feeling permissible. My closure with God at that period was due to the fact that, as I expected, according to the word of the Bible, I was damned. That lasted a year and a half to two years in my life and I really believed that. And then I thought, I don't believe this God any more. At the end of it, however, I was still reading and still thinking about religion. Eventually I came to the conclusion that I actually don't think that this authoritarian interventionist God exists.

For how long did you join the Protestant Church?

It's funny talking about it now, because it really must have been only two years, but it felt such a longer period in my life. It must have been two years, because I was in my fifteenth year. I remember that was when I made a decision that I didn't believe in God.

Did you tell your parents about joining the Protestants and how did they react?

Yes I did. They reacted very badly. They were shocked, they didn't believe it, they said, "what the hell are you doing!..." I was trying to explain to them what Protestantism... I could have said I had become a Hindu and it would have been exactly the same reaction.

How did it help you joining the Protestants?

They introduced me to philosophy – in no other way. It was a really destructive thing in every other way.

Do you think it is more stressful and traumatic for Greek families to deal with the reality of homosexuality than other ethnic groups and why?

I remember when I was eighteen, there was a friend of mine, Lisa, who was Greek. Her mum grew up in Athens but her parents were from Asia Minor, I think. We were very good friends and her mum told her, why don't you have an affair with Christos, he is a good boy. And Lisa said to her mum he is gay! So next time I was around to Mrs S's place – she was a great woman, with a cigarette in her mouth, a glass of whisky in her hand – sitting at a table, she had cooked for us, she offered me a whisky and said: "Christos, Ms Tammy told me she thinks you are a poofter. Look, my father has fucked men, my brother has fucked men, my husband has fucked men. It's natural, that's what Greeks do..." And then I said, "But *Thea*, they have fucked me ..." When she heard that she froze, put down her glass of whisky and said, "This is different! ..." So there is something about masculinity in Greek culture, in relationship to what you were saying before, off the record, about lesbians who are more acceptable in Greece...

For Greeks masculinity characterises usually the dominant, not the passive partner, regardless of whether it's a woman or a man.

It's not only for Greeks but for people in the Middle East too. If you ask me, I think it's actually a residue of the Ottoman culture. So for me, trying to make sense of all that – what it is to be a man – was very difficult, so the identification I made at that time was with women. I became a very strong feminist, because I think that was the first glimpse of how to challenge the culture.

So, how exactly did you speak to your parents about being different?

Basically my mother really asked me, when I went to visit her, she said, "*Eisai poustis?*" ("Are you gay?").

How did she know?

She had understood, because I had already told my brother and my cousin. So I answered "yes", and she was very angry. She said at the time, "Don't say anything to your father because he will kill you." But I actually did tell my dad a few months later, because I just thought it was unfair. My mother knew it, he didn't.

What did he say?

Dad was much more understanding than my mother. He is not a man of very many words at all, but he was disappointed – it was very clear. He said, *"Na prosexeis... To mono pou tha sou zitiso einai na prosexeis..."* ("Take care... I will ask one thing of you: to be careful..."). My father would find it very difficult to talk to me about sex, even if I were straight, let alone... It was very hard...

So when exactly did you leave home?

When I was a first year University student.

Do you think that Greeks are stricter than other ethnic groups in terms of homosexuality?

I would say that Greeks are not dissimilar to a whole range of Eastern Mediterranean cultures I met. In terms of degrees, I don't know if it would be harder if it be Lebanese, or another nationality.

What about Australians?

I think Australians are easier to deal with it, although we are talking about generalisations now. I think that in Australian families there is more independence. Because they are not migrants, there is not an investment in a child as there is in Eastern Mediterranean cultures. Maybe I'm very critical of Greek culture, I have to say. And I'm still very critical of the lack of courage in a lot of Greeks, not only in the Greek Community of Australia but also back in Greece. Greeks don't have much courage.

Things have changed now, of course, but still one wouldn't dare stating openly one was gay and expect to be employed.

It's not just in terms of sexuality. I think there is a lot of dishonesty in the Greek family and how people relate to each other. It was really tough coming out in that old period in my family, especially in the beginning, but now it's not so hard for mum and dad. But I think I have a very mature relationship with my father and my mother and that includes my relationship with my partner. Actually it's a much more mature relationship than with most Greek-Australians that I know of around me who are still hiding things from their parents. They are forty-three, forty-five year olds and they are still hiding things. I find that incredible.

That courage and truthfulness has helped you to overcome hardship and cope with life better.

It can harm you less.

Costa Taktsis, a famous Greek novelist, the "patriarch" of homosexuals in Greece, was always feeling guilty for being gay. He actually believed strongly that homosexuality was an unnatural thing, a "disease", and condemned it throughout his life. How would you explain his stance?

You've got to remember our generational difference and the fact that I'm an Australian who grew up in Australia. I can understand completely where he comes from, although I don't believe what he says. For me, I don't have that religious obstacle any more. For me that whole question of masculinity, passivity and who's the dominant partner, hasn't been part of my life. From the start of my sexual exploration I was both whereas, it sounds to me, Taktsis was really feminine – that makes a difference in the sense of shame. I do, of course, have a memory of guilt and I understand some of his criticisms of homosexuals. I understand him completely. But a whole generation of different politics, of different cultures has been formed of how we understand sexuality now. But tell me something: why did Patrick White never like Taktsis?

Because of his unorthodox lifestyle, especially as a transvestite.

That's very conservative of White!... When I started off as a writer, there were a lot of people who were older than me, both straight and gay, male and female, who were involved in the sexual politics of the sixties and seventies. That is a period I never experienced first hand but it was really influential on me. There were people I loved and admired really deeply, but I also realised I didn't want to be part of that world.

There were a lot of bitter feminist and gay activists, a lot of doctrinaire people who had sacrificed love and family – things that were and still are important to me. That is why I became very interested in forging my own path as a man and as a homosexual man in this culture.

That's very important as each individual is different.

You know, I initially gave *Loaded* to a gay and lesbian press to publish. They sent me a letter saying that they liked the writing but they couldn't publish it because they thought it was racist and homophobic – which says something about where the politics was at the time.

Whereas they should have been the first to publish it...

They didn't because they had such a rigid definition of what was correct about homosexuality and feminism, and that's how you get those problems. But the more you talk to me about Taktsis, the more fascinated I am by him as a person.

He was a very fascinating person indeed. And so many years after his death, he is still very popular with the public. His famous novel The Third Wedding *has been staged once again in Athens by the National Greek Theatre Company with huge success.*

One thing that's important to say, in terms of my relationship to someone like Taktsis, is that the homosexual writers that I have responded to best and had the biggest influence on me – and I can't separate those two things – have been people like Pasolini, Taktsis, Jean Genet, John Rechy. They are people who did not have a correct line or a non-contradictory relationship to sexuality. I find less interest in the work of a lot of gay writers who are much more popular.

Do you think there is any meaningful relationship between art and homosexuality?

I think that for a long time (and I'm not only talking about Australia but broadly in culture), the *outsider* position has enabled us to write about or perceive or represent the world in very interesting ways. And I think the homosexual, for a long time, has been an *outsider* in our culture. That's why I think it's been a position of importance to artistic expression. Now the more homosexuality is becoming less challenging, more "domesticated" – that's the word I want to use – that relationship between homosexuality and art is not as strong. I think it's the *outsider* position that makes the difference with homosexuality.

Some great writers and artists in history have been homosexuals. Do you think that being homosexual enhances artistic achievement?

As I said before, what it does is it allows you to have an *outside point of view,* which is useful. Does it make you a better artist? I don't know. It may make you, in the Greek context, a courageous artist.

Why do you think religions are so strongly against homosexuality?

I think that Christianity and Islam, which are sibling religions as they stem from Judaism and are monotheistic religions, make a mind-body split which is pivotal to those religions. They are in that sense dualistic religions: the body is the side of corruption, the mind is superior. I think Judaism was in a great crisis with the coming of Roman power and Greek thought. Jews thought that they had a more ethical system that made them a nation above all nations, a nation of God, the only nation with an ethical, moral system. And what happens? They confront the sophisticated ethical world of the Greeks and the complex legislative state of the Romans, which smashes them. And I think part of the reaction in the Judaic-Christian and Islamic religions is to be a pagan world and sexuality embodies the pagan world. It's historic. There is nothing about God per se, there is nothing about religion per se that makes homosexuality a sin. It's an accident of history.

How do you explain the sex scandals in the Church?

For a lot of people the Church was an escape. If you thought that your sexuality was suspect, for a long time the Church was where you would go, because no one would ask the question. Now if you are a priest, you have the clout of religion to cover up your deviant sexuality. My feeling about it is that homosexuality is considered negative because it's a minority expression of sexuality – the majority expression is heterosexuality –

given that procreation sustains and reproduces itself. The whole religious edifice which is built around sexuality is very specific to history rather than faith or God.

In one of your interviews you've said that "The root of everything is to be found in the nature of shame and sexuality in civilisation [...] History, biology, art, everything talk in favour of and honour the reality of multiform sexuality." What exactly did you mean?

What I meant was that, if you look at the natural and cultural world, we have produced the reality we know from whatever religious or moral restrictions there are in a multiple sexual world. This is undoubted. On one level that's as simple a statement as possible that I wanted to make. But in terms of Eastern culture, because we have such a shame and such confusion about our sexuality, there is part of me that I would hate to see all that shame go, because it has actually created some of the best art in our culture.

But there are limits. Can you tolerate incest, for example?

Yes. I mean as an adult you can't make love to your child. You've got to separate incest from paedophilia. To answer your question honestly, I don't know that I have an issue with incest that a lot of people do.

If you had children, would you make love to your children?

No, I wouldn't make love to my children, but I'm not so sure that I see a moral problem in a brother and sister making love to each other, if they are adults. I don't want to sound like being cavalier about it, but I find it very difficult to make definitive black and white statements around these subjects. I know that I have, from a very young age, incestuous desires – even though I don't act on these. That's the point I want to make. I won't come out and say all incest is wrong. I'm not someone who supports adult-child relationships but when it comes to adults, the whole thing changes for me, as the desires are so much more complicated.

What has been your relationship with women and what part have they played in your life?

Women have played a very important role in my life from the

beginning, I think. I would not have survived or I would not have found the strength to do things if there hadn't been women in my life. My closest friends have been women. They supported me morally and in camaraderie in those really important ways. The sense of the injustice that women are subjected to is a real pivot in me rebelling, about a lot of things to do with culture. I would hate to live in a world of men only.

Did you ever have any sexual relationship with women?

Yes. It has been a long time though. I used to have sex with women more often when I was younger. I think one of the things that happens when you are homosexual is that you don't have the fear that heterosexuals have. I've never understood gay men who have been misogynists. I've always loathed those kind of men. Sex is really pleasurable, you know that, and I think when you grow up homosexual, you don't have the fear of heterosexuality, because it's the norm. I never had a physical aversion to women's bodies or the notion of heterosexual sex. When I first had sex with a girl, it was pleasurable because it felt nice. But my desire wasn't strong, that's the difference.

What role has love played in your teenage years? Was it more useful or harmful?

I'm really grateful for the experience of love. My life would have been a less meaningful life if it hadn't been for love. It wouldn't have been an interesting life. Love made me curious.

Haven't you suffered because of love?

Of course I have. But that suffering is part of being in love. If you ask me at the moment when you are feeling the most abject and tortured due to the experience of love – which feels like a prison you will never escape, which makes you like the most destitute as a human being – I probably would say no, fuck love, it is no worth it, it kills you. But if you ask me at the moment of falling in love, when you are so elated from that experience, then I would have a different answer. So that's why I'm saying, if I'm going to weigh the negatives and the positives, I would suffer again and I would be happy to suffer again for love. But I think the most horrific things have been justified in the name of love as well. I'm not a romantic in that sense.

As a teenager, did you have an idea of what you wanted to do in life?

No. That I wanted to write maybe...

Were you anxious about things such as studies, career or financial independence?

I thought about how to be financially independent, it was important, but I didn't think about a career. When I tried to imagine myself in particular careers none of them made sense, none of them felt right, none of them felt like worth striving for.

How would you imagine making money?

I always knew I had to work, but I didn't think a lot about these things. I knew that I was going to work, I knew I needed to make a living, but I never thought making a living was connected with the important things in life. I knew from early on I didn't need a lot of money to survive.

Was money an important issue for you?

No. I mean yes when you have to pay the rent, but I never became obsessed about money.

Weren't you anxious about the future?

No, no. I knew I had to work, but I never worried about what will happen if I get sick. No, that wasn't part of what I thought at all.

In your books you are preoccupied almost obsessively with sex and drugs. Why is that? Were you ever a drug addict yourself?

I was for a period. I did have a problem with amphetamines. It was serious enough that I went into rehabilitation. I started using those drugs almost at fifteen, sixteen. For the first few years they were recreational. But there was a period when I was definitely addicted, I would take them every day.

How did you overcome this problem?

With the help of professionals. I did go to a clinic in Collingwood, for a period, and I saw a fantastic woman there who really helped me a lot. She was great.

Is it because of these experiences you've had that the presence of drugs is constant in your books? Or is it because it makes interesting reading?

I lived in a particular kind of world that is not an everyday world. My sense is that people's sexual lives and drug lives are much more common than we assume in the Australian middle class. There is also a huge separation between the stories we tell of ourselves and the reality of what ourselves are is. That's what occurs in *The Slap*. Yes, more characters take a lot of drugs and have a lot of sex. You've got to realise I am creating a situation at a point of conflict and tension. At that point you tend to partake in extreme behaviour. I feel that the experiences I'm talking about are – I wouldn't use the word *common* because I don't think they are – but I don't think they are unreal or forced either. And I think that is the reality of how we use drugs in this culture.

Isn't it an easy way out for you as a writer to deal with your characters' problems?

I see what you mean. I'm much more interested in and fascinated by how you convey these experiences of sex or drugs, because those experiences are still part of my life – I just want to give expression to them. I'm a little bit unclear about what you are asking.

Are these things a ready made formula for you to use to get around a difficult situation?

I hope that's not what I'm doing. That's not how I see it. I do write realistic fiction but I never saw myself as a mainstream writer. When I was sitting down writing *The Slap*, I wasn't thinking, well, how do I make this palatable? I want to write about this world that I know of. And I've gone to those parties where very middle class people are taking drugs in the laundry, they may have thirteen year old kids, but they are still doing it. They may not do it every day, but they do it. I've witnessed such events. They are real.

How important were music and films as a teenager and how have they influenced your literary work?

Films, for me, have helped me more than books. They first triggered my passion for art. The cinema was my first love in that way. From very early on I would see very great films by the mid-century Europeans when that cinema was in its creative peak – so that was a huge influence – understanding edits very early on, as with writing. Music – when I write I tend to think about the musicality of what I'm writing. So, in a sense, my metaphors are cinematic and musical rather than literary. They have played a very crucial part in my writing. The initial working draft for *Loaded* was a soundtrack I remembered, because to me writing that novel was making a mixed-tape.

In secondary school, did you read a lot of literature? Which writers and books did you like more and who has influenced you the most?

I read constantly from a very young age. The Americans, the ones that stand out for me, are writers like Cousin Cullers, Ralf Ellison, the African-American writers and people like Norman Mailer and Henry Miller were a big influence. Then I was very fortunate because, when I was in year nine, I had a Czech teacher, Mr Havir, a very erudite man, who saw that I really liked reading and he basically introduced me to European literature. He introduced me to Dostoevsky, to Stendhal, to those figures. Yes, I was a constant reader and I wasn't just reading high school texts, I was reading much more widely. In *Dead Europe* this teacher is actually represented as a character there.

What other interests did you have as a teenager?

Cinema was my passion. I would go twice, three times a week, to the films. Cinema and reading were my passion. I wasn't a sports person. Those were my interests really.

How good were you with composition writing, for example?

Mr Havier was a very big influence, as I said, and it was not only that he encouraged my reading but he encouraged my writing as well. I've been writing from very young. In that way that you start thinking maybe I can do this, maybe I can start writing stories. When I look back, I was so influenced by what I was reading at the time. I remember there was a Scotch lady teacher who was a bitch. I was in year eight, so I was quite young and I remember her – it was quite a humiliating thing to do to a child – holding up a piece of writing and saying, "Chris Tsiolkas has written this. This is filth!" and tore it up. But it was me attempting to write in the style of Henry Miller and she was very offended. Look, for me, because I didn't come from a literary background, it took a very long time to feel at ease in expressing myself, and that is not unknown for a lot of people from our background. Because it's not seen as something legitimate. So I've been writing all through late high school, I've been writing in my University years. But, as I said, it took a very long time to say I'm a writer.

Apart from the Marxist ideology, what other ideology or philosophy had attracted you in your adolescent years?

Apart from Existentialism, a big influence on me was Feminism, not as much as a philosophy but I guess as a philosophical way of understanding the world. At high school, my best friend's mother was a strong feminist and I remember her giving me books to read, especially when she went to University, like a whole series of feminist writings. For me Feminism was a way of also understanding my gender confusion, confusion around sexuality. And I think, inevitably, as in any time a male engages with Feminism, it was both a really positive force and a really negative one as well. Positive in the sense that it made me understand my relationship to my mother better, it made me understand the nature or the role of women in the culture I grew up with. It gave me an understanding that there were alternative forms of sexuality, alternative forms of choices you can make around your life. The negative came from the puritanical element to Anglophone feminism. So I became quite confused about my masculinity through that kind of engagement in this world. Almost felt guilty for a while about being a man. Part of my writing has been trying to understand that relationship to feminism. A lot of feminists would say I got it wrong...

What was your greatest revolt as a teenager? To what extent does your protagonist Aris, in Loaded, *reflect his author?*

What I remember as being the most significant moment which occurred within the family was when I made a decision not to study Science in high school. I must have been about sixteen. My parents had that drive and ambition for their children to be very well academically trained to get out of being working class. So they wanted me to follow a vocational career, and I decided to say *no*. Now that seems a very small thing, but I think it was the first time I really challenged my parents defiantly and the first time I actually said no, I don't agree to this. So I chose to do History and Literature, subjects which I thought would not lead to that kind of professional life. That was the first kind of defiance I remember. The other thing was moving out of home but that was after I left high school. That was probably the most important thing I did. I don't think I would have been a writer if I've stayed at home.

Of all the above we've discussed, what has been the most tormenting and the most exciting thing in your adolescence?

The most tormenting, the most difficult thing, was when I decided to leave home. The most exciting time was when I made a decision I no longer believed in God. That was a thrilling moment, it was quite a frightening moment too, but it just felt like suddenly – because I was being influenced by the Existentialist literature I was reading – I could make my own mind in the world. It felt like having a great freedom. It may seem controversial, but I would say that the first time I took drugs was also exciting. It's no longer probably a good thing to say, but it was thrilling. You felt as if you could alter consciousness, you could play with consciousness in an alternative state to normality. I know a lot of people who have said to me that they are scared of and don't want to take drugs because they fear losing control, but I never had that fear. That moment of rejecting fate and God and trying drugs are around the same period. The latter would not have been possible without the former and it was that sense of freedom, as you said, that was exciting. That sense of, well, everything I've been taught is of re-examination. And drugs for me was part of that question.

Comparing your childhood and your adolescence, which of the two was the most significant in your life, both as a person and writer?

As I said last time, I have a nostalgic relationship to my childhood and a very painful relationship to my adolescence. In that pain comes the material and the struggle in writing. So, in that way, I would tend to think that the adolescence period is more important. But you know, I'm a middle-aged man now and as I get older I tend to be thinking more and more about my childhood, so that makes me reflective in the next phase of my writing. You know, until very recently I feel like I've been trying to come to terms or understand or still battle those demons from adolescence. And I feel some negotiation there, some overcoming of those demons, not all. So I've been thinking a lot about my childhood recently.

Do you think that writing has helped you to deal with and heal some of these old wounds?

If I didn't have writing I would be spinning out of control because the material has been quite dark. In a way the craft of writing is teaching you how to manage that, you learn how to create a narrative, a story out of it.

If we accept that our childhood is our lost paradise as they say, would you agree that our adolescence could be characterised as our lost and rediscovered hell?

I think the institutionalised nature of the family and school, even though I had a loving family, even though I had some very good teachers, I felt for a long time that I was literally pushed on the wall. If I could have an image of my adolescence, that is a head pushing me under the water. If there were a benevolence in my schooling or in my family at all, that was the opposite of freedom. It wasn't true of childhood but it was certainly true of my adolescence.

Clifton Hill, circa 1996. Christos working on The Jesus Man.
(Photo by Effy Alexakis)

3
ADULTHOOD

In one of your interviews you spoke of a "sense of family responsibility" when you started university. What kind of responsibility was that?

It was in my second week starting university. My uncle Costa – who is not really a blood relationship, but has a very strong bond with my father, and he was one of the prime adult figures in my life when I was growing up – came over and drove me to Melbourne University. He pointed to one of the buildings and said, "There I laid the stones to that building." He was a brick-layer. He tapped me on the back of the head and said, "Don't ever forget we are very proud, your parents are very proud that you are the first of your family to be at university but you have a huge responsibility now..." For a long time it was a responsibility that I felt I had betrayed, by moving out of home, by not pursuing a vocational study.

When you started university, were you still with your parents?

Yes I was. I left home after seven or eight months. I didn't actually become eighteen until October of that first year at university, and psychologically for me it felt like I knew it was going to be such an enormous challenge to my parents but I wanted to feel that I had the legal weight of adulthood.

How does this responsibility relate to the fact that you were not a model student, as you were involved in activism, sex and drugs? Were these activities part of your overall life education?

For me that time was anything but study. It was exploring. I don't actually have any regrets about that. That was what I wanted to learn and experience, that's how I wanted to live. I look back on it now and

I think I would be so much a better student if I went back now. But you've got to remember that I have been reading all this time. It wasn't like I went to university and went, oh my God, I've discovered Sartre or I've discovered Gide, because I had been reading those writers in high school.

Your parents wanted from an early age to instil in you a love of learning. This is typical of all Greek parents. Did your father actually want you to become a cultivated person or just want you to move up the social ladder?

For my father, his notion of education had much more to do with status. It was my mother who introduced to me the notion of education also having a further function. She certainly had that, whereas for my father it was very much opportunity, that's how he saw it.

How did you see it yourself?

I think that, from quite early, I saw it as a way out. So, from high school, I saw education as my ticket out of town, out of the suburbs. But I was also very much a product both of those attitudes to education. I also saw it as a way of becoming a better person. It was never a question about status or money. I didn't care about that. But that notion, that if I didn't get an education what would I do? I would be trapped in a lifestyle that I felt it was unfulfilling, I had a notion of that. So there was a sense of cultivation of self. I'm talking now in retrospect, but I was very conscious that I was learning, that I was reading, that I was able to start moving in circles where I could speak about those things. I had no idea about the whole of the culture, class, etc.

Why did you decide to study Arts?

Look, I didn't have a very concrete understanding of what I should do. As I said, I wanted an education. It wasn't career targeted. I was doing Literature, I was doing History as part of my high school life. So Arts seemed to be the area to go. I'm not making this up, my dad would vouch for it. We had this career teacher, Mrs Pope – my friend Catherine at high school, who is still my closest friend, can testify to this – and I remember her coming out of a meeting and saying, after spending ten minutes trying to convince me, not to go to university because you would come under the influence of Communists. That was the level of career counselling then. So when I sat down with her trying to work out what I would do for my future, I remember her giving me information about applying to the Banks. In that way it wasn't a school geared to encouraging non-vocational ideas of study. So I had no idea of how the academic world looked or felt, how it worked at all.

What did you major in at university?

Politics and History.

What kind of History?

American history. I was fascinated by American history, still am, still read it.

Don't you think higher education is a waste of time as it produces future unemployed graduates? If you had children, would you encourage them to go to university?

If I had children I would encourage them to explore whatever the joys of life. Because I've worked as a teacher, I think one of the great mistakes of the education movement in the sixties and seventies was to decimate the apprentice system and to make higher education the only kind of legitimate path for people. I know there is a whole history of economics that comes into play for why these decisions were taken. But if I had children I would just encourage them to read, to be active and to just pursue their joy. I was too young when I started university. I had, as I said, no concrete understanding of what I wanted to do. I think there were opportunities that I got at university that would have taken me a long time to make use of hadn't I been to university.

Throughout history many great minds had never gone to school and were educated at home. Wouldn't you agree that the education system as a whole should be abolished and be replaced by something new to serve the real needs of young people?

I agree. A friend, who has been a mentor of mine – Sasha Soldatow – has said to me that you're going to have to work hard in your writing to remove the trait of the academy, and I think that's true. It took me a while to rid myself of that kind of what we call "instrumental kind of writing," which is a factory producing a particular kind of garbage.

George Seferis, the Greek Nobel laureate poet, has said that erudition can be negative for a writer, because he or she ceases to be innocent.

I don't disagree with this. My only caution there which derives from my experience is that, I've grown up with people who were never educated, who were not even given the basics of learning (how to read and write), as was the case with my aunt, and that lack of knowledge has blighted her life. So sometimes it can be a romantic sensationalism of that innocence that people like you and I can make, because we had the luxury of being given knowledge. But as I said before, adolescence was like being in prison – that's what I think school is. You ask most kids over there what the experience of school is... I reckon there is nothing like doing a bit of a stint teaching in Northern and Western suburb schools to make you a fatalist, especially when they take children away from their parents at a young age.

When did you actually teach?

I started doing a Diploma of Education in the early 2000, much later, after I graduated from the University. I was still writing. It was during the time I was working on *Dead Europe*, because I've always been working to support myself. So I've done some mentoring, which I really enjoyed, and I have a huge respect for teaching as a vocation. So I started a Dip. Ed., thinking, maybe I could be a teacher... But because I wanted to work in the State school system, I was working as a volunteer at Northern Secondary and also doing some stuff in TAFE, in the northern suburbs. I realised it was a choice I had to make and you can call it selfish, but there was no way I could be a full-time teacher and be a full-time writer.

It must have been a very good experience for you as a writer.

It was great being around teachers and having those conversations. It was really disturbing and depressing being around teaching some of those students. I wanted to shake so many of them who had no real understanding of what they were into, or what they were choosing to do. The most favourable part of that job was actually doing literacy with fifteen and sixteen year olds, who had gone through the whole of high school and still didn't know how to read a word at sixteen.

Of all your activities at university, which would you consider the most beneficial for you – activism, debates, editing Farrago, *reading literature, intellectual discipline?*

I would say it's the people I met, it's the intellectual challenge. What I used to love about being a student, and it didn't necessarily happen on campus, was part of the life of being a student. I used to love to just walk to a friend's place who were all students, sitting up drinking coffee till five o'clock in the morning, talking about literature or politics. That was where I felt most privileged and alive. And *Farrago*, for example, felt like a continuation of that. The reason I got into *Farrago* was to meet people who were working in newspapers and felt like a continuation of that aspect of university life which I adored and I still feel lucky that I had that. So that's why I said before I didn't care I was a terrible student, because I was up until five in the morning and missing my lectures.

After you left home, who supported you financially?

I did. I was working at Food Plus doing shifts.

Were you a full or part-time student then?

I went actually to part-time right at the beginning, because I was quite conscious of what I was doing. I started off as a full-time student and then, from early on, I realised that I wanted to move out of home. So I went down part-time as a student and I was doing shifts at Two-plus. I'd been working there since I was fifteen, right through high school. The guy who owned it was Greek, with whom I got on quite well and he trusted me.

So by the time I was seventeen he would give me night shifts – which were between eleven at night till seven in the morning – because I was getting paid double time back then. It meant that I could start to save some money.

Until you graduated, how many part-time jobs did you have?

Too many, quite a few. Also to support myself, in the second and third year at university, I took a full year off, to work pretty much not full-time but to work pretty hard just to get some money.

After you graduated, where did you work?

My first job, after I graduated, was at the mail room at Coles-Myers which I hated. So I only stayed there a few months. And then I got a job working at RMIT in the Student Union, which was through a contact, through a friend of mine who was working as a student counsellor. I was there for a while. From that job at RMIT I got involved with the Union Movement.

What was your involvement with a veterinary clinic?

In my mid-twenties I was at the State Film Centre in East Melbourne. I had been overseas and came back, and I got a job over there. The State Film Centre eventually became ACMI (Australian Centre for the Moving Image), that's the history of it. So I was working through that period. And then, while I was working on *Dead Europe*, which is a very difficult book, all through this time I'd been consistent about working part-time on the curatorial film program for ACMI. I was also one of the shop-stewards, at a time when there was a huge restructuring. I was working on this novel, which was a huge mother-fucker to complete. I was in a very creative but very intense job. I was a shop-steward, as I said, at that time when most people were losing their jobs, so we were meeting every second day. I was part-time and ended up working full-time. But there was so much going on, I was trying to juggle so many balls in the air, that I would be waking up at 3.17 every morning.

And how did you find time to write?

I was slowly falling apart, that's what was happening. Eventually I quit that job or there was a redundancy, but I still knew I had to work. One of my best friends was a veterinarian, so I said to him, "Look, I'm in between jobs at the moment, I've resigned, I've got a bit of money and am working on *Dead Europe*... He said, "Come in and I'll give you some work." It was the best job for me, after all the intellectual fiery work, just being in an environment that was so different.

What exactly did you do there?

I got trained to be a nurse for animals, as I don't have any science background. It was in Northcote, I live in Preston, so it was like a half hour walk to my work. I really enjoyed the people I was working with. I'm not a sentimentalist at all about animals, but it was an interesting job to have to look after animals. You are also dealing with people who are in grief. Coming from a Greek background, I think we have a very different cultural relationship to animals. It was a great place to work. I'm not a sentimentalist, but I have a great respect for animals. For me it was a perfect job as a writer.

4

LITERATURE AND CRITICISM

Is it true that, when you were little, you said to your mum: "I want to become a writer"?

She is the one who remembers that incident. She says I would have been ten years old. It was probably a conversation that a parent would remember much more.

At what age did you decide that you would definitely become a writer and what exactly prompted you to that decision?

It was in my mid-twenties. I had been working for a long period, by then, in a variety of jobs. I used to work for the Union Movement – this is straight after university – and then I got a job in the State Film Centre. At that time, in Victoria, it was a great place for someone like me to work because I was a film archivist there, but I was deeply unhappy working full-time. So many things were good in my life – I had my relationship, I had a good job, I had good people around me but I was frustrated. So I made a decision to go from full-time to casual and part-time work. So I remember sitting down with Wayne, my partner, and saying, I would like to do this, I would like to see if I can be a writer. I've never had done any writing courses, but I had the itch – that desire. And I did it. It was the best thing I ever did. I went down working three days a week and the other two days were my writing days, which I treated quite seriously. We were renting in Richmond at the time and that bedroom became my study.

When exactly did you become a full-time writer?

In 2010.

How easy or difficult was it for you to become a writer in a country with a small population like Australia?

This is what I wanted to do. I am a writer because this is the only thing that I can do. You know, part of wanting freedom is for me to be a writer. I have been very clear, when I made a decision to be a writer, that I had to work. So the question of audience was never really an issue for me.

Didn't it worry you that you wouldn't be able to earn a living as a writer?

That was one thing we talked about back then, in my mid-twenties, with my partner Wayne. That it would be possible I would be bringing in a very small pay-cheque as a writer for the rest of my life. But that's what Wayne wanted me to do. I also realised in my thirties that if I were heterosexual and had children, things would be different, it would be almost impossible for me to be a full-time writer. That is why me and Wayne decided against becoming fathers to a lesbian friend's child. It obviously was a concern that had to do with our decision. So I realised very early on that I was going to write, but I would never make a living from it. Sometimes I can be really frustrated when I meet creative writing course students who seem to have no awareness of that. They seem to think that two years of creative writing and they would be on top of the world. And when I tell them about my working life they don't want to hear about it, they don't want to hear that they may have to work and discipline themselves to find time. But a lot of writers love their work, they are working all their lives in a whole different kind of jobs.

The fact that you had a migrant background and wrote about multicultural issues, was it a disadvantage or an advantage and why?

I think it was an advantage, because I had stories to tell that were fresh. Look, regarding that whole question of the politics around multiculturalism and migration, I'm fucking lucky that I was reading the Americans when I did. Because you yourself did American Politics and you understand my obsession and fascination with the American culture. In America they have never had to go through this kind of questioning about authenticity, about whose stories to tell, because it's a migrant culture. Their big cataclysm is the race stuff, that's the wound in America. But you know, I was reading Jewish writers who were second, third generation, or Italian writers who were second and third generation, and they were telling their stories. I felt quite frustrated about the whole question of multiculturalism when it came to writing. Because it felt like, on the one side you had a dominant Anglo-culture, that was prescribing what real and authentic writing should be, and then on the other side you had the multicultural Community going, this is what a Greek writer should be. I was lucky to meet people who were so encouraging, like George Papaellinas and also Sasha Soldatow, who sat down and talked to me about the state of literature in Australia. But really, the best conversations were about the ethnicity of the writer.

Not many years ago multicultural literature and writers of migrant background were considered marginalised. Now it is considered trendy to be such a writer. As Carlos Fuentes has said, and I quote from memory, "the eccentric world is now central [...] and the only way to be central in the future is to be eccentric." Why do you think that has happened?

You are asking a question of history. I grew in a country like Australia, very conscious that I was a wog, an outsider – that's very true. And that gave a certain fire to the belly, it gave a certain urgency to the kind of writing I was producing. As far as the history is concerned, I feel now that I don't have an answer. I don't know if my generation now is the centre or whether I am. I refer to it as a "pet" of the Australian literary scene. So as long as they have Christos Tsiolkas, they can say that they are representative of different voices. I'm still exploring that, I'm still not sure about that. I don't think things have changed. I'm suspicious because I think the literary world in Australia is still quite conservative.

When you first started, did you realise there was any racism against you as a writer, given that your first book was rejected?

I was thinking of one of your previous questions in our last session, "why are your characters Greek?" Now, if I weren't an Australian writer, would you be asking that question of me?

I don't know, maybe not.

Yes. Because there is the core of all this. There is still something unsettling in the Australian identity, about what "Australian" means.

Isn't the same in Britain, with their colonial writers?

Yes, although I think there is a greater confidence by people of colour in England than there is here, but this is an outsider's perspective. Here we are really still suspicious and unsure... To give you a concrete example: Talking to a woman I know – she is from an Anglo-Australian background – who has been working in theatre in the UK for the last ten years, but came to live back here in Australia last year, she said she couldn't believe how wide our stages are. She couldn't believe how tokenistic the work is. So yes, I think there is something different to the Australian culture beyond what is happening in Europe. And I wonder if that is partly due to our notional distance from the centre, the traditional centre being broken down. As Greeks we have it too – that we are far away from where the real culture happens, the real world. There are a number of times I'm frustrated with bloody Greeks who are whingeing and whingeing about, oh I would like to be in Athens... Well, get the hell out of here and go and live in Athens!... This is never going to be Greece, Australia will never ever be Greece, it will never ever be England, it will never be fucking France! If you want that, go there! I've been emotive about that because I myself experienced the same thing. When I was writing *Loaded* I was feeling that way. Now I feel a different kind of urgency. It has nothing to do with that question any more. I am Australian. In the end I can't do anything else.

Nevertheless you can never entirely eradicate these questions as they are deeply rooted in human nature.

I know and I agree with you there.

What has contributed to your success as a writer, from your very first book?

If you look at Australian publishing over the early ninenties, which is when *Loaded* got published, a whole generation of young women came into the publishing scene, who were more eclectic and more adventurous. That was what fundamentally shifted things in the early nineties, that allowed these voices to go in. The eighties was a particularly arid period in Australian writing because, you know, when we were talking about the influence of the academy, God the eighties stank of it! So I think ten years earlier a novel like *Loaded*, which has never been contemplated as mainstream writing, could never have been put out by Random House and, maybe ten years after *Loaded*, there would have been not another book about similar issues. It was the moment of time I think. Also, I'm hoping, it had to do with the writing, it had to do with the voice in it. The film by Ana Kokkinos also helped of course. In a way I have to step aside from that question, because I can't answer it. Why do you think it happened? Was it the right timing, what they call "the perfect storm"?

Sometimes in life things happen accidentally.

They do, exactly. Which is why I keep saying I'm fortunate, I feel very blessed about it.

Look, your best novel is Dead Europe, *but* The Slap, *which is very good too but not your best novel, sold like mad. Why? You can't explain it.*

That was an accident! There was obviously some hunger to read about these contemporary lives.

How would you determine "talent" and literary "merit" and how important are they for you?

That old cliché, ninety per cent perspiration and ten per cent inspiration is fucking true, we all know that. And to know how to be a writer – and I'm still learning this – is about doing disciplined work. I do think there is something about an instinctive talent to things that – I don't know what it is but it is there. Sometimes you see a young child taking a paint brush and begin to paint. I think that there are writers who have that instinctive ability to sit down and write. But without that actual work, that talent doesn't mean very much. And it's the same, whether you use the sports analogy or the arts analogy.

There has always been this strong belief that popular and best selling fiction (thrillers, crime novels, etc) does not belong to the cannon of serious literature but are second class. In which of the two categories do you belong?

As a writer I belong in both, because *The Slap* is certainly in the popular category but *Dead Europe* is not. Can I just say that one of the things that I'm very thankful is that, for me, it's a spent question. That's because I grew up with a different relationship to the popular culture. I just don't live in a world that divides between the *high* and the *low* any more. I feel I wasn't even born into that world. So when it comes to music, for example, that question makes absolutely no sense to me, because I don't have a classically trained mind.

But isn't music a different kettle of fish?

Why? Some of my most favourite writing includes Céline, whom there would not be anyone in the world who would judge him as a popular or populist writer.

Do you consider The Slap *as being serious literature?*

For me, yes, it is serious literature.

Would you prefer to be a best selling rich writer or a great but poor writer?

A great but poor writer. I want to be a great writer – of course I do. I've dedicated my life to this vocation. The self doubt of being a writer is there constantly. So there are moments of real unhappiness, that is part of the writing life when you think, I've got no talent, I'm a fraud, it's not real. So when you ask me what would I prefer, I would prefer to be a great writer. I mean I've been very fortunate with what happened with *The Slap*, but *The Slap* is an anomaly, it seems to me. The proof will be in the books that I'm writing now. But I do think that with that question you have to be very careful. For me, the elitism of the literary world and some of those concepts about what is a real book or authentic literature are not worth criticising and are really dangerous positions that are taken. Because what would you say about *Pride and Prejudice* or Dickens?

Perhaps the most striking thing in your fiction is the "energy" it radiates. Where does that "energy" come from? Is it true that when you write, sometimes you get up and perform by imitating your characters?

Yes, when I was working in the theatre with actors and seeing how actors prepare for their role, has made me think about how you create a character. So there is something that I learned from the theatre. As for the *energy,* I think it comes from the fact that I think musically, that's where it comes from. So the metaphors I use for writing are musical metaphors.

Does this explain why your writing is reminiscent of script-writing, with the use of direct speech, dialogues, etc? Have you ever studied script-writing?

I never studied it. I got involved with script-writing because I love cinema. I do also think filmically and that is reflected in the writing as well. So maybe my music and visual imagination have contributed to this form of writing you mentioned. I'm aware of it too. To be really honest, I'm one of those writers who are overly descriptive. That's my style. I will also use the term *vigour*. I like writing that is vigorous, which is why I'm not very good at all with the English. I'm good with the Americans but not very good with the English. Because I find them – it is a problematic term but I would say quite effete, I'm not captured by the language of a lot of English writing or contemporary English writing.

Is it because English is more of an intellectualised form of writing?

Yes, exactly. I completely agree. I've done mentoring in the last fifteen years, working with young writers and I said to Andrew Hutchinson, who was writing a very different piece of writing, "Mate you've got to write with your dick on this one!" And he always talks to me about this... I think he's got genuine talent and discipline, so I hope he finds his voice.

Do you think that writing can be taught?

No, but you can teach reading. I never did creative writing. If I was doing a writing course, the first year I would sit my students down and would not allow them to write one word. They would have to read for a year. That's the most important thing you can do.

That's exactly what Borges has said: unless you are a very good reader, you can never be a very good writer either. One presupposes the other.

Because that's where you learn your craft.

Do you think that, for a writer, physical fitness is equally important to intellectual fitness? Do you exercise at all?

I don't run but I walk fast. For me walking has been part of the discipline as with writing. Part of what I do is walk from Preston to Brunswick.

What time do you get up in the morning?

Six o'clock.

What time do you go to bed?

Usually around ten thirty or eleven. Usually the first couple of hours, when I get up, I'm writing. Then I take an hour of exercise, and then I go back to the desk.

Let's talk about your work practices and habits. First of all, do you think that writing is an easy or difficult task for you?

The beginning is wonderful. I love the beginning. It's actually the most pleasurable part of writing for me. What I have to do the work at is to sustain that interest.

So overall, do you find writing an easy task?

Overall yes, yes.

Have you ever experienced what is called "writer's block"?

Never. Knock on wood, because I know it may still happen... I remember a female friend of mine who, some years ago, said, "Just work, work like a demon, because you never know when the block may come," and that has stayed in my mind.

As a writer, have you ever thought of or experienced the limitations of language to express deeper emotions?

All the time. I can't imagine that any writer worth their salt has not thought of the limitations of language and has not thought of, sometimes, language as a cage that you are banging against, trying to escape. I can't imagine that there isn't a writer who hasn't fantasised, as I have, of being a musician. Because there is a way of creation that is not bound by language.

But isn't this limitation itself the real challenge for a writer?

For me the whole craft of writing, what I'm learning, is that it is precisely that. That there is the book that is written in my head – because there is a writing that happens in my head all the time – and then there is the writing that I do with the pen or on the computer. And the craft that I'm trying to learn is how to mediate between the two. That is what the writing is. And the reason I still love writing with the pen is because it is a physical act, it's not just a mental act. I think you get trapped and language feels most as a cage when you forget the physical act of writing – the manual work of how you put that on the page.

How long do you carry an idea in your mind before it takes form on paper?

That's a very good question. The process for me is when I'm at the end of a novel, I'm writing the next one. So, for example, at the moment I'm doing a second draft of my new novel, and I've already started thinking of the idea for the next one.

Isn't that interfering with your current writing?

No, because I haven't started the actual writing. But I've started taking notes. The novel I'm working on is *Barracuda*. But I've got an idea that is there. So what I've started to do is read things that are connected to that story. When I do a second draft I don't feel this new idea will intrude into this one. The other thing that happens with me is that, because there is a long period I haven't worked between theatre or film and novels, I feel that I'm good at separating the different types of work, or I hope I am. That's part of the process. I would never work on two novels at the same time, I never have, I wouldn't do that. But I can work on a play at the same time when I'm writing a novel and sometimes I find that a relief to work at another form. Because different literary forms are different writing forms. For example, I think short stories I'm very inadequate at, but I enjoy sometimes to write a short story just to learn to be better at it. So it doesn't feel an interference.

Of all the ideas you have in your mind, how do you decide which ones are worth materialising?

If it's an idea that excites me, then I don't have difficulty working. For example, there was another idea that I had earlier in the year, for a book, and it was sitting there. I was thinking about it, I put it aside and I hadn't come back to it. Part of the writing life is doing those walks. Part of the writing life is actually when you are walking and thinking about those things.

Before you write a novel, do you do any research or other preparatory work?

I don't have a rule. It all depends on the novel. It depends on the material. It depends on how lazy I am sometimes. The important work for me is the working on a structure for a novel, that's quite key. Until I have a structure, I can't begin work, and part of that sometimes is research, in notes, where I go, this is the form that it will take. Once I have that, then the real work begins.

How fast do you write? I mean, how many words do you produce a day?

I try to write two thousand words a day. If I write two thousand words, I feel like I've been doing the work.

Do you have a regular work pattern?

As I said before, it's the first time in my life that I have been able to live completely on writing. There was a period, at the end of last year, really distracting, because in the past I've been fixing my day around my working life. And so suddenly I had this freedom to write and became a little bit lost. That's why now I'm renting a studio in Brunswick, because I needed the discipline of going into work. At the studio I feel I can begin work, and when I'm there I'm focussing on the writing. Then I have one day a week at home, which is what I call "my administration day," where I just go through emails, correspondence, etc.

Do you write in handwriting or in the computer?

Yes. All *The Slap* was initially done in handwriting. When I first started writing I was working at the typewriter, not at the computer.

If you were not a writer, what else would you have been?

A film-maker or involved in the film industry, most definitely.

And if you weren't an artist, how else could you enjoy life?

I think I could possibly be dead, as there would be a search for excess...

You remind me of Márquez who has said that, if I couldn't be a writer I would have committed suicide.

For me it would be a slow suicide through drugs or through excess. Because I can't imagine being happy otherwise.

What exactly does a writer need to be successful: inspiration, imagination, talent or hard work?

All of the above, I would say. And being a successful writer does not necessarily mean being a *successful human being.*

For you, what exactly is successful literature?

I'll paraphrase what Jean Cocteau has said: "What's in a man of art that astonishes us?" When I read that, since a very long time ago, I've always thought that that is a great definition of what you want from a great artist – that which keeps astonishing you. And I think the books that I still love, or the films that I still love, or the pieces of music that I love still do that. You come to them again and you are astonished by what this artist has done with words or whatever.

Do you think that an element of great art is its duration in time?

Shakespeare is a great writer, in my experience, and that's more important than the notion of how long his works have lasted. Of course Shakespeare is a great writer but that's because he can still astonish us. Harold Bloom, the great American critic and author of *Shakespeare: The Invention of the Human* wrote, you look at Shakespeare and so much of who we are is in Shakespeare, the archetypes of who we are and the language we use. The same goes for the classical Greek writers.

For you, who is the greatest writer ever?

What comes to my mind is the writer of *Job* in the Bible, because it still fascinates me every time I read it. Thinking as a novelist now, I have to say Tolstoy.

Really? Why is that?

Because he is still the master of what we call the novel. My favourite of his works is *Anna Karenina*, but I think the greatest work is *War and Peace*.

I found it boring when I first read it as a young man.

You should read it again. However, I love Dostoevsky more. I will change my mind and say Dostoevsky... But in the end, the greatest writer ever is Shakespeare, given that I too write in the English language. I recently saw a production of *Hamlet* which wasn't a great production but it was a reminder of how much this language is dependent on that man. It's astonishing. [...] I also love Stendhal, because I read him at the most opportune time and had been influenced by him.

Do you know that his novel The Red and the Black *sold only one copy when it was first published in France?*

Really! I didn't know that. We should write a story about that one person who bought that book...

Would you agree that your fiction derives mainly from your experiences and it is not so much an intellectual exercise?

I wouldn't necessarily say that I'm not an intellectual writer at all.

Don't you think it's more popular to read about somebody's experiences rather than to intellectualise a particular story?

The best answer for me is to say that I'm a new world writer not an old world writer. For me the separation between what's the intellectual and what's the body is either or. I had the same problem when I was recently in China. I had the same confusion that I had in Western Europe. I have a different relationship to those questions. I'm not side-stepping your question but I think that, for me, there is a lot of things I think about. When I'm writing a novel like *Dead Europe* or *The Jesus Man* I may not have a philosophical language, I may not have a maturity as a writer to express. But I certainly don't see it as a purely personal novel, I think there are ideas there as well. But I also understand how Europeans may think.

Are you saying that the individual is also universal?

Yes. But also the ideas are also understood through the body-bound Ideas are not only bound. In a sense I'm a pragmatist. I mean I may like philosophy, but I also know that I am a shitting, pissing, eating man, and that's just as important to me to make that the centre of consciousness, as is intellectual speculation.

That comes out loud and clear in your books – your obsession with the body and its functions. Obviously you don't do it out of perversity but because you strongly believe it, it's your philosophy.

It's the way I've come to understand myself in the world.

Some people consider philosophy and literature as nothing more than "mental masturbation." What's your opinion on this?

I don't have a problem with... masturbation. It's going back to what we were saying before. You treat that comment quite seriously, so I'm treating the question quite seriously by asking: What does "mental masturbation" mean?

In his introduction to Zorba the Greek, *Kazantzakis says that real life ("flesh and blood") is much more important than writing ("paper and ink") and you can never replace the first with the second.*

Yes, I fully agree.

Do you think that literature can change people's lives?

On the level of the individual, there are books you read that do start a period of enlightenment and transformation – that's possible. I'm thinking particularly when I was a younger man, being introduced to literature and ideas was a transformative experience. But can books change people's lives? I've become less convinced that a writer can change the world. What literature can do is to open up pathways, so it can be a heartened experience and enlightenment. In terms of the big question, the suffering of the world and the politics in the world, I'm not so sure any more that the pen is mightier than the sword.

Let's talk about fame. How has fame affected your life and where do you go from here?

Certainly the biggest change for me was with the success of *The Slap* – that there is economic security that I have now that I didn't have before. So that *is* a change. Now, how would that play out in my future is difficult to predict. But having economic security is something I'm very grateful for. And I realise how fortunate I am. There was a period – just after *The Slap* went enormous in a sense, as it started selling overseas too – where I lost a little bit of direction, just because in a way I had understood myself as a writer outside of the mainstream and suddenly I was placed in the centre, which was confusing. It was good, especially when at that period I was given a three-month residency in Scotland, in 2010 – after *The Slap*. What was fantastic about that was that I was based on the west coast, north west of Glasgow, away from the big cities. It was this remote but beautiful part of the world where I just started writing a new novel there. That was a period of grace for me. I just realised that doing the work makes me happy. That's the source of happiness I like. It is not so much fame and fortune – these things are ephemeral. Doing the work is what matters to me. The other thing is that I hope I'm grounded within my relationship with Wayne, within my family and my friends. I think there is an element of the notion of retreat that I learnt in Scotland that's really important. That you need to step away – even when you may become mainstream and be part of the centre, you don't have to live in that world. So I am happy to do literary things, I'm happy to do talks, but I don't want to make my life centred around the literary world, the literary community and be in the city of the literary world, whether it be here or somewhere else. Maybe that's got to do with middle-age as well. I've become more and more interested in the space of retreat. The other thing that happened too is that I no longer pretend to be the *enfant terrible*. As I said to you the other day, the one thing that I'm very sensitive to is that I don't want anger to become bitterness – that's something I really have to struggle against.

What are your plans for the future?

To keep writing. I would love and hope to write a great book one day.

How did you feel for failing to win the Booker Prize? Was it a big blow for you?

No. Part of not wanting to belong to the literary world and wanting to keep a certain distance from it, is to be aware of the manufactured elements of those prizes. It is great to be nominated, it's great to win prizes. I would be a liar to say the opposite. For your confidence, for your ego, all those things matter. But you also realise that in those prizes they are not necessarily picking the best writing. To give you an example from another art form: I imagine winning something like an Academy Award would be a wonderful thing. But I've seen Academy Awards for years and I know they don't pick the best films – that the best films occur outside that system. And I think there is a similar system with the Booker Prize. But to be even short-listed, for me was a surprise and it was a very wonderful moment when I heard about it. I think if you start chasing those things, you end up chasing your own tail. And also they start changing your writing. You start thinking, am I writing the books that I want to write or am I writing for this audience?

Would you like to discuss your new book?

It is not an accident that I started writing *Barracuda* just after *The Slap*. The book is about how a swimmer deals with failure. It is about a working class young boy's life, from thirteen to his middle thirties, who has a phenomenal talent at swimming. Growing up in Australia, it's impossible not to think about sports. And I have always thought about sports people that I both admired and envied. Because a writer may win a Booker Prize, may win an award, but that voice of self-doubt never goes away, as he wonders, am I truly any good? Whereas with a sports-person, a swimmer, if he is the first to hit the tiles, he knows he is the best in the world. That's what led me to the story. So the book is about a swimmer, but it's also about success and failure and how you can come back from failure.

So, have you departed from your familiar themes? Is your hero Australian?

There is still a connection to my past. I don't think you ever completely break from it – that hasn't been my experience. My hero's mother is a second generation Greek and his father is Irish-Scottish-Australian. In a way I thought I wanted to create a character that had a foot in the old world.

Let's talk a bit about criticism now. Would you attribute various negative reviews and criticism of your work to the fact that you are a popular writer, given that usually best sellers annoy critics and they make them suspicious?

You've got to remember that I've been doing this since my early twenties. This is what I do, this is my craft. I still read criticism, because I'm still a reader, and as such I think criticism is important. There is nothing criticism can teach me as a writer. I know I'm talking to someone who is a critic, but as a writer what can I learn?

One negative review about The Slap *said that, a gay person with no kids cannot speak convincingly about family life and bringing up kids. How do you respond to this?*

That review, which I read, epitomises for me more the distance between the critic and the writer than that particular point of view. Everybody who works as a writer of fiction knows that what you do is you exert, you use your imagination. Obviously this lady reviewer was trapped in identity policy versus authenticity that no longer makes sense for me, and has not made sense for me for about twenty years. I don't think you have to be a gay man to write about Taktsis, for example. I don't think you have to be a female to write about a woman. I'm happy to write about Aboriginal characters. I think there are certain politics that come into play when you write about difference. But really those arguments are so spent and they have been so destructive for creative and imaginative writing. They have been so destructive for political argument that I just want them to be laid to rest. I am not interested in those politics any more.

Of all the reviews and criticism written about your books so far, has nothing at all been useful for you?

No. Criticism generally has. I still read criticism but it hasn't helped me in my work. Because, firstly, it takes you years to be able to read every positive criticism objectively. Secondly, you can't separate critical responses from those very things you were talking about before. The dissolving of the space between your ego and the critical view may be very fine. I can't do it. You can't just do criticism of yourself objectively. I can read criticism of anyone else, I can learn criticism from that way, but in terms of your own writing it is foolish to expect that artists are going to respond to criticism as anything but a kind of personal loss.

So how do you react to criticism overall, regardless of whether it is positive or negative? Does it leave you indifferent?

No, it's not that it leaves me indifferent – and maybe this is a weakness in me, I have to be honest – but I feel that, whether it's a glorifying or a negative review, in the end the experience is the same – it is a distraction. It just makes me think how much of this is true, how much of this is authentic and I do take on. As I said, I can't read it objectively. This is not a criticism of criticism. By my bedside table at the moment I've got three books of literary criticism which I read, because it engages my mind, it makes me think about what I do. But it is difficult to read about your own work because you can't have that objectivity you need to reading it. It's not useless to the reader of my work, but for the writers themselves it's of little help. And in the actual craft, in the actual working day of your life, it doesn't contribute anything. And so the decision I've made is that I actually read as little about myself as possible. I never Google because you get distracted from the actual work, you get distracted by questions of ego and other similar questions.

Doesn't criticism reflect, in a way, the public's attitude, the average reader?

I'm not writing for the average reader. I'm writing for myself, from the very beginning. Every time I hear a writer saying they are writing for someone else I think that is crap. If I were a selfless man I would be a teacher.

So you don't care how the average reader reacts, whether they like or dislike your work?

It's very satisfying, of course it is when you get readers who respond to your work. Of course. I would be a liar to say I'm not enjoying that.

You may enjoy the act of writing as such, but you don't write in order to read yourself, you write for other people to read your work.

That's true, but I don't have an average reader. I mean I don't go, this is the average reader. The closest I come to is my partner Wayne, but even there... The reader, for me as a writer, is unknowable. The reader is a stranger. Of course I want a book that is going to mean something, that is going to have an effect, but it would be a lie to tell you I sit down and think of the reader. Because the danger you have with the reader is this: you then start compromising your work with this chain of thinking, which can really poison your work, it can poison your intentions.

5
IDENTITY

Did you go to Greek school?
Yes I went to Greek school where the well known poet Dimitris Tsaloumas was my teacher for a while.

Let's talk about the issue of "Greekness." Reading your novels one has the feeling that – consciously or subconsciously, directly or indirectly – you are attempting to do one thing: to explore and define your ethnic and cultural identity. What exactly is "Greekness" for you?

Remember this: given that for a long time my notion of "Greekness" and what being "Greek" was so bound up with the notion of the family and could not be separated from it, when I felt I had to become independent, to reject or to cut away myself from the family, it felt inevitable that I had to separate myself from "Greekness." By which what I really meant was that I had to cut myself of from the family, for a period, in order to survive. That was a very hard thing to do, but it was necessary. Otherwise, I felt, I wasn't going to survive. Because I didn't have the tools and I didn't have an understanding of where that separation laid between those two categories, that was a struggle. So, for me, "Greekness" was family and family was "Greekness." And part of what's being happening in my books it is me trying to trace what that separation might mean. Sometimes I respond to realities of Greece and "Greekness" and sometimes I respond to the notion of Greece and being Greek. Does that make sense?

I have a feeling that you are still trying to sort things out, regarding your cultural identity, because it preoccupies you all the time in your books. Where do you attribute this obsession?

You've got me in a really interesting moment now, because I was just thinking about the book I'm working on now, where the character is still Greek because his mother is Greek...

See what I mean? Most of your characters are non-Australian...

But what exactly makes an Australian character?

I mean you overdo it with the Greek element in your books, despite the fact that you were born here.

The *Jesus Man* deals with an Italian family, but I use a lot of Greek elements there too. It is completely instinctual. This is the cultural world I know and that's coming through.

Why don't you use Australian characters? Don't you find them interesting?

I do find them interesting when they are put up in relationships to other things that go around them. For the movie *The Slap*, three of the characters are Greek, five aren't. Maybe that's a really interesting question that you are asking and one of the responses to it is to ask, who has possession, who has rights to this notion of "Greekness." But it's true that I can't get away from it.

Which means that, regardless of what you claim (i.e. that you are neither Greek nor Australian), deep down you are Greek.

The important thing to realise is that it's always subconscious when you come to actually drafting and writing. It's not that I'm sitting down going, ah I want to write about ethnicity – there are things that come to me. But you are right. There is still something I'm exploring about what it means to be Greek and Australian. I mean, I can't separate the two. The next novel I'm thinking of writing is a historical novel set at the beginning of the twentieth century. That maybe a way of freeing up myself from those concerns. Because I'm at a stage of my life now where I've had certain contentment and I don't feel the urgency of those questions as strongly as in previous years. Now there are other urgent questions that I'm beginning to explore.

If you are neither Greek nor Australian, could it be a deeper existential problem, or is it perhaps an interesting literary subject you are cleverly exploiting?

I'm turning in the last couple of years to a lot of books that were really important to me when I was a late teenager. People like Camus, Sartre, and I think Existentialism is the central philosophy that had really an influence on me. There was a long period where Existentialism was almost a dirty word in Australia. I don't know what the situation was in Greece but I think postmodern and poststructuralist criticism were really dominant in the late eighties and nineties when I came to adulthood as a writer. I was very suspicious of Existentialism or I read it suspiciously but I got influenced by that kind of thinking. Now, for me, all that reading I did for 15-20 years is ephemeral, it doesn't actually say anything. What I return to is the question of *how to be a good man in a world without values and principles.* This is a fundamental question for me that I want to explore through my writing. So, in a way, I'm quite proud to take on that question of Existentialism. As I said, it was conceived for a long period as a spent force, as no longer an important issue. I no longer believe that. I think it still is a central question for me in a world where I have lost my faith in Communism, where I lost my faith in God, where there is no certainty. How do I live, how do I live an ethical life, how do I become an ethical man, how do I become a good writer?

It is obvious that you dislike labels. But do you truly believe that people can actually live without identities (ethnic, cultural, racial, sexual, religious, etc) when this has never happened in recorded human history? But even if we could have in the future a "uniform humanity", how would this help humankind?

You've got to make a very clear distinction between Christos Tsiolkas, the man, and the Christos Tsiolkas, the writer. As a man, I think that of course identities are important, in the sense that how else do you define yourself and make sense of who you are and how you live. So they are crucial, in order of creating a narrative for yourself, in order just to communicate in the world. But as a writer, what I was reacting to was that, within identity there are borders and barriers that it's important to challenge, to break these barriers and also to question, to challenge.

The point of my question was this: Let's assume that barriers are broken like the Berlin wall was brought down. Do you think that humanity will be freer and happier? In other words, what's the benefit of a globalised world?

For me, when I talk about the barriers of identity, they are not necessarily akin to a globalised nirvana of a borderless state. I don't think that exists and I don't know how that would be possible.

But traditional characteristics are collapsing and are being replaced by multinationals like McDonalds everywhere. So where are we going to end up?

I don't know where we are going to end up. I'm trying to think through the young man who wrote *Loaded*. My feelings about labels and my feelings about identity at that time were that they were straight-jackets. So I was reacting against a uniform notion of what it was to be Greek or homosexual, of what it was to be working class. So it's in that light that the struggle against identity was important to me. You are asking a political question now about globalisation, which is not reducible to questions of identity. My intention was never to say that what I wanted was some kind of multi-*gelati* world. It doesn't matter what you are, it doesn't matter what you believe, it doesn't matter what your values are, everything is the same. I was saying that I wanted a less straight-jacketed a way of being in the world. On that question of globalisation, one area where it is confusing for me is – because I'm a child of migrants and because Australian identity has never been clear-cut, and because of growing up here feeling like a wog, and feeling that I was not Australian – has meant that the question of where do I belong has never quite left me. And I do feel like, maybe, a person of my experience is only conceivable within a globalised world.

Would you feel comfortable being characterised as cosmopolitan?

I'm not going to give you an answer, yes or no, to that one. I don't think the term "cosmopolitan" is enough to describe the experiences and the politics that I'm talking about. I think where for me the notion of "cosmopolitan" is interesting and complicated and has value, is that I do think that my experiences are very urban experiences. Both from my sexuality and from being questions of *migration, diaspora* and *class* – that it is in the urban centres where I feel most at home. I think that there is something about the *urban* that fascinates me and goes right back to your question about the city. Because it is the cities where outsiders fled to across history. The cities are a very interesting site of friction, collision and collaboration. In that sense and only that sense do I feel affinity with other writers who use this term. But in and of itself, I don't think it's enough to define yourself as "cosmopolitan." Again it comes back to questions of *class*. It's a very hard thing to feel that you have that freedom to exist anywhere in the world, it's not a possibility that is given to many people. I just think that there is something for me in the notion of being cosmopolitan, but I tend to be very suspicious of how a lot of other writers and critics have used that term. Where my suspicion comes from is that cosmopolitanism is a very bourgeois notion of identity. But the question of the *urban* is historically important for me. That you create, subconsciously, places to escape.

6

THE STATE OF HUMANITY

(Decadence, materialism, spirituality, ethics, racism, animal liberation, intellectuals, media)

Today not only Europe but the whole of the western world is in decline. How and where do we have to turn to for a new renaissance

There is a great famous quote – that I heard about a few weeks ago and has stayed with me – which was that, it is easier for us to imagine the end of the world than it is to measure the end of Capitalism. So I think it is very true a kind of "bereavement", that's the word I would use here, which comes to that notion of the decline. We are through the end of empires that collapsed at the end of the 20th century through two very devastating global wars and it's not a surprise. It is going to be a very painful experience.

What do you attribute it to?

I attribute it to the end of Imperialism, a consequence of which is that Europeans are going out to redefine the world. I mean, Capitalism has infected writing and art. Is it possible to think of a non-commercial space for art at the moment? I'm very suspicious about that, because it seems we are all affected by the materialistic spirit. I think if you talk to writers or artists, they feel trapped – it's like a miasma in the world. For me, it's not anything profound. I'm not a seer, I can't see the future. One thing that I have begun to do is to start looking up to Asia – to start reading Asian literature, to start thinking about a culture that existed pre-Europe and is different to Europe. That's just at an individual space that has been really important for rethinking about my project and what I am as a Greek-

Australian or as an Australian. To be honest, I find an excitement in being in Asia at the moment that I no longer feel when I'm in Europe.

But even in Asia, people are not indifferent to materialism. The worship of money has infected them too.

Of course. I accept that, even in a Communist country like China, Capitalism is the way that works. Markets are incredibly liberal in making money and that is the main concern of the government, of the state. I guess, what Asia doesn't have is the kind of imperialist project. It feels different to the way the Europeans think, the notion that it was our destiny to recreate the world and that we are the centre of the world. I think there is a freedom away from that that I experience when I'm in Asia. Maybe that's because I'm a non-Asian in Asia, but I find it incredibly refreshing. It doesn't feel as arrogant and it doesn't feel as dominating. Even though I have an internal and an ongoing battle with notions of spirituality, of God in my head, there is something about the eastern traditions that are really important. I think one of the reasons why Kazantzakis is a hero for me, is because he comes from Greece, from Crete, and he battled with his demons of what God is and battled with God in his writing. There is something tantalizing about that and a path that I think I want to take in the future. But I've grown up in Australia and the notion of being more Asian than European started to get some meaning. I noticed, last time I was in Europe, and while coming back and being in Bangkok was just such a relief – the smells, the food, the faces – I thought thank God I'm near home. And I thought, does this mean that's where I've shed my European skin then?

At other times artists and intellectuals were more influential in their societies and the world, but not anymore. Why is that?

Again, it is the age of the markets – the merchant is king. It's not the poet, it's not the priest. The merchant cast is the dominant cast. Don't forget too that this notion of the philosopher, intellectual, artist, I wonder how much of that was a product of modernism as well. I mean, you look back, before the 18th century, and most artists made their living by having a patron. I'm just wondering if what we are seeing is a transformation in the role of what being an artist means. But that role has been transforming the centuries, the experience of the 20th century man of letters who believed that he or she would change the world. For me, coming to adulthood in my writing, part of the problem now is that after the failure of Communism, after the failure of these great narratives that were meant to answer the evils of the world, they created their own evils. And it's harder for me to assume that public space. I understand why artists may want to step away from that kind of role. I think that role – to be public figures – is still important. I genuinely understand their reservations. Sartre was a good example. Some of his writing on the Soviet Union is rubbish. What I mean is that although I was born a generation after that, I still accuse myself of this all the time for prevaricating, for not being forthright in my opinions. So, all I have is questions, lots of questions.

But you've been involved quite a bit in public debates, much more than other writers.

Of course. I still want to do that, but I also want to make sure that I'm not seduced by the cult of celebrity. One of the things I hate at the moment in the English speaking world, is the dominance of opinion in the press and the media, where writers, filmmakers or actors come on and give us their opinion on what is happening in Syria. And you know these people have no fucking idea of what is happening in the Middle East! So, you've got to be very careful that you are not seduced by the media.

So where do you draw the line between your devotion to your private artistic work and your responsibility to social issues?

In some ways that line shifts for me. The first thing that came to my head was that you have to be sure, as an artist, that when it comes to the role of your public life, that you are speaking from a position of knowledge. That is not the same as speaking about fiction. So if I do have knowledge of the issue and the issue is important to me beyond 24 hours or a week, and is something that animates me, then I will intervene. But I am much more comfortable in my private space, concentrating on my work. Even though I have great respect for those intellectuals who become part of political culture – and I mean political in the broader sense – I don't think I have those skills or talents. But there are issues that will make me come out of silence. And I hope that never changes.

It is true that most media want to take advantage of artists, for marketing purposes – to sell newspapers, etc.

You can't imagine the number of times I had people from the newspapers contact me, to give my opinion on something... You could do that. But who would really need to know Christos Tsiolkas' opinion? If it were about education, I would turn to speak up, because it's actually important to me. If it's about racism I will speak up, because that's very important to me. But, just to give you an example, the other day it was about young people and violence in the city. And I thought, well I have an opinion but I don't want to be into that debate, because that's a 24 hour issue.

In your books you seem to be a defender of the marginalised, the poor and unlucky people of this world. But when some of these people somehow manage to become powerful, they tend to become equally unjust and oppressive to their fellow humans beings. So how do you justify your position – especially now that you yourself have changed roles and have become a celebrity?

I think *The Slap* was very much a novel that emerged from me, realising that, even though I am very proud of my left-wing and working class heritage, I could no longer claim that, as the fact is I'm a bourgeois man now. I think *The Slap* was the beginning of that process of me writing a different world. It doesn't mean that I've changed ideas, but I am much more conscious that I can't speak with an authority or an authenticity that I may have felt when I was younger about certain things. However, the notion of the outsider and the marginal has been such a kick and such a fire, in terms of the writing I do, that I don't think I will ever defect from that. The worst thing to do is to betray that.

In one of your interviews you've said: "Another sign of our world's decadence is that we can slaughter animals with such a grandiose, horrible, massive and effective way, without looking them once in the eye." Does this mean that you are in favour of animal euthanasia or the prohibition of animal slaughter?

One of the most profound essays I've read was Peter Singer's about animal liberation, and even though I'm an hypocrite and I don't live the ethics of this, I think he is absolutely right. I'm not someone who believes in a transcendental, an anthropomorphic God who has created us in his own image. I let that go a long time ago. So, the suffering that humans cause on animals is truly horrific. I have told my mother, and she has laughed, that I would have loved to have my own animals and slaughter them – and she said, you would be terrible at it!

How do you mean?

Because that's the most humane way of doing it, rather than having these big abattoirs and factory farms.

But isn't killing the same?

It's about the way they treat animals. I don't have a problem with killing animals. That's part of how you treat the world. But you have a huge problem when treating another being abominably. It's as simple as that. There's nothing very profound in it, but I'm very wary of the hypocrisy.

Because the other argument is that, when there is so much human suffering in the world, animal suffering seems unimportant.

That's my argument. I'm not a vegetarian and in the end the suffering of humans is more important. All I'm saying is that there is a profound truth in Singer's essay. I've had lots of arguments with atheist friends of mine about that essay, because they believe that humans are more important than other animals. I tell them, well, yes, you can hold that view, but in the end that's a theological, a religious view.

Do you think human principles and values are eternal or variable?

I believe we need to be instructed by history – and history teaches us that change is the very essence of society – but I do still struggle and want, or have to act in a way that I believe there are things that are universal. Are they eternal? That's not necessary the same thing. As an artist I want to believe that I can speak to something called the "universal." That I can talk about love in a certain way that anyone who reads it can understand that action – the notion of social justice. I think morality is so bound, culturally and historically, but the striving for good is human, is universal. Our definition of what the "good" is can change, depending on history, culture, geography. But the notion of struggling for the "good" is something that we all acknowledge. I have found, in my own life, that I'm returning more and more to the ancients, in terms of guidance. When I was answering questions to you last time, you asked me about anger in my writing – especially in *Loaded*. And just recently I read Seneca on anger – a phenomenal read. He is very influenced by Stoic philosophy, which is Greek Hellenistic philosophy. Maybe ponder your question, because he is very suspicious of anger. He doesn't think that good reasoning can arise from any anger. I'm long winded. What I wanted to say was that, for me, is quite heartening to go back to ancient writers and discover that their work makes sense of my contemporary reality. It does make me think that there *is* something called the "universal." The second thing coming from your question – especially when it comes to religion or notions of spirituality – is that we are so used now to a "supermarket" mode of belief that, look, I'll take this from Buddhism, I'll take this from Christianity, I'll take this from Aboriginal philosophy and the things that I don't like I'll discard. I think that's really dangerous, intellectually vapid and arrogant of us. When I read the ancient texts, when I read religious texts, I have my intellectual arguments with them, but what I'm most conscious of is my shortcomings, my weaknesses. So you read the Stoics and there is so much of Stoicism that I think is fascinating and instructive for me, but I'm also constantly aware, reading them, of how I fall short of their philosophy. That's also true when I read Buddhist texts, it's very true when I read St. Paul.

In your books you talk a lot about racism and condemn it. However, racism does not characterise a particular race or culture but everybody. It is ingrained in human nature, like hate, injustice, etc. So, why this blame game?

I think you have got to the very heart of something that is an obsession of mine and I'm still trying to work through in my writing. I was very surprised in a lot of the reactions in Europe to *The Slap* and its translations. English, Scottish, French and German critics were asking me about why are my characters so racist, which was confusing to me. This comment, I think, comes from a certain bourgeois liberal ascendency in Europe, about how they view themselves and the world by not admitting to their own xenophobia or fears, etc. Now, in terms of racism, I'm becoming more and more aware of how the fear of the stranger is another universal characteristic that you see when you travel through China. You will also see it in Japan, you will see it in so many cultures. It's something that troubles me, because it remains unresolved as they are trying to generalise that everyone is racist, so why does it matter? I was brought in a country that did a particularly horrific misappropriation of territory and destroyed a culture because of racist politics. So the racism of someone calling me "wog" is not equivalent to that of someone stealing a child, because a mother is Aboriginal. It's within those rifts that I'm still fascinated by racists. To use the European example, I don't think someone being insulted for wearing a hijab is equivalent to being put into Auschwitz. But trying to work out what those differences and similarities are is still an animating project for me. That's where racism is still important, because I look back in my life and go, oh well, I got called a wog a bit, I experienced some of it, but really it wasn't the end of the world. But I also know that sometimes racism can actually create the most inhuman of crimes.

7

RELIGION AND DEATH

In your books you give the impression that you are an atheist and nihilist. However, in some of your interviews you've claimed that you try to retain some of the conventions of the Greek Orthodox faith. What exactly is happening – do you or don't you believe in God?

I am an agnostic. I am trapped in a relationship to God where I want to believe.

Why don't you believe in God?

The reason I'm hesitating to answer is because this is a huge question and I feel I will never answer it. I have come to an understanding that there is no monotheist God and I don't believe in that. I don't believe that there is a transcendental God high in the heavens who is a rational being and has judgement of the world. I don't believe that. But I have a sense of the soul and what I'm trying to discover is what my understanding of that aspect of humanity is. What is the soul, what is owed to the soul, what is a calling that emerges from that understanding?

Do you believe that the soul is eternal?

I think I'm still trying to answer that question for myself. I know that my soul, what I understand of it, is not eternal. I understand that. I think a lot of people actually confuse that – the notion of the soul with their own individual relationship to the soul. I'm trying to explore that issue. But maybe the best thing to say to you is I don't know yet. I'm still exploring it. And I want to explore it because I think that there is something there worth exploring. I worry that if you let go of any notion of faith and the soul, you open a door possibly to inhumanity. I'm not sure of that either. I'm still exploring it as well. I'm just trying to explain to you why that question is still important to me.

For you, to have read thoroughly books such as the Bible and the Koran, it means that there was a deeper need in you to discover various things. However, this uncertainty and dilemmas, about believing in God, are obvious in The Jesus Man.

I think that's partly because I grew up in the Christian tradition where there was a struggle with the body that always led me to take a heretical stance against Christianity and Judaism, as those two religions are so against the body, desire and pleasure. And I think the young man who wrote *The Jesus Man* and *Loaded* was really struggling with that very profoundly. Whereas now I'm probably less curious or less angry.

How do you explain that in a holy book like the Bible, there is such a purely erotic book like The Song of Solomon?

I went through a period where I had rejected all spirituality and Christianity. So going back now to the Bible, as an older person and hopefully a little bit wiser, you realise that this was not written by the hand of God. There are contradictions in the Bible and I enjoy those discoveries. I don't need them to make sense. One of the things that I love in the Bible is because it doesn't make sense. And because it doesn't make sense, it makes me believe that there is a possibility of a reconciliation with God, if you like. Because God is not the truth of the God I grew up with.

How has your reading of the holy scriptures influenced you, and how does religion influence our lives?

The returning to the Bible and the reading of the Koran were also part of looking at the language. The language of the Bible, the language of the Torah, the language of St. Paul's letters, the language of the Koran is a particular kind of language which I wanted to think about when I was writing *Dead Europe*. The other thing is that, as I said, there had been this break for a long time with the notion of the spirit and the notion of religion, and within that break there was this void that was filled by something that was called Marxism, Communism. As I became an apostate with that faith as well, that led me back to thinking about religion again. Both politics and religion helped me to understand the similarities between them and what I was searching for from the beginning, and possibly that I was going to find it in religion rather than in politics. So that's the world that I approached when I was writing *Dead Europe*. I think *Dead Europe* is a lament, it is about the loss of faith. You want to go back and rewrite your books. What I was trying to do was to say that political faith and religious faith are so entwined in European history that it's impossible to separate them.

Were you baptised?

I was baptised (*laughter*).

Do you go to the Greek Orthodox Church at all?

I do go. Because I find that being in that space and praying is incredibly important to me. So, for example, my dad being ill recently, I've gone to church and I lit the candles, I perform the rituals and I find them incredibly comforting. But at the same time, having being to other parts of the world, if someone's is ill I would go into a temple or a mosque and I perform a prayer. But of all the religions, the Orthodox Church is the one I understand better and it's most comfortable going in. In my mid and late twenties, and in a very difficult point in my life, I was working across the road from a Cathedral. As I was a very unhappy man at that point, I remember one lunchtime going in and allowing myself to pray, it was such a comforting experience. It wasn't just comfort. It was so important to me, perhaps because it was the beginning of the seed of wondering if I had being lax with attending to the question of the soul.

How can an agnostic pray when he doubts about the existence of God?

Because what I realised at that moment – and I think the eastern traditions understand this much better than the western traditions – is that prayer is in some ways a form of meditation. I'm not an expert, but I would think that some eastern philosophers would say that the act of meditation, while you are experiencing meditation, is independent to the question of whether God does or does not exist. Whereas for us, coming from a Christian and Judaic-Christian-Islamic tradition, it is something hard to understand. Sometimes I wonder whether growing up in Orthodoxy, and because of the history of Orthodoxy, it has made us more open to some of those Eastern notions of prayer.

Of what I know about Eastern traditions, they do believe in the existence of a supreme being – even if they don't necessarily call it "God."

I know and I understand that. What I mean is that if a Buddhist monk in Bangkok saw me meditating, he would not ask me, do you believe in God my son?

Do you think that, overall, spirituality is beneficial for people's well-being?

One of my big concerns is that, at the moment, there is a very strong atheist movement and this belief that the scientific and rational world view is the right view for a globalised secular age, according to people like Richard Dawkins, Christopher Hitchens and others. My worry, as I said before, is that if you don't annex spirituality to human concern, you leave a door open to an inhumanity, and that really worries me.

What is your stance on death?

I'm not afraid of death. However, I'm now a man in my middle-age and conscious of the frailty of the body, that the body is decaying. And I really want to grow older with Wayne – that's important to me. I don't have the fear of death. For all my spiritual wavering and obsession with these questions, I do believe that whatever happens in afterlife is of no use to me, as Christos Tsiolkas. I have been raised in a culture – and I mean Australian rather than Greek culture – that is not very good talking about death; something which is really true. And maybe because my father is dying at the moment, I've been thinking about this question a lot. I believe it's really important to come to some peace with the notion of death.

Do metaphysical issues, such as life after death and heaven or hell, concern you at all?

No, no, not any more. When I was younger I was terrified of hell, but I think they are myths. Very strongly now I don't believe in the notion of heaven and hell. And there is a bit of that in *Dead Europe* where Colin is talking to Isaac in bed, which probably comes closest to what I believe. I actually think that if I do die and there is a hell, I would take hell over heaven, because I would have no faith in a God who created these two distinct worlds. There are some myths from religion that I do feel at peace of having discarded, as they no longer frighten or animate me. I no longer have a fear nor an interest in them; and heaven and hell is one of those.

What is the meaning of life for you?

To be a good man. To try as hard as I can to be a man who is honourable in his relationships with other people. The two things I really fear are greed and bitterness. Those are the kind of things I want to struggle against, because I think they are poisonous for the soul.

What do you mean by "bitterness"?

That you are owed more than you have been given. One of the things I have learnt – even small as it may be, having observed enough people and older people around me – is that I do think that bitterness is a very destructive and poisonous element. And greed is the same too.

Would you like to be remembered more as a good person or a good writer?

Of course I want to be remembered as a writer, because there is the ego. I would be a liar to say the opposite. But then I want my nieces to remember their relationship with their uncle, or Wayne to remember his relationship with his partner. I want those things. So I do hope I will be remembered as a writer.

Why do you think there is so much suffering in the world and whose fault is it? Do you believe in the original sin?

I think it has been a relief to no longer blame God for suffering.

In your earlier novels you attribute suffering more or less to the original sin.

As I have said to you earlier, in some ways I see those first three novels as a trilogy now which are about the loss of faith – political and religious faith. Now I'm talking to you as a forty six year old man who is disturbed by the question of suffering. But what I'm saying is that, at this point of my life, I no longer blame God for it. And this is again where I've been influenced by Eastern traditions – I think suffering is part of being human. So we all must learn how to make our way in a world of suffering. But I also think that there are unjust, evil and malevolent creations of suffering that are human made.

Isn't suffering necessary to make us better human beings?

Understanding suffering in that context is really important, but then there are examples of suffering which none of those arguments apply. One of the most outstanding examinations of that would be certain accounts of being in death camps such as those of Primo Levi (*If this is a Man* and *The Truce*). What does starvation teach a four year old child in a refugee camp? We should strive to be good, to not allow metaphysical concerns around suffering to blind us and prevent us from changing, ameliorating ourselves.

If you had the power to change something in the world that would make a noticeable difference to people's lives, what would that be?

The nature of such a question makes you confront exactly what is happiness and what true happiness comes from. The thing that comes to my mind, as an answer to that, is linked to the notion of real education. That I would want everyone in the world to have the experience, for at least a period of time, of a real education – not a compromised education. If we had the opportunity to do that, it would be a very different world.

8

LOADED

How do you explain the following contradiction in your introduction of the Greek edition of Loaded?: *"When I was writing this book, I realise now, I was writing it for a Greek readership and I was writing angrily"?*

When I wrote that "Introduction" I was very conscious of the fact that the Greek edition of *Loaded* was coming out and I actually asked if I could do such an introduction. Why? Because I knew my parents were going to read it for the first time and, in a lot of ways, that introduction is directed to my parents. Does that make sense now? That was the audience I had in mind – Mum and Dad. Because I knew it would be a very shocking book for them.

You've said that you wrote this novel in a state of anger. Is this true and why?

In many ways it is difficult to recollect exactly the man I was when I was writing *Loaded*. I was angry, certainly, it felt for a long time that anger was the necessary fuel, the necessary fuel, if you like, by which I could make my "escape" from the traditional patriarchal network of Greek familial and social ties. The anger I carried was certainly destructive but at the same time it was also paradoxically productive. I think we are scared of young men's anger – and this is now not only something about being "Greek" or "Greek-Australian." Certainly the fears we have are legitimate. We all know the violence and aggression that young men can wreak to others and themselves. But anger can also allow one to move forward, to take control of one's life, to not acquiesce and be subservient. It is only with the onset of my middle years that I can see that more clearly now. When I was writing *Loaded*, I was closer to Ari's age; I could see the necessity of the anger but I didn't know how to control it, how to tame it. (My problem, however, was never directing that anger and fury to others, I internalised it and hurt myself). I watch my friends with young sons now and I want to say to them two things: Don't be so hard on them. Teach them how to manage anger.

In the introduction to the Greek edition of Loaded, *as if apologising for some of its violent scenes, you write: "If I sound polemic it is because some things are dealt only with anger." How did you mean, given that anger can relieve tension but cannot resolve problems – it can only make them worse. I mean, what did you have in mind, what reaction did you expect from the reader?*

I know you have questioned me on this before, but I am sincere when I tell you that when I was writing *Loaded* I wasn't thinking of the reaction of the reader at all. I wanted to know if I had it in me to write a book, if I could do it. And when you are writing your first novel, you don't imagine it occurring again. So I put in all of who I was at that point in my mid-twenties. I wrote it in almost a euphoria. You are right, anger can't resolve problems, it must be tempered by empathy and insight. But if I hadn't utilised the depth of my anger I would have never left home, never confronted the homophobia of the Greek and the Aussie communities, I would have continued to hurt and despise myself. I should acknowledge that at around the time I started work on *Loaded*, I had read Celine's work. That was powerfully influential for me. Even though I hope my personal ethics are a million miles removed from Celine's fascism, I was so excited to read a novelist who could make art from fury, from anger. There is a fearlessness there that I still respond to.

This novel continues to baffle me a bit. I mean the book is not of a polemic nature. Although Ari is facing multiple identity crisis (cultural, sexual, existential), he is not exactly an angry but rather a timid young man who feels more comfortable in being apathetic and inactive. This self-confessional narrative is both a protest and a cry for help. Why this ambiguity and why isn't he trying to help himself?

You have to understand that in many ways my first three novels were written under the sign of the collapse of Communism. I chose the left and left politics from a very young age, from the middle of my high school years, and I was heavily influenced by Marxist theory and radical politics. But by the time I came to writing *Loaded*, Communism had collapsed and the certainties of politics had been crushed. It felt false, at that historic moment, to create a way forward, to invest in hope for Ari. I wasn't feeling hopeful, I was feeling crushed. I have referred elsewhere to *Loaded*, *The Jesus Man* and *Dead Europe* as a kind of trilogy where I was working through my despair with the collapse of the revolutionary project. That of course sounds too grand for what is, as you say, a self-confessional narrative, but I am trying to think back to how I came to write in the way I did. The truth is that Ari doesn't know how to help himself because at that point in my life neither did I.

Ari is also ambivalent in his sexual orientation. He is presented as both straight and gay. What exactly is he and why this ambivalence?

O, maybe I am not made for these times. I do believe that we are truly polymorphous perverse creatures and that bisexuality is a possibility for all of us. At the time I was writing *Loaded* you must understand that an older sexual politics was being challenged by a new "queer" politics. That was a very strong influence on me. Also, Ari is a very young man, just leaving adolescence, and the truth of that period in a young homosexual man's life is that one is still wanting to assert their masculinity and masculinity is identified strongly with heterosexuality. Ari's struggle is reconciling his masculinity with his sexuality and so there is a part of himself that desires to be "straight" because that is how he proves his masculinity. Even at forty-six years of age I don't think I have completely overcome such an equation in my own life. I still – sorry to be blunt –

have a problem with being "fucked", am much more comfortable with being the active partner in intercourse. I am not proud of this, I think it speaks to my not overcoming my masculine conditioning. But that is the truth. Ambivalence is exactly what I wanted to convey in the novel and I think in all my work.

Ari admires his close friend Johnny, who is a transvestite and considers him his guru, but disapproves of his extreme behaviour. Where do you attribute this and many of his other contradictions?

Johnny-Toula is the real hero of the book, I have always said this. Johnny is the brave character, Johnny is the one who lives their reality – including their sexual reality openly. Ari doesn't have the courage to do that. I think the transvestite/transsexual is always the bravest of the sexual outlaws. They do not pretend and they do not hide. Ari's disapproval indicates something of his moral cowardice. I think he is wrong to object to Toula's daring. One regret I have about the novel is that I made Toula a "victim", suggested a level of incest and abuse that I think was now a mistake. The damage of "abuse" doesn't need to be there to "explain" Johnny. I'm still glad I wrote that character.

Would you agree that the major causes of Ari's existential crisis are (i) boredom (which derives from a lack of purpose and meaning in life) and (ii) loneliness (that is, a deeper lack of communication)?

Ari's problem is that alternatives and possibilities for challenging and rejecting corporate gendered, racial and sexual identity have proven failures or proven impossible. You are right, he is timid. George presents a possibility for transformation but Ari refuses to seize that possibility. I have a fantasy of returning to Ari one day as a character, to write a kind of sequel. He is an alter-ego. I think I have said this to you already. But I have been fortunate in my life to discover love. It is through my love for Wayne that I have learnt to negotiate the contradictions that tear Ari apart. But, as I have said above, at the time of writing *Loaded*, with the collapse of politics, I didn't know how to write a love story without it seeming sentimental or false. That is still a challenge for me. I want to write that book one day. Do not forget that I wrote *Loaded* having experienced the recession of the early nineties and that Ari is an unemployed young man. After so many years of economic prosperity in Australia, I think we have forgotten how destructive the possibility of permanent unemployment or under-employment can be. Ari can't see a future, because that was the truth for so many people I knew back then. It was literally soul-destroying. People suicided, used drugs, became mad, in order to find a way out of that experience. I have just come back from Greece where I am reminded of the tragedy of unemployment again. It corrodes the soul, my friend. In a capitalist world the idea that you will never experience a fulfilling working life is a kind of death. Don't forget that too is part of Ari's experience.

Ari is an introvert but not a loner, who doesn't trust language and communication because he is afraid to expose his sacred inner self (soul) as he says. Is this why he prefers escapism as a stance and/or reaction to life's adversities, through bodily experiences – sex, drugs, alcohol?

Yes, because when all political solutions have proven spent or empty, when all that is left is material excess and consumerism, then drugs and casual sex and the euphoria that comes from such experience feels more *real* than anything else around.

Ari is of the view that "we are screwed since childbirth", humanity has no hope whatsoever and the planet is doomed. I assume many people think and feel that way, regardless of their age. The number of psychiatric patients in the western world is a testimony to this. What is your view on this now?

I have learnt the importance of tenderness. Are we all fucked? Part of me still believes this, of course I do. I think we are all living a moment of abject disillusionment where even the word democracy has been fouled and corrupted. I think Ari would still hate this world. But age brings an awareness of complicity and age brings – if you are lucky – a certain human understanding. Tenderness and compassion are now important to me in the way they weren't when I was Ari's age. I understand what it means to fail now. Ari doesn't know this.

I know your passion for films. Loaded *has been made into a feature film. Do you sincerely believe that those novels that make it to the big screen – apart from adding to the writer's fame and promoting the book – actually justify the novel as such? My understanding is that rarely do we have a successful marriage of fiction and cinema. In most cases novels have been betrayed by the cinema. How comfortable do you feel about this intervention?*

Ah my friend, I can think of a dozen exceptions already. *Jules and Jim*, great novel, great film. *The Leopard, Les Enfants Terrible.* It's a good film. I was very fortunate.

In Greece, the scene which enraged most in the film Head On *– and resulted in vandalising the cinema – was the one where Johnny, the transvestite, tells a Turkish taxi-driver that "your great grandfather raped my great grandmother" and afterwards burst into laughter. Was this deliberately done to provoke?*

I find it laughable and I find it pathetic that such a scene can cause such an uproar. It is still one of the passages I have written that I am proud of – and as you must know, as a writer, we are our own worst critics. For me that scene, even as I wrote it, was a way of expressing something of the pleasure that I think is important to celebrate in growing up in a multi-racial, multi-ethnic urban environment. I am so glad that I went to a primary school where my friends could be Turkish, where I could go into their houses and realise that the racist stereotyping of the Turks by the Greeks was not the truth. Migration, in that way, is its own country and I am glad that I grew up in that "nationhood." Who are the people who object to that scene? They are the same cunts who vote for New Dawn in Greece. It was never meant to be provocative. It was meant to be joyous, it was meant to convey how in a multicultural diverse world we can shrug off the baggage of hatred and enmity that so blights our world. For that reason I am still proud of that scene.

9

THE JESUS MAN

In this novel you were trying, in many respects, to construct a more ambitious fictional composition. However, somewhere along the way you've lost the plot.

The problem with *The Jesus Man* in that respect is that I didn't have the necessary skills and craftsmanship for a writer at that point. My failure with *The Jesus Man* is that I should have done two, three or many more drafts to actually try and get to the essence of what I wanted to communicate in that book.

How many drafts did you do?

I can't remember. It was a handful and it should have been more. It should have been a work that I spent another year at least on – that's what I'm saying. But you learn from your experience. I didn't really know that at the time. *The Jesus Man* was where I learnt that. So one thing is that I should have spent more time with it. The other thing is that I concentrated more on the actual language. There were so many ideas flowing in my head and I didn't actually concentrate on the grip of what writing is – the words, the language. That was another lesson I took from *The Jesus Man*. What was I trying to do there? I'm going to be very honest with you. It feels such a long time ago that anything that I'm going to say about it would be with hindsight. I said to you already that the first three novels in a way, for me personally, feel like a bit of a trilogy about faith. I was trying to find a way in *The Jesus Man* to fight against a certain self-righteousness of my culture. To actually say that history has an effect on us all and we are products of history. And people do the most abject things, but it is important for a writer, for an artist, to understand the humanity of people in those worlds. So for me, Tommy is really damaged and he lacks courage, he is not a good man. But Lou, his younger brother's story is about coming to understanding the humanity in the man. I would also say that in a very strange way, this is where I don't think I was very effective. Because I didn't know enough about all this as a writer. I was trying to work out something about Christian ethics in the novel. That's why it was called *The Jesus Man*. Of course I was experimenting. I didn't want to write a straight-forward autobiographical novel, in the way that I had done in *Loaded*. I wanted to do something different.

But there are quite a few autobiographical elements in The Jesus Man.

You've got to remember that, for me, there is an element where you always do reach into yourself.

In this novel you are posing too many questions (existential, religious, metaphysical, philosophical, ethical, political) but without answering them. Instead one would say that you are creating even more questions along the way. Why do you avoid taking a stand?

It is true that I have tried to pose too many questions. With that book I was very conscious that I did want to leave a reader with questions – not that there was an answer to the questions I posed. But, in a way, I dealt with too much material in that. I was also wanting to write a book about economic rationalisation, as well as a book about the loss of faith, as well as a book about history and the dynamics of how it plays out in a family. There is enough material in each of those for one novel. And I didn't have the necessary skills and experience, the necessary talent at that time. There is an element where I will always feel a certain affection for *The Jesus Man,* because it is the child that is most ignored. This book got published in France this year. I was interested in that, because the French were responding to it in a different way to an Australian audience. In terms of my writing life and my life in general, I think it's good to have failure. *Dead Europe* would not be the novel it was if I had not experienced a humiliation that comes from the work that is rejected. There was a choice, I remember, right after *The Jesus Man* where I thought, do I give up writing and do something else, and I didn't make that choice. I made a choice to write and I'm really glad I did, but that experience of shame and humiliation is a really important thing to go through. If you are going to take this art seriously, you are going to have to be prepared to fail.

For the first and only time you introduce the "suicide" element in this novel. However, you don't give the impression that you condone it as a resolution to human problems. Can you talk a bit about this controversial issue? Where do you stand on the issue of suicide?

I'm speaking as an individual now. The experience of suicide is the thing that connects all of us as human. The experience of your choosing whether to end your life is something that we share across culture and across history. When I was young, I had a Greek friend of mine suicide and she wasn't given a Greek burial. I was only young but I saw the shame her parents had through that experience. I remember that was one of my first breaks where I realised, I fucking hated religion for what it did. So suicide then, from very young, became something that I may not necessarily have given myself over to, but I thought that the ethics of what suicide is became really important to me. Over the period of writing *The Jesus Man* two people that I was very close to, one suicided and one tried to kill himself. The question of who owns our lives is a fundamental human one. Suicide cannot be separated too from the question of sacrifice.

However most cultures and religions are against it, as they believe God gives life and God has the right to take it away.

My answer to that theological question is that God may have given us life – whatever God is and whoever God is – but has no right to claim it. I object to that Christian and Judaic ethics. If there is God and has given us life, he cannot ask of us that our lives belong to him any more. I'm with Prometheus. Gods may have created us but that doesn't mean we owe anything to them.

Do you think suicide is a brave or a cowardly act?

My experience of having lived through people's suicides is that it is an act of courage. That doesn't necessarily make it always a commendable act or a right act or a just act, because of what you leave behind. But to get to a point where you put the gun to your temple or the rope around your neck or the knife into your vein, to snuff out your life, requires an act of courage.

In The Jesus Man *you also introduce for the first time the "family curse" which is an ancient Greek motif – something which you explore even further in* Dead Europe. *Why does this element interest you so much? Do you see it as an interesting fictional device to utilise or is there much more to it?*

The notion of the "curse" is a very interesting device. What it allows you to play with is the idea of legacy and blood. It was through exploring with *The Jesus Man* – and again I probably didn't do this very well at all – the notion of a historic curse, because of the legacy of the Australian nation founded upon Aboriginal blood. I think there is something being Australian that I at least carry, which is accursed, because of this terrible historic event. One more reason why it's interesting for me to play with the "curse."

You also introduce here for the first time the political element, talking about how appallingly the Australian working class was treated by the conservative governments of the Liberal Party. Although it is implied that they are in a way responsible for Tommy's demise, because of creating unemployment, the overall handling of this political element in the novel seems awkward. Do you agree?

Again, for me those first three novels are about a loss of faith. And one of these losses was the belief in the working class and the belief in a Communist politics. I was trying to deal with that, as well in *The Jesus Man*. That's why I started off with the Whitlam period because that was, if you want, one of the great myths of socialist Australia. And by the time of Tommy's death and Louie, that myth no longer resonates or has the historic power that it did. And in fact the working class, by Louie's time, is the Hansonite class. I think you are absolutely spot-on – I didn't do it very effectively, but that's why I was trying to do that. The other thing that I learnt with experience is that it's very difficult to write within the contemporary moment. You need the distance of time to be able to fully explain something as important and difficult as Pauline Hanson's One Nation. And I was writing within that time. So there is a perspective that I didn't have.

You mean things had to mature enough inside you?

Yes. Part of the problem with *The Jesus Man* – because I have not thought of the novel for a very long time – is that there is an element of that, which is reportage rather than fiction, of reportage couching fiction.

We know that sex and drugs are permanent features in you work. However in The Jesus Man *you overdo it with scenes of pornography, voyeurism, masturbation, rape, etc. How is this overkill justified?*

I refer you to what I said earlier about not concentrating enough on language; so that's why I think it failed in most passages. In defence – and it goes back to what we were talking about when you asked me about prizes – I would say that a lot of critics don't read the books that I read and don't believe in the kind of writing that I espouse. It's wonderful to get a great review in *The Age* but this newspaper does not review the books that I want to read. They have different expectations of their readers. I started writing *The Jesus Man* at a point when the internet was slowly developing and I could already see then the danger of pornography – about how you could easily lose yourself in that world. *The Jesus Man* was partly me writing about that fear. So, pornography becomes Tommy's world. What is disturbing now is that probably *The Jesus Man* is quite tame, in relationship to what you can see on the net.

You are doing some very interesting and clever things in this novel – especially in the Preface and at the end, with Louie adopting the role of a thesis writer, talking about writing, how he sees his shortcomings, etc. Were these narrative techniques and devices to justify your overall weaknesses in the novel or just experimentations?

No, no, it wasn't to justify anything. I think I'm quite genuine there. It was me trying to experiment. What I liked learning in *The Jesus Man*, as in all my novels, is the scenes of voice as counter-voice. *The Slap* is a much more confident novel, obviously, but I could not have got to *The Slap* without doing *The Jesus Man*.

Finally, in The Jesus Man, *as in all of your books, you end up again with a nihilistic stance. Why is that?*

At that time I thought nihilism was the only answer or response to Capitalism – to be blunt. I thought that either there was to be a full acquiescence to the capitalist system and to the market, and nihilism was the only response that seemed to have a genuine resistance to it left, with the collapse of Communism, with the collapse of socialist ethics, with the collapse of those kind of hopes. Any loss of faith – and I learnt this when I lost my faith as an adolescent – has to come through the fire of nihilism to the other side. And I learnt that from Nietzsche, because I've been returning to Nietzsche and to the existential writers. You read them in a particular way when you are adolescent, you read them in an adolescent manner. And it's been interesting to read them again as an older man and to actually find the wisdom of the past that they were showing me. I spent far too much time in the eighties reading the postmodernists than I should have reading the existentialists – that's what I feel now.

10

DEAD EUROPE

In this novel you focus on the dark side of Europe. You present it as a barbaric, cannibalistic continent by silencing the great culture that it has produced in the past. Two questions: (a) why this negative view of Europe and (b) if Europe does not produce culture any more, which continent does?

To the first question: I was killing my father, my parent, with this book. So, of course the response had to be harsh – that was what I was doing with *Dead Europe*. A necessary murder, I have to say, to free myself of an adolescent, romantic attachment to this continent as I'm a child of the New World. My experience of Europe is that it is cannibalistic, in the metaphorical sense. Now, to the second point, it is a novel of extremes. I'm not saying that Europe cannot produce anything of value or of greatness any more – certainly that's not what I feel. But I find so much of what European produces at the moment sterile. Where do I look to now is definitely the East, the Middle East and Asia. The other place that I think is really still fascinating for me are the Americas, both the North and South. The best writing from the European legacy is coming from South America – from Argentina, from Brazil, those parts of the world. I love Europe but, fuck, how class-bound all that society is, from Greece to the UK! I'm used to hearing about the UK, but it's everywhere, in Greece too, it's everywhere in that continent. This book was written after having travelled through Yugoslavia, just before the collapse into wars and how could you not see the savagery of that continent... On the one hand Europeans are patting themselves on the back, because they've put up shrines to the Holocaust and, on the other, they are allowing the most horrific violence to reoccur.

In Dead Europe *there is the same nihilism as in* Loaded. *Why this constant pessimism and nihilism? Are you endorsing Fukuyama's* The End of History*?*

The novel is about a particular death, an annihilation that did occur. The peasant class in Europe was killed, as part of the European project. Communism ended. Not that there aren't positive things about that, but a certain annihilation happened in Europe and I am expressing it. As for Fukuyama's book, even when I read it, when he was writing back in the nineties, I was angry about it. In a way *Dead Europe* is me trying to write against that thesis and saying no, it won't be perfection, it won't be some kind of idealised science fiction, nirvana, that the European project also contains real silences and dangers. In fact I would claim for *Dead Europe* – this is where I'm nervous because I'm the author and the author is dead – that I am in that novel, saying that history does not end but continues.

A Greek reviewer wrote about this novel: "It is an ambiguous work designed to cause controversy and debate. Is it a political commentary for a Europe which, according to the writer, is dying slowly, together with Capitalism, or a novel about sex tourism in Europe? Is it a political work or the delirium of an homosexual?" Of all the above, what exactly is it?

I like the phrase "delirium of an homosexual!..." I would argue that this reviewer's particular questioning is precisely that – I'm not a European writer. Isaac is a New World character. His responses to what he sees around him emerge from his New World. I'm not European and I don't have a European mentality. One of the frustrations I have with the Europeans is that they want all of us to have that mentality. Europe is trapped in an intellectual space where they can't see outside itself. It's one of the weaknesses now that Europe is facing up to, in a kind of globalised digital world that we are living in. Talking to Europeans about China, for example, I find it so interesting, because they can't see beyond some kind of underdeveloped peasant picture that they have in their head. I am a child of Europe, but anyone who grows up in Australia must know that we are a bastard child. We are not a legitimate child. And the bastard is never going to write something that will satisfy the parent. I find similar responses in the UK as well. I'm also illegitimate in the UK.

You've said in an interview: "In European modernism, homosexuals, as well as Jews, were seen as offenders and subversives and that's why they had an important role in the margins of culture." Does this explain your interest and love for the Jews?

I don't know if that fully explains my interest and love for Jewish culture. It is one of the things that led me to Jewish culture, definitely. The Jewish-American writing was so instrumental for me. That's how I understood the Jews, not so much as homosexual but as outsider, for so much of a modern European history and probably about my anger about the homosexual and the Jew for abandoning that role more recently. It's an unjustified anger, a seeming resentment. But for a long time I was angry about the taming of the homosexual, that we became just another good citizen of Europe and the world. Whereas I was attracted to the idea of the outsider. I realise now that it is romantic. I still understand that desire but most people just want to be safe. We are writing within history. That role of the Jew and the homosexual that I was referring to in that review, is something that had its great expression before the formation of the nation states and up to the end of World War II. And then the Holocaust completely changed the nature of Jewish identity, the civil and sexual rights, and the politics of the sixties completely changed the nature of homosexual identity, so it no longer holds. I'm very influenced by the writer Hannah Arendt. And her book *The Origins of Totalitarianism* was really influential when I was writing *Dead Europe* in terms of teasing out these possibilities, because she writes with the formation of a nation-state, about the role of the Jew and homosexual in culture at those points.

In this novel you seem to be preoccupied with anti-Semitism. At the same time you are ignoring, for example, the plight of the Palestinians and also the powerful Jewish lobby in America which, for many, govern the world financially. Isn't this a biased stance?

It's funny, because some people have accused me of being a vile anti-Semite. Again, I'm hesitant, because I'm the author and what does the author know? But one of the central moments for me in *Dead Europe* when I was writing it, is where Soula, the Muslim woman says, "am I a Semite?" She is in the square in Paris and she says that to Isaac when they are discussing anti-Semitism. For me, I didn't have to mention the Arabs, I didn't have to mention the Palestinians by name. For me that was the crux. This continent which prides itself on having got rid of anti-Semitism is doing the same thing once again in its history. Aren't the Arabs Semites? Now, I'm assuming that the reader is intelligent enough to make those connections – to say why is that in there? That's my defence. One of the motivations to write *Dead Europe* also came from that observation, of the hypocrisy of seeing, as I said, Europeans patting themselves on the back for somehow coming to terms with World War II and proudly saying that anti-Semitism would never ever have a foothold in Europe again. And then treating the refugee and the Muslim outsider in despicable ways, or being scared or terrified of them, or anxious about them.

Although in this novel you raise various political issues, you don't express a clear political view on them. You attempt to create an epic narrative for Europe in decline but without completing your debate. Why is that?

I can answer that with a question: Why is that problematic? I'm sorry to repeat myself, but it is to understand my first three novels in the context of the loss of faith and *Dead Europe* is part of that process. Because when you lose faith – whether spiritual or political faith, or even faith in someone you love – it is literally falling off the cliff. You are in the air, because you don't know where and how you are going to land, because previously there was a safety net for everything – whether of ideology or of God or certainty – and those three novels were written in the act of falling. And it's out of falling that things emerge. What I was most fearful of doing was to be false, to provide an answer that I no longer had faith in myself, to cheat the reader in that way, and I saw sentimentality as a danger to that. If I neatly resolved these novels, I would be cheating the reader, because it would not come from a genuine imagination or will or belief. Whereas, by the time I came to *The Slap* – when I first started plotting, sketching and thinking about the novel – I was going to have Richie suicide. And as I was writing it and discovering his character and his world, I thought, no actually fuck it, I'm going to be hopeful, I really like this kid. I don't have to be destructive, I don't have to be nihilistic. But the reason I could do it in *The Slap* was because it was genuinely from within myself, I wasn't partaking on false ending.

Once again, Dead Europe *describes in more depth the identity crisis that individuals and ethnic groups go through, by talking about a false or deformed homeland (e.g. Greece) and a continent in disarray (e.g. Europe). Does the current European crisis make it a prophetic novel?*

The only legitimate answer I can give you is that I'm not a seer, I'm not a prophet, and the novel is what it is. In certain ways the novel is outdated already because it is about a Europe before the crisis. What I was foreseeing, if you like, is that history is not going to end. But I had no idea of the nature of what the future would be. But I did know that things were going to change. And I could see that these were unresolved, unanswered questions about the nature of European identity. And that's the important thing of being an outsider. All the late part of the 20th century in Greece, when I travelled there and the early 2000s, but it was the 1990s which was the crux of what I experienced that came to *Dead Europe*. Being an outsider, I was constantly asking questions about this European identity and what it meant, and it seemed to me much more precarious than the Europeans themselves were identifying. So, it was not a crystal ball that I had, I was writing a narrative.

How do you see Dead Europe *now?*

Artistically I would still say that Europeans are still not responsive to that book, because, as I said, they don't want to hear what a bastard child of Europe has to say about them.

Why does it annoy them?

Perhaps they think that I don't have a right to write about Europe. That's my sense. Europe is quite closed at the moment, and that is part of its danger. And you've got to remember, I travelled through Eastern Europe and the Eastern European experience is so different from the Western European experience. Not that there aren't similarities, but in terms of a notion of "Europeaness" that superiority that Europe has is part of the European consciousness and it's an arrogance. And you can see it in the Greeks here in Australia. But I don't want to feel a pleasure in people's suffering with what is happening in Europe today.

You've talked about the three kinds of deaths of Europe – that of Communism, that of the agrarian society and that which derives from war and racism. Is there an Australian death and, if yes, what is that?

The death that shrouds my conception of Australia is that of its Aboriginal history. It is of an almost primal experience of growing up as an Australian – knowing that there is this awful history and the fact that we have to reconcile ourselves to it. In terms of the future, maybe there is an element where I have to understand that this is an island. The parochialism of this country is what is always frustrating. Is it a death? It's not that kind of death if I'm imagining, if I was to write about it. It would almost be a death that comes from being so bloated that you explode – that's how I feel about Australia at the moment. We are in danger of just becoming the most obscene kind of consumers. That's what all our culture will be – a culture of exchange and the market. That's my fear about Australia. It's a death of poison, because that's a poisonous kind of culture.

You've said in an interview that Dead Europe *started, in a way, with the Macedonian issue. Would you like to expand on this?*

For me, the experience that I was referring to was that I grew up with Macedonian friends. And it wasn't till the breaking up of Yugoslavia that suddenly it seemed to become a defining aspect of Greek-Australian politics and culture. And that's what astonished me – the swiftness of that experience. I'm not making this up, but whereas I had all the relatives who a week before were joking about using Macedonian terms, suddenly they were stabbing their fist on the table and saying there is no such thing as a Macedonian language! How can you say that when, just the other day you were talking Macedonian to me...

Has this issue influenced you in any way – especially writing Dead Europe*?*

I would not isolate the Macedonian issue with my whole feelings about the responses to the break-up of Yugoslavia, which was a sadness for me. Whatever the history of the regime, there was a possibility of hopefulness in the federated Slavic nation that was destroyed in the wars, and I think that is sad. I still stand by that. It's hopeful when you have a belief that nations can transcend themselves to create a union of possibility. Again it comes back to the hypocrisy we were talking about before. Here it was Europe, at one point, claiming for itself an ability to transcend history and create a united continent and, at the same time, supporting the destruction of another confederation. They could not see the connections between those things – here in the Balkans we will allow this kind of division around ethnic and linguistic lines but we won't claim it for ourselves in the West. So it's not so much about Macedonia and Greece, as it is about Europe.

In this novel, in particular, there is a strong sense of guilt and, at the same time, a quest for an ethical proposition. If so, where can we trace the roots of this guilt, and do you think writing is a way to redemption?

The short answer to the second question is that, for me, there is a way of reaching towards atonement in writing. Where does this sense of guilt come from? Growing up in a culture where I felt a real sense of shame and guilt for a long time has obviously infected my writing. It's one of the things I had to deal with in order to become an adult man.

Was it because of homosexuality?

I think so. It must have been, it must be ingrained in that experience. You are heterosexual but you have a sense of shame and guilt coming from that background as well. The other thing, again, is that I come back to that colonial history of Australia that creates a notion of shame attached to it. It was travelling to Europe that I felt a certain shame being Australian because of the history of the Aboriginal people. So, trying to understand Australia is trying to understand that history of shame. Trying to understand myself is trying to understand that experience of shame. When it comes to my writing, I am trying to make sense of that. That's where the sense of atonement comes from. In *Dead Europe* the centre, in a way, is that conversation that Isaac and Colin have in bed. And what it came to was a very political answer – that love is the one experience I've had in my life and through my relationship has been able to lead me away from shame. Not that I haven't experienced shame within a relationship, we all do, but in a way it's not a very profound conclusion at all. At the end of *Dead Europe* where is the retreat? The retreat is in love, in Colin's garden. It's as simple as that. I have no grand answer.

Would you agree that in Dead Europe *the proposition you are making is two-fold: (a) free choice of an individual regarding their identity, and respect and faith in the other human being and their weaknesses and (b) rejection of the ideological systems and religious dogmas. If so, isn't this a humanistic anarchism?*

That's very spot-on. Because I think what happened with me over the long period that took me to write *Dead Europe*, was that I actually came to an understanding of humanism again. That had been a long period in my intellectual life where I was rejecting humanism for nihilism. I had this wariness of humanistic ideals, because I thought they were false. Coming to *Dead Europe* I reconsidered my fallacy. That's why I said that, in a way, I returned to existentialism which I still see as a philosophy of humanism.

11

THE SLAP

There are two slaps in this novel – that of Hugo and that of Richie – but you make very little of the latter. Why is that?

Because readers have become so lazy in our culture that they have to be reminded that they have to do the work as well. I'm so frustrated with this and because you've given me the opportunity I just want to say that I'm fucking sick of people going, why haven't you explained this, or why aren't your characters more likeable – that kind of ridiculous reading which wants everything laid out in simplistic terms. Whether you think I've failed as a writer, you must see as a reader that there are two slaps in that novel. You must assume that the writer must have made some kind of choice and that it wasn't accidental, if it were to work. Part of the way I had Richie's slap in the book is to indicate that that slap doesn't carry the resonance of Hugo's slap. That's because it comes from a moment of love of a frightened mother who – as we have seen in the respective chapter "Richie" – is a really good person. Whereas Hugo's slap happens in the context of people who have not spoken the truth to each other. They are together and they are lying to each other. They lack the courage to be honest with each other, and that's why that first slap is much more dangerous, difficult and obscene than the final slap.

Don't be surprised if students do postgraduate theses on this second slap in the future...

It's interesting that no one talks about whether Tracey was right or wrong to slap Richie at that point. Probably because we all understand that she did it in a human moment of terror, because deep down she loved her child. It's not what happened with Harry.

The slap of Hugo simply intensified the various pre-existing disputes of individuals and families. This incident highlighted the hypocrisy of family relationships and the eternal war between the two sexes. How would you explain this hypocrisy, especially of the middle class? Why can't people be true to themselves and to others?

We can't be true to ourselves because that would take a level of courage. We find it much easier to pretend, to lie, to try and get along, to not reveal, to not really challenge our marriages, our relationships, our families, our world. I'm hoping I'm not cruel in my depiction of these people, but they are not courageous people. And that seems, to me, to be something that is true about the world they are existing in. In terms of the battle of the sexes – which is equally interesting as the issue of the Europeans we were discussing earlier – I think the bourgeois class assumes that we are anti-racist and anti-misogynist, but I wonder how genuine we are about that. I say "we" because I'm including myself too, as I no longer can pretend I'm working class, despite my heritage. I also think that sexual politics has got to a stage where we find it difficult to be honest with each other about the way men and women are in relationships – there seems to be a sort of acceptance of a certain ideology around gender. So, we find it easier to just accept that without challenging it.

You mean that we prefer to live in our comfort zones?

Of course we do. It was really important to me to reveal in the novel not only the hypocrisy of men but of women as well. I'm going to talk as an Anglophone writer and not as a writer in another language. One of the things that has happened in the English language novel – partly because the main readers of fiction are women – I fear that, sometimes, there is pandering to this readership who doesn't want to be challenged around femininity and how that works in culture. So Aisha, who is I think a much more capable character than Hector, is equally hypocritical. And I was really surprised by the number of female readers who were outraged at me for expressing that. What I'm interested in is the ways culture has changed, because we are all prey to the idea of progress. Of course there is progress. The situation for women, for example, is much better and much different than what it was forty years ago. After writing *The Slap* I was away and I reread a novel that I had not read for decades, which was John Updike's *Couples*, set in the late sixties. My God how honest and unsentimental that man was about heterosexual relationships! And, I thought, something is happening to the reader that has made them more conservative in the English speaking world. So readers have become more conservative in what they expect from fiction.

All characters more or less re-examine their lives after Hugo's slap incident. Does this imply that modern Australian family is in crisis and, if yes, what kind is that?

It was useful to be reminded of this while reading Updike. I think relationships and families have always been in crisis. It has been the grist of so much great literature – you go back to Anna Karenina, for example. There is nothing new about this. What is interesting but also dangerous in *The Slap* is the Australian complacency – the fact that that group of characters are so unwilling to be challenged, as they are so righteous in their beliefs.

However, you are not against the family as an institution.

No, no. Genuine, honest relationships are what we all desire, aren't they? Part of this is accident. I'm not saying it was fully formed consciously, but part of it obviously comes from all this thinking that I've been doing about the family and what the family is. And going to that second slap, you may ask, is it accidental or is it conscious? I can't tell you the answer to this. Probably the healthiest family relationship in that book is between Tracey and Richie – a single mother and her boy. I think the family is incredibly important – in my life it has kept me centred. But, at the same time, great damage can be done within the family as well. So I'm both a critic and a supporter of the family in that way. Because how do you simplify something as vast and dynamic and as shifting as the family?

In The Slap *materialism, consumerism and easy lifestyle are presented as an obstacle to true happiness. How can we overcome this "effluenza" problem?*

As I said to you before, it is easier for us to imagine the end of the world than it is to imagine the end of Capitalism. So, the only way to do that now is to try and imagine, to try and do that active imagining. How we do that is going to be incredibly difficult and I have no easy answers to that. But I have found, in my own life, that resisting and saying "this is enough, I don't need more" is really important, both individually and collectively, as a culture.

You mean exercising self-discipline and constraint is important?

You look back at your work and you see your mistakes, but I am proud of the "Manolis" chapter, because I think that character, who belongs to my parents' generation, is a very distinct voice in fiction.

I too think this is your best chapter.

Thank you. To me the crucial thing in that meeting of Manolis and Aisha in the cafe, is the revelation that there are things within that older culture – things to do with honour and civility that we have lost in my generation. That's so central to me, in terms of how I saw Manolis. I mean that we need to take a step back and reclaim some of those experiences, because my generation does not know about civility in that way. And it doesn't know how to have enough or how to be satisfied either. In fact, self-entitlement is the Australian disease. Of course if you travel through America and Europe you realise that it is a much more general disease than an Australian disease. And the Greeks are suffering from that too. Wayne and I were in Greece last March and we were having a whisky in Athens. Wayne hadn't been in Greece for a long time and he said, Chris, is it that they've forgotten how to have a good time without money? Last time I was here, Greeks weren't wealthy but they knew how to be content. And I wonder if there is a certain truth to it. Now they expect everything as well. Wayne was surprised by how much more materialistic they have got in their expectations.

Is it just materialism to blame for humanity's plight or is it because there is an imbalance between materialism and spirituality?

In *The Slap*, the ideal balance is reflected in the characters of Bilal and Shamira who actually transcend some of that materialist culture through a spiritual choice that they've made. And, at the same time, they are looking for property – a house. But they are making choices that are emerging from a sense of sensible entitlement. They are the poised characters in the book, and that's partly because they have a spiritual sense that the other characters don't have. They are the most Aussie characters, after Rose and Gary, because Shamira is white Australian and Bilal is Aborigine. But that character of Shamira is Anglo-Australian and she has made a choice to become Muslim, which means that I'm saying something about spirituality.

Most of your characters in this novel are well off middle class people but don't feel content. They feel a sense of emptiness and discontent. What exactly do they lack? Is this a criticism against the conceited Australian attitude of the "Lucky Country" syndrome? Do Aussies need some kind of disaster as that of America to shake them up?

I think there is a certain complacency that comes from being well-fed, not having to worry about shelter, all those things. And I think there is something too about Australia being an island nation where you don't have the friction of borders to concern you. Even in a digital age, geography is important. We are at the end of the world – and I don't mean that in the negative sense. It's just the reality of where we are physically on the globe. The thing that concerns me about Australia is that with all this good fortune, we are becoming a less egalitarian nation, we are becoming a less kind nation, we are becoming a more anxious and frightened and selfish nation. What is interesting is the question – what causes that? What causes us to be so self-centred? That's what I'm trying to examine in this book.

Is this reflected in illegal migration and the boat people?

I was reading this morning in the paper that Jordan accepted 150,000 Syrian refugees. Yes, this is reflected in a neurosis – and it is now only a neurosis about borders. The tendency to nostalgic memories is something to watch out for. My feeling is that Australians were kinder when I was younger, but maybe I'm just romanticising the issue. But it feels like we are becoming a less kind nation. I don't think you need to be a Marxist to see that consumerism and materialism actually create quite negative characteristics in human life.

Obviously many characters in this novel live with illusions. But aren't illusions, like dreams, necessary for people to keep on living?

Yes, provided you have the maturity and self-awareness of being able to understand what is possible – because without that understanding there are dangers. Dreams are important, but they have to be tempered by an understanding that you have to share those dreams and illusions with a community, with people around you, they can't be constantly only focused on the ego and the self. And I think that's the difference in our culture at the moment.

I have not been entirely convinced as to why you resort, again, to sex acts and drug use in The Slap *too.*

Those experiences are part of my contemporary life. Maybe, in a sense, it is because of my own experiences clouding the world I'm creating. Partly it is because I like writing about sex and I like writing about drugs.

I can understand about sex – it is part of life. But what about drugs?

It's a good question. I don't know if I can answer it. In the latest book that I'm writing, the hero actually takes drugs. As for my previous books, I do think drugs are part of Australian contemporary reality. Do I overdo it? That's a moot point. But think about all the anxiety in Australia about alcoholism. We are a culture that does tend to have a good time. I don't think that's false to the reality of Australian life.

In the "Manolis" chapter you touch upon two interesting and important issues: (a) The right of old people to love and sex (and not being marginalised and discriminated against because of this need) and (b) the fact that society tends to see old age as a form of disability or the first stage of death. How can we change this attitude, given that life expectancy will keep increasing?

It's going to be something we are going to think more and more, because the reality is we are living longer. I think in our culture there will soon be a crisis between our fear we have of age and death and the reality of people living to a point where they are going to still want relationships, and I don't think we are dealing with that possibility very well at all.

Did you touch upon that subject deliberately?

I don't think I set out to do it deliberately, consciously, but I'm starting to think for myself about my body. While writing *The Slap,* I was reflecting a lot about my parents and all those things. Looking at their lives has strengthened my bond and relationship with both my parents because they've talked to me honestly about their lives. So all of that went into the novel. That's how "Manolis" emerged from that.

WORK

1

LOADED:

To walk the tight rope over chaos
(A young nihilist's manifesto in the "Lucky Country")

Introduction

The first work of fiction by Christos Tsiolkas *Loaded* (first published in 1995 – all my quotes from Vintage edition 1998) could be characterised as a twenty-four-hour "chronicle" of the life and stagnation, the activity and passivity, the relationships and loneliness, the little adventures and inertia, and, finally, the views and beliefs of a nineteen-year old Greek-Australian gay man who lives in multicultural Melbourne.

Ari, who has finished secondary school unsuccessfully, having failed to gain entry into university, as was his parents' wish, is interested in neither going back to school nor trying to find work or do anything else with his life. Even though he seems to want to change the world, effectively he has no dreams, ambitions, plans or aims in life. He wishes to do nothing at all, except to have fun (mainly by listening to music, which he adores, but also through alcohol, drugs and sex) in order to break his unbearable boredom, justifying, at the same time, his aimless existence as well.

As a problematic person – mainly because of the way others (parents and friends) regard him, due to his wavering stance (neither committed conformist nor committed fringe-dweller, who does not go to extremes, as, for example, is the case with his transvestite friend Johnny) – it is natural that he is trapped and wavering in a soul-destroying borderline from the impasse from which he cannot escape. And it is here that the great irony, as well as his drama, lie: In the fact that, whereas he hates the miserable, absurd, unjust and inhuman world he lives in and would like to change it, in the end he is not convinced whether such an effort would be worthwhile, at least on his part. That is why he comes to the convenient and painless conclusion that, such a venture would be not only impossible but also futile. For the very simple reason that humanity is in any case doomed due to its "original sin." Therefore humanity should accept that "to be born human is to be born fucked up" (101).

The reason he draws this conclusion is apparently because he realises that, while he is unable and unwilling to (even try and) change himself, by changing subsequently his own life and fate (as it is easier and more convenient to depend upon others, such as his parents), it would be futile and utopian to expect the rest of the world to change.

Thus, through this cynical, pessimistic outlook and inert, passive attitude of his, it is quite natural that there arises an angry, damning indictment – on everybody and everything – of a seemingly misanthropic, reactionary, anarchic, marginalised young man who, essentially, is nothing but a timid figure (as e.g. he does not dare to reveal to his parents that he is gay), a guy with hang-ups (due to his homosexuality which he loathes, as well as his Greek descent) and a confused, volatile teenager, where it suits him fine to espouse a simplistic, black and white approach to things by adopting an overall nihilistic stance: "... there is no way out of this shithole planet. [...] That's why I like the idea of it all ending in a nuclear holocaust. If I had access to the button, I'd push it" (64). This stance does not, of course, stem out of some specific philosophy, but simply because it is the only way, the only weapon available to him – through this provocative, libellous, so to speak, informal "manifesto" – to react, protest and let steam out by declaring and justifying his existence in the world.

It is an angry and, at the same time, desperate cry of protest of a disoriented, volatile youth who is in despair, emitting – through this unorthodox, confessional outburst – an indirect and disguised but nevertheless clear SOS for help. Because behind this raging rant at the world, there is the latent painful self-pity of a personal impasse, with no prospect of resolution in sight. But this is natural, after all, since young Ari seems to be searching for "something" in life – judging from his reasoning and reactions. However, this is something that he is neither conscious of, or if he is, he avoids confessing it – as it would undermine his nihilistic premise – or, most likely, he does not know what he actually wants, what this "something" he is looking for is. In any case, he lives through a small hell from which he attempts to escape whenever and however he can – by resorting to "having fun" and pretending that he is carefree and happy...

The first thing one notices about this young hero, who is the central character of the novel and around whom the story revolves exclusively, is that he has a first name (Ari) but not a surname. This may not be coincidental. On the contrary it may be interpreted as a symbolic indication of a more general and multiple identity crisis that the nineteen year old Ari goes through, that is: ethnic, cultural, sexual, existential. It is about a youth of Greek migrant parentage even though he dislikes the "Greek-Australian" label ("I... can't stand [the word] Greek-Australian", 115) who leaves school at the age of eleven and since then – that is for a whole year – he remains idle, as he does not wish to study further or to work. In order for him to kill time, he occupies himself obsessively with music, sex and drugs. Indeed, it would not be an exaggeration to claim that the whole book, with its first-person narration, its strong confessional tone and intense polemics, is not much different to a (personal) manifesto against all the well known conventions of life: studies, job, marriage, family, etc. But even though the book gives the impression of an outrageous text of extreme accusations written by an angry young man, yet it is not characterised by a polemic texture, for the simple reason that the young hero has not actually revolted against anything in particular. On the contrary, he remains fearful and timid (for example his reactions against his family, even against his friends such as Joe, who scolds him for his indifference and hopelessness), preferring the security of apathy and inaction. That is, he prefers to compromise with his reality through his addictions and passions because, apparently, he is afraid to react to this state of paralysis that his inaction has brought about.

In this respect, his confessional text constitutes a desperate cry for help from a young man who is in a great crisis, even though this deafening cry is somewhat subdued. Ari, of course, is too proud to confess such a thing. After all it is not something that his age and temperament would allow, as he would never dare to publicise his fear, embarrassment and impasse. However, his overall confessional testimony can only be interpreted as a frantic distress signal, that is, as a desperate attempt on his part to be understood by his social environment and perhaps an attempt to understand his own self too. But let us examine one thing at a time.

Identity Crisis (ethnic, cultural, sexual, existential)

(i) Ethnic and cultural crisis

Ari's discord and conflict with himself appear to have their roots in his ethnic and cultural identity. Although nowhere in the book is this explicitly stated, it is implied from the context that he is an Australian-born youth of first generation Greek migrant parents, with whatever that entails: double heritage and cultural identity (Greek-Australian), which consists of the two halves, one from each side, and which places him somewhere in the middle, on the borderline between the two or perhaps nowhere at all. As for himself, he does not know exactly what he is or how to define himself, let alone how he should feel. It is indicative that at a party which his friend Joe gives in his house, Ari identifies the term "dag" with that of "wog", saying disparagingly to Joe's girl-friend Dina "-I don't think you're a dag. [...] I do think you're a wog" (39). To her question which follows ("-And what are you?") he does not have an answer. Instead, he reacts with the following silent thought: "I don't answer. I'm not a wog, I'm not sure what I am but I'm not a wog. Not the way she means" (ibid.). Ari adopts the same neutral stance, one of non-committal, when he is asked in a Greek night club in Brunswick how he feels about his ethnic identity:

> -Are you proud of being Greek? she [Ariadne] asks. The whole table is looking at me. [...] The question makes no sense to me. I'm glad I'm Greek, I answer, but I'm not proud of it. I had nothing to do with it. The married woman laughs. That's the most sensible thing I've heard all night, she says to me.
>
> -Are you proud of being Australian? The old man's question feels like an interrogation. The answer is easy. No, no way. Proud of being an Australian? I laugh. What a concept, I continue, what is there to be proud of? The whole table laughs at this and Ariadne gives me a hug. (72)

The fact that Ari avoids committing himself verbally about his identity and how he feels does not refute nor does it hide what he is or what he feels. On the contrary his stance may emphasise it even more. It is not just that Ari almost always associates with Greeks, likes Greek music, eats Greek food, speaks Greek frequently, likes making love with Greeks because, as he claims "Sometimes, however, I see a Greek man, not necessarily someone particularly handsome, and I want to feel their body against me, to use dirty words with them, to have them whisper Greek obscenities" (57). The fire of his "Greekness" also emerges tellingly and spontaneously from the passion he exhibits when performing and experiencing Greek dances, as we witness straight after the "interrogation" he is subjected to about his identity:

> The band finishes a song and the bouzouki begins the sad cry of the Vamvakaris song. I jump up, leap on the dance floor and begin to sway to the music. Ariadne joins me, and we twirl and move around the floor. I mouth the tortured lyrics. *Your two beautiful hands will destroy me.*
>
> Ariadne moves sensuously, coming in close to me, and I drop to my knees before her, clapping my hands together in time with the

rhythm, encouraging her in the dance. She motions for me to rise and I leap onto my feet, turn twice on my left foot, twice in the other direction on my right foot. I block the rest of the pub out; do not see the other dancers around me and Ariadne, do not see the band, the crowd. I shut my eyes, Ariadne disappears except for the lingering scent of her sweet perfume, the light trace of tea-tree oil in her hair. I fall and stumble in the hashish rhythms of the song, chasing the agonised cries of the clarinet. (72)

This does not imply of course that Ari is not indeed going through a cultural crisis. This crisis, however, consists more than anything else of the fact that Ari does not trust words – perhaps because he sees them as traps, perhaps because he considers them as being of no substance. That is, that they are a pretext rather than a useful tool for a deeper and more genuine communication and therefore essentially useless. That is why he trusts only his body, by preferring bodily rather than emotional experiences, as he confesses: "I'm not much for conversation. Even with girls (and it's easier to converse with girls) I don't seem to have much to say. The more they talk the more you realise you are not the same" (108).

Finally the reason Ari avoids committing himself verbally, regarding his identity, is not only that he is unsure of whether he is Greek or Australian, nor so much that he does not trust the language to communicate easily. It is mainly because he refuses categorically to reveal what he considers to be the most valuable, holy and sacred "inside him", as he confides: "There is a small part of myself, deep inside of me, which I let no one touch. If I let it out, let someone have a look at it, brush their hands across that part of my soul, then they would want to have it, buy it, steal it, own it" (10-11).

(ii) Sexual identity crisis

Another element in Ari's personality which is unclear and nebulous is his sexual orientation. In the somewhat fragmentary life-story he narrates, it is of course apparent that Ari is bisexual, as he has sexual encounters mainly with men but occasionally with women too. But as in other aspects of his life, it is entirely unclear as to how his homosexual-bisexual inclinations have come about. Whether, that is, it was a matter of conscious choice or triggered by a random incident. In the subtitle "I became a slut", although he confides that it is the latter, the whole phrasing, regarding his initial sexual encounter with both sexes, is ambiguous since he presents those two sexual experiences as identical with the narrative use of "First time": "I became a slut. It just happened. First time, the first time remains crystal clear. A middle-aged guy in a tracksuit blowing me in the bushes at Burnley Oval after school. The first time with a girl, a bedroom at some party" (107).

The doubts as to his sexual preferences (98) – which could be interpreted also as a split or sexual identity crisis and even as perversion – can be ascertained in another sub-chapter of the book entitled "Every time I look", where the narrator-hero reveals:

> Every time I look at a gay man, even if I think he's attractive, I can't forget he's a faggot. I get off on real men [...] I sleep with faggots but they always disappoint me. The desperate effort to hide his effeminacy always betrays him. I can see it in myself. But I do a good job of talking-like, walking-like, being a man. I've got the build, the swagger, the look. [...] Faggots love sleeping with me, they think they've scored a real man. Being a wog is a plus as well. [...] it's vanity, I know it's nothing more, but I get a buzz out of faggots thinking I'm straight. (91-92)

However, notwithstanding any of his sexual discords, ambivalences, eccentricities and perversions, Ari never goes to extremes – by becoming a transvestite, for example, as his Greek mate Johnny has done – even when he considers him to be his best friend-guru, about whom he brags as follows: "Johnny taught me about movies. [...] Johnny taught me about music. [...] Johnny gave me attitude, a sense of style, an arrogance to take on the world. We wagged school often. I had Johnny, I didn't need history, geography, mathematics. I didn't want to learn how to be a conscientious clerk, an effective part of the assembly line. I didn't want to be a good lawyer, a good doctor, a good accountant" (98-99).

For Ari there is always a red line which he cannot cross. Thus, when he realises for the first time that Johnny dresses up like a woman, he is somewhat shocked and this is his reaction: "What do you think? He asked me. I groaned. Johnny, Johnny that's too much" (99). Ari, notwithstanding Johnny's instigations ("-Never, ever, ever think anything is too much", ibid.), remains in mid-air, on the borderline of rebelliousness and passivity. He is even afraid of revealing to his own parents that he is gay (141), always thinking like a little boy when he returns home late: "Mum and Dad are going to kill me. [...] The walkman is screaming at me that I have to fight for my right to party and all I can think of is that Mum and Dad are going to kill me" (138).

In the final analysis, Ari's sexual identity is only a part of the numerous other "crises" which constitute the wider "crisis" he is going through. This does not mean that the sexual crisis is not important, given that the three axes around which his life revolves are: sex, drugs and music. For him, at least, there is simply no point in trying to sexually define himself by naming it in words, as he points out succinctly, underlining once more his uncertainty as to what exactly he is. Thus, when asked by his foreign girlfriend Serena, whether his parents know that he is gay, he is in doubt and reacts as follows: "Am I? I want to say. I want to tell her that words such as faggot, wog, poofter, gay, Greek, Australian, Croat are just excuses. Just stories, they mean shit. Words don't stop boredom. Instead I shake my head. No, I tell her, they don't know" (141).

Notwithstanding all this, in a desperate attempt to eventually define himself sexually, just before the end of the book, he summarises his overall identity and his purpose in life, by making, without evasions, the following categorical statement:

I'm not Australian, I'm not Greek, I'm not anything. I'm not a worker, I'm not a student, I'm not an artist, I'm not a junkie, I'm not a conversationalist, I'm not an Australian, not a wog, not anything. I'm not left wing, right wing, centre, left of centre, right of Genghis Khan. I don't vote, I don't demonstrate, I don't do charity.

What I am is a runner. Running away from a thousand and one things that people say you have to be or should want to be. They'll tell you God is dead but, man, they still want you to have a purpose. They'll point to a child and say there it is, that's purpose, that's meaning. That's bullshit. A child is a mass of cells and tissues and muscle that will grow up and will become Jack the Ripper or the president of the world. Maybe. More likely it will grow up and become a dole statistic. Worse, it will grow up and become an accountant. A child isn't a purpose, a child isn't meaning. A child is an accident that occurs when a piece of sperm bumps into an egg.

They'll point to someone working hard, point to my Mum or my Dad and say, look that's purpose. Work hard, dignity of labour. They'll point to two weak human beings who haven't got the guts to walk away into a lonely happiness, who year after year stick out jobs they hate and a marriage they can't breathe in for the sake of making some rich boss richer. They may have a house but the prick who owns the factories they work in has two houses, three houses, sixty fucking houses. There is no dignity without choice and there is no choice. I didn't choose to be a runner.

I like music, I like film. I'm going to have sex, listen to music and watch film for the rest of my life. I am here, living my life. I'm not going to fall in love, I'm not going to change a thing, no one will remember me when I'm dead. My epitaph; he slept, he ate, he fucked, he pissed, he shat. He ran to escape history. That's his story.

Press stop. Tape is terminated. (149-150)

(iii) Existential crisis

The most important crisis that Ari experiences could be characterised as existential *par excellence*. Although this word is not mentioned anywhere in the book, it does not stop the hero from experiencing it first hand and tasting it completely, as it is apparent in every exasperating and painful word he utters in his confession. It should be remembered that Ari is one of three children in the family. His parents belong to the working class and, naturally, they face financial problems. That aside, Ari's father detests his life in Australia and dreams of returning to his homeland. As for his mother, even though she is Australian-born, she suffers from loneliness, as well as the rift with her husband and children and turns to alcohol for consolation. The elder son, Peter, had already been in a rift with his parents and left the family home, but has not broken ties with them completely, whereas the younger son Ari – although he is a wreck in their eyes, due to dropping out of school, with no apparent intention of doing something with his life – continues to live with them, living at the same time his own unorthodox life, something which his parents are ignorant of. In short, even though it is not a broken family, it nevertheless remains problematic or better still dysfunctional, simply because instead of a genuine mutual respect, there is only a rather formal relationship between parents and children. Indicative of this is the way Ari sees his parents and the love-hate relationship which exists between them:

> Dad has an excuse, he was born in Greece. A different world. Poverty, war, hardship, no school, no going out, no TV. It's a world he'd prefer to go back to and a world I have no fucking clue about. Singing around coffee tables, sleeping in the afternoon, walks in the evening and celebrations in the night. He should never have left, no matter how bad things were back there. Here, under the Australian sun, he's constantly sniffing the air and looking disappointed. He can't really breathe here, he says.
>
> But Mum's different. She was born here and is as Australian as

me. Shit, with the nasally squawk she speaks in she's more skip than me. She butts out her cigarette and lets fly. Where have I been? Why don't I ring? I stare into her forehead. The questions continue and I don't answer any of them. She starts a rave in Greek, calls me a fucking animal, a pig in the mud she stresses, throws a tea-towel at me and starts crying. I go to her, put my arm around her shoulder and kiss her on the cheek. Hi Mum, I say, I'm hungry. She slaps me slightly on my arse and, grumbling a little more, starts preparing lunch. [...]

-I used to fight with your grandfather all the time, Ari. I scoop the meal in my mouth, wrapping the feta in bread and swallowing it in large bites. But I always respected him, Ari. Always. She says the last words in Greek.

-I respect you too, Mum. And Dad too. It's a lie and maybe she knows it. I love my parents but I don't think they have much guts. Always complaining about how hard life is and not having much money. And they do shit to change any of it. Dad would like to go back to Greece some day, he thinks that life will change for him then. But Mum wouldn't leave us behind and I don't know if Greece would make her any happier. (12-13)

Generally speaking, the book is permeated by the sense that the parents feel betrayed by their children and whatever dreams and aspirations they had invested upon them. Conversely, their children hold the parents responsible for their own failures for having provided a non-conducive family environment. A small example:

My father screaming at me, you failure, you animal, and my soaking in the contempt, suffocating in my guilt. Then watching my mother throw the same words, the same expressions to my brother as he is walking out of the house. Seeing him drenched in the stench of her venom. Not believing them for my brother. Not believing them for my sister. A glimpse, a slither of light in the darkness of the Greek family drama. Thou art not responsible for thy parents' failure. (100-101)

For Ari then the existential crisis – which is basically manifested as a lack of meaning in life – obviously pre-existed due to the reasons already mentioned. However, in the unfolding of his story, it is presented as if this crisis begins to culminate by becoming openly official when Ari fails his final year exams, something which is a great blow, not so much to him of course but mainly to his parents. This is how this dramatic family scene is depicted:

> The night I received my final year results Johnny came and dragged me away from my parents who were screaming abuse. So he failed, Johnny told them, you've got one son at university. How many do you want there? My father started screaming at him as well. We left the house and he told me he had a surprise for me. We went back to his house and he lit me a joint and left me sitting on his bed flicking through movie magazines. He went off into the bathroom and emerged, twenty minutes later, in a red dress, thick make-up, his hair up in a bun, looking like a woman in a black and white photograph, a scared young woman on foreign soil. What do you think? He asked me. I groaned. Johnny, Johnny that's too much.
>
> -I'm disappointed in you, Ari, he retorted. Never, ever, ever think anything is too much. He sat beside me on the bed. This life is shit, man, uncompromising. He put his arm around my shoulder and I smelt perfume. Haven't we always said, he continued, that what we hate about the wogs is that they are gutless? They don't take chances, don't upset the status quo. He fiddled with a strand of long black hair. Well, Ari, it's not just the wogs. It's all of them. I'm not scared, he shouted defiantly in Greek. (99-100)

Thus, according to the narrator-hero's reasoning, the more problematic the family environment, the more problematic the child will become, as happens with the case of his Greek mate Johnny who reacts by going to extremes and becoming a transvestite, as he explains:

[...] Johnny's mother died when he was a young child. He carries her photo around with him all the time, a photo of a young, scared woman. A black and white photo of a young girl just having landed on foreign soil which she was to detest and in which she was to be buried. Johnny grew up with an alcoholic father who had no idea of how to look after a child, who gave him over to aunts and neighbourhood women to raise, women who had their own kids and their own husbands and their own work and houses to look after. [...]

Johnny dropped out of school early, first chance he got. We got drunk together at the back of the high school, celebrating his decision, throwing our beer cans into the river. He told me that his father had started sleeping with him, getting drunk, coming home smelling of cheap spirits and getting into bed with Johnny. (97-99)

The main causes of Ari's existential crisis could be summarised essentially as two-fold: (a) *boredom*, which is caused by the lack of meaning in life and (b) *loneliness*, that is a deeper absence of communication. Let us examine these two aspects more closely:

(a) Boredom

It is indicative that even from the second page of the book, when young Ari has just got out of bed in the morning, he cannot hide the boredom he already feels: "I've just got up and I'm already bored. I wouldn't mind a joint" (3). Nowhere in the book is there the slightest indication that Ari suffers from any mental disorders such as depression, anxiety, etc., which could be blamed for his negative mood; on the contrary he seems to be in perfect health. Notwithstanding the way he speaks as to how he feels and sees the world around him is not different to that of an exhausted elderly person ("Nearly twenty, I sound exhausted", 141) who is in the twilight of his life and is besieged constantly by pessimism and depression. The hero himself does not claim of course that he feels that way twenty four hours a day. On the contrary he confesses that even when "Straight, I can approximate *kefi*..." (23). However he seems to be afraid of this feeling of boredom ("Speed evaporates fear" he says, 23). That is why he makes sure he faces up to it with the use of drugs, as they bring about some mental stability and make him feel more "normal." That is why, as he says, "I'm always conscious of fighting off boredom. Speed doesn't let you get bored" (23) and proceeds to combine it with sex too (ibid.).

Ari's boredom stems from the "original sin" and is a result of "Realising that to be born human is to be born fucked up" (101), consequently there can be absolutely no hope that humankind will change its fate since the planet is either way doomed:

> Pol Pot was right to destroy, he was wrong not to work it out that you go all the way. You don't kill one class, one religion, one party. You kill everyone because we are all diseased, there is no way out of this shithole planet. War, disease, murder, AIDS, genocide, holocaust, famine. I can give ten dollars to an appeal if I want to, I can write a letter to the government. But the world is now too fucked up for small solutions. That's why I like the idea of it all ending in a nuclear holocaust. If I had access to the button, I'd push it. (64)

This attitude explains his categorical refusal to get out of his state of inaction and passivity and do something with his life. It is not so much that Ari suffers from a lack of self-confidence or self-respect. He is simply convinced that there is no point, nor is it worth keeping to the beaten track and the compromise, as his friend Joe did and most people do, given that nothing will change in his life or in the life of humanity, as nothing had changed in his parent's life either. That is why he considers it more honest, dignified and right for him to be unconventional, by going against the current, instead of mimicking like a monkey the stereotypes that others have put in place for him. This explains why, although he is nineteen – an age at which presumably a person's creative life begins – he stubbornly refuses to plan anything for the future. In his mother's question-query-protest ("-Ari, why don't you go back to school. You are going to be twenty next year. An adult and you still don't have a plan to your life", 27) he reacts as follows:

> I butt out my cigarette and sit back in the kitchen chair looking at my mother. I don't know what to answer her. I could go back to school, I could try and get some shit job cleaning toilets in a hospital somewhere, or disappear in some office labyrinth in the city somewhere, doing a job that a computer could do faster and better than me anyway. A computer wouldn't have an attitude problem. I try to put some words together, and though I know what I want to say, I can't make my lips move. (27)

Generally it infuriates him immensely when he is asked whether he has found a job ("-Got a job yet? Joe asks me. I hate that question", 8) for the simple reason that he is not at all interested in any work ("I'd hate any job," he says, 17) and the prosaic commonplace attitude and conventional life-style of his close friends like Joe worries and saddens him greatly because he himself is unwilling to end up with a "mortgage"; which basically means a "mortgaged life" as he explains:

> Joe has got his world worked out, or so he likes to think he has. He's got a job, got a girlfriend, got a car. Soon he wants to get married. I think it's a mistake but I figure that it isn't my business to tell him such things and I don't. He's an adult. But it seems to me that there are two things in this world guaranteed to make you old and flabby. Work and marriage. It is inevitable. The faces of all the workers and all the married people I see carry the strain of living a life of rules and regulations. Joe's face is still young looking, he still has sharp bright eyes. But he's changing. Doing the nine to five on weekdays. No dirty T-shirts but a shirt and tie and a briefcase by his side. He keeps his crew cut because he

still wants to dip one foot into the pool of freedom, but even that will change once the wedding ring is slipped on. They won't let him walk up the aisle without at least two inches of hair, not in a Greek church. It's his cop-out.

Unless you're a smart thief everyone has to work, or scrounge around saying yes-sir-no-sir-can-I-have-a-raise-sir-can-I-have-the-day-off-sir-my-grandmother-is-sick-sir-dad-can-you-lend-me-twenty. We all have to sell ourselves. But you don't have to get married, you don't have to sell all of yourself. There is a small part of myself, deep inside of me, which I let no one touch. If I let it out, let someone have a look at it, brush their hands across that part of my soul, then they would want to have it, buy it, steal it, own it. Joe's put that part of himself up for market and he would be the first to say it's because he can't put up with the demands. Parents, friends, bosses, girlfriends, girlfriends' parents, cousins, aunts, uncles, even the fucking neighbours. They all want to sell, buy, invest in the future. And now he's just waiting for the right bid, and I know what it is. Once his parents and her parents offer a house, or at least a hefty deposit, the deal will be clinched. The marriage will be arranged. Joe will have joined the other side, just another respectable wog on a mortgage. (10-11)

It is natural therefore that his friends' reactions, such as those of Joe, hurt him deeply and bring him close to a rift, but they fail to knock some sense into him or make him change attitude:

-Man, what did I do, what did I do? Joe finishes his piss, shakes his cock, flushes and turns around to me. Grow up, fucking hell Ari, grow up. Get a job, I'm embarrassed to be seen with you. I study his face. Notice the light layer of fat forming under his chin, the small strands of wrinkles around the eyes. Get a life are his final words to me and he walks out of the toilet. A young boy comes up beside me and washes his hands at the sink. How are you doing? he asks in Greek. I don't reply, walk into a cubicle, close the door behind me, gather my fingers into a fist and smash into the cistern. The sound, a loud crash, reverberates around the cubicle. Mad motherfucker I hear the boy say and hear him leave the toilet. Alone, smelling urine, shit and cheap cologne, I spit into the basin. Fuck you, Joe, fuck you, you cunt. The words keep repeating. Fuck you Joe, fuck you, you cunt. I repeat them twice, three times, they become a chant. (66-67)

This inactive, passive stance of his – much as it may seem paradoxical – is, from his own perspective, a form of resistance. Perhaps the only weapon of protest he possesses.

(b) Loneliness

Loneliness is the second most important cause of Ari's existential anguish and crisis. This may sound odd or even contradictory, given that during the confessional narration of his story rarely does the young hero give the impression of a loner, a recluse, withdrawn from life and the world. On the contrary we see him not only being constantly in the company of other people but having elevated entertainment into a full-time occupation, as he participates in frenzied parties where he is involved in individual and/ or group sex and drug orgies. In the face of it, this seems true but in essence it does not reflect the full reality. If we listen attentively to this agonised self-confession of Ari, we realise that behind the lustre of his extrovert, frantic and unrestrained life-style hides a frightened, lonely person in despair, because he has very little communication with the rest of the world and this is eventually his greatest drama. Which means that, even when it is assumed that communication is taking place, the dialogue is missing, as we can witness in the case of Ari and his sister Alex: ("Alex is talking away at me, telling me gossip about her friends and I'm not very interested, I keep turning away from her, looking out the window at the passing shops. She doesn't care, she's just happy to talk", 35). The lack of substantial communication lies in the fact that Ari is hardly understood by others around him – even by his own family and closest friends like Joe – but also that he rarely understands them. Thus, even when Ari is hobnobbing, associates and entertains with others, or even when he makes love with them – regardless of whether they are women or men – there is no deep and genuine relationship between them, but only a rudimentary, mechanical communication, as a huge – psychological – rift separates him from the others. This absence of communication is due to a serious shortage of any positive sentiments, given that Ari feels essentially dry of feelings of love as he confesses with a concealed sadness and bitterness: "One day I'd like to meet someone I felt so strongly about that I would get up at dawn to play them a love song. Not to worry about what the neighbours say, what his parents will say" (37).

This lack of communication, however, is not something that characterises Ari alone but almost everybody whom he mixes with, given that we are dealing with a more general socio-political phenomenon at hand, as he points out: "In the East, in the new world of suburbia there is no dialogue, no conversation, no places to go out: for there is no need, there is television" (43). But the people who associate closely with Ari also feel an unbearable loneliness, such as his mother, for example, who feels alone, forgotten and cut off from everybody:

> It doesn't look like Dad is coming home in time for dinner and I can see she's getting tense. She keeps rubbing the vein on her forehead.
>
> -Are you going to go to *thea's*? I ask. She doesn't say anything. Go Mum, Alex says, what the hell are you going to do on your own on a Saturday night.
>
> -My children could stay with me. Her eyes cloud over. My children could keep me company. Alex makes a face and gets up from the table. I don't want a lecture, she says, and goes off into the lounge. My mum gets up, follows her, and they begin an argument. I grab a magazine, one of my mother's, and flick

through it. I hear snatches of the argument. Alex is too young to be going out. I read about a woman who is married to a man who bashes her. Alex says the house feels like a prison to her. Mum says she's worked hard all her life for us kids and we've all let her down. Alex yells at her that she should live her own life, not live through her kids. I put down the magazine and go to the bathroom to clean my face. I comb my hair, put some aftershave on my armpits. I grab my cigarettes, the speed and my wallet, and march into the lounge room. Mum is on the sofa crying. Alex is in her room. I take Mum's hand. Come on, we'll walk you over to *Thea* Tasia. (32-33)

Escape-flight

Under the aforementioned conditions, it is natural that Ari is not only possessed by a desperate desire to escape from the joyless and unbearable reality of the world he lives in, but that this escape has become something of an obsession for him, as he constantly says. Primarily he feels being suffocated by the oppressive family environment from which he dreams of escaping. Hence, referring to the dysfunctional relationship he and his brother have with their father, he says: "Then he looks sad and I wish I could walk straight past the gate back down the street and away from him, my family and the world" (12).

His tendency to want to escape, however, is not only in relation to his family but also to the country in which he lives and which oppresses him with its daily routine and boredom, hence his desire to live for a period in Greece: "It wouldn't be forever, I answer. I cannot envisage forever, I'm thinking more a couple of years living in a different country, meeting new people, getting excited about unfamiliar sights, sounds and smells. Also a couple of years away from the family and all their hang-ups and expectations. I can't say that of course" (27). For Ari it is impossible not only to compromise with the world and its ways but even to think of desiring what his sister confides in him she would love to have in life

("-A big house, a big backyard, a dog, a good job", 38). So his timely and expected reaction does not surprise us: "We pass an old couple walking their dog. – You want to be like them? [...] You don't ever want to get out of this city, do something different with your life?" (38).

But because there is no way in the world that Ari can realise his dream of fleeing from his family, the city and the country he lives in, as he is unemployed and has no money (26), the only choice available to him is to escape through three possible avenues: (i) drugs, (ii) sex and (iii) music; sometimes individually and at other times in a combination of all of them.

Drugs (alcohol)-sex-music

We need to be reminded from the beginning that although Ari's overall unorthodox life-style may give the impression that this is a fringe-dweller individual, this is anything but true. Not because he does not want to belong to that class, but because he is apparently afraid and prefers the security of the family home on which he is dependent. Let us not forget that Ari, as a child of a Greek family (from which children break free at an advanced age, if at all) finds it extremely difficult to become independent. A proof of this is that, even though his brother Peter, who was brave enough to leave his parental home, Peter was still in need of depending on somebody else, namely his girl-friend Janet, as the narrator-hero admits with brutal honesty: "Then Peter met Janet and he walked out the door. She offered him a way out. We are weak, lazy, useless, we can't do it on our own, we need the strong back of another" (76).

The last comment of course applies more to himself (Ari) who is not brave enough to break free from his family. Notwithstanding all this, however, or because of this, Ari admires the fringe-dwellers whom he considers the most interesting and creative elements of society and, to a degree, he tries to imitate their philosophy and the way they live, even though in the final analysis it is, more than anything, an impulsive, cheap imitation. His admiration for the fringe-dwellers and the reasons behind it are summarised in Ariadne's reasoning, which the narrator-hero cites and which he seems to identify with completely: "She is arguing for a new left, of young people, artists, deviants, troublemakers from all the communities to get together. She wants something new, something radical. [...] I want to be involved with the deviants, the mad, the creative, all those people that the Greek community despises, all the general Australian community despises" (71).

Therefore he considers it natural, on the one hand to have this illusion of being a "fringe-dweller" by mimicking their way of life and, on the other, to live in guilt, having a secret life, unknown to his parents. A testimony of the fact that he wants to convey this impression – of being a "fringe-dweller" – is that his self-confessing narration has as a starting point – in the introductory chapter – the following characteristic scene, consisting of an amalgam of sex-music-drugs: "The morning is ending and I've just opened my eyes. [...] I yawn. I scratch my groin. I feel my cock and start a slow masturbation. [...] A robotic voice is squealing over a brass-beat on the CD. [...] My head hurts and I wish I was home. Peter slips me a smile and asks me if I have a hangover. I nod and Janet laughs at me. [...] I've just got up and I'm already bored. I wouldn't mind a joint" (2-3).

Drugs

Ari is not exactly the classic type of junky. On the contrary he is afraid of hard drugs which he uses only on special occasions. In any case he is a frequent user of (mild) drugs and alcohol, not because he is addicted but as a recreation and because they help him escape from the unbearable daily reality from which, as mentioned, he has no other way out.

He thinks of drugs as a kind of remedy which will help him transcend the environment he lives in, relieve him of his boredom, alleviate his anxieties and impasses and make him feel well, by transforming and embellishing the world around him:

> I take three strong drags [...] Long, strong drags. [...] The smoke is making me high and the kitchen seems bigger than before, full

of unfamiliar objects. [...] My mind is drifting. I reach for one of George's cigarettes and light it. The nicotine straightens me out a little. (5-6)

And elsewhere:

Drugs mould the club, drugs initiate the dancing, the search for sex. The smell of amyl, the boys with clenched jaws on speed, the girl in the middle of the dance floor waving her long arms towards the disco ball, lost in an acid dream, the alcohol that lubricates our movements around each other, the joints rolled in dark corners. Without the drugs the music would be numbing, monotonous. Without the drugs the faces would be less attractive; wrinkles, bad teeth, double chins. I sniff the smell of marijuana and I'm happy. (89)

Another reason is that drugs, as well as alcohol, facilitate communication or anyhow an elementary understanding with his mother, as he claims: "When I'm speeding, when Mum's drinking, we can converse like normal people, without getting heated and uptight with each other" (26-27). Besides, it is not at all by accident that, alongside with Ari, both of his parents resort to alcohol as a way out of their problems, as of course is the case with the father of Ari's friend Johnny: "He calls his son and I whisper to Mum that Mr Petroukis is drunk. Good idea, she says and goes to pour herself another shot" (29).

Sex

Apart from drugs, or in combination with them, Ari resorts obsessively to sex as well. This happens not because Ari is a degenerate pervert but because he sees it as a substitute to the genuine emotional communication he is missing. In the sub-chapter "I became a slut", he initially claims that this happened accidentally ("I became a slut. It just happened", 107) without giving any specific details, whereas subsequently he exposes his promiscuous behaviour to all forms of extreme and sometimes dangerous sexual activity, with both men and women. He actually seems to detest such activity for when he returned home after such an unbridled sexual activity, he had "a shower to get rid of the smell of perfume, of aftershave. Getting rid of the smells that linger from a five-minute thrashing of bodies" (108). He concludes by emphasizing that this unreserved, excessive sexual activity is a desperate, mechanical act of momentary bodily satisfaction, due to a lack of any emotional communication and satisfaction, as he says: "The more they talk the more you realise you are not the same" (108). In other words it is a desperate substitute for "human communication" from which the "human" is absent and what remains is only the "illusion" of *communication* as a beastly act. Here is how he describes this process:

> Coming home, late from school, Mama asks Where you been? You answer, out with friends. Having a shower to get rid of the smell of perfume, of aftershave. Getting rid of the smells that linger from a five-minute thrashing of bodies.
>
> Fucking, not falling in love, I'm not much for conversation. Even with girls (and it's easier to converse with girls) I don't seem to have much to say. The more they talk the more you realise you are not the same. Sometimes, it happens, you are in the middle of a fuck-looking into the eyes of a girl on top of you, her hair framing her beautiful face; a young guy on his knees in front of you and he looks up and smiles-and I have felt a certain tenderness, have felt I want to just lie on a bed and talk to this person, share jokes, fantasies, share some time. A tenderness that while he is sucking me, she is thrusting her groin down on me, I think, this tenderness, this must lead to love. Then I blow, I come and the tenderness goes. Then all I want to do is go away. Put on my pants, wipe my dick and go away.
>
> I ask myself how many people I've had sex with. I've lost count. I've become a slut. (108)

Music

The third ploy via which the narrator-hero pursues his "flight" from the daily reality is *music*, which could have proven useful and beneficial for him had it not been combined with drugs and sex. Ari has a craze for music and is a passionate devotee of it ("More than that, I love music...", he says, 19) but not exactly as most music lovers do or even because it's fashionable for his age to be preoccupied with it, but for the added significant reason that, as he says, "keeps me at a distance from the people brushing past me" travelling him to other worlds, something which, as mentioned before, cannot be realised with conventional means. The importance of his relationship with music is explained by him as follows:

> The Walkman is my favourite toy. It creates a soundtrack for me and lets me slip into walking through a movie. The tape I've got on at the moment I put together the other week at my cousin's house. A few sad songs, a few fast songs, a few songs I never heard of but I liked the look of the CD covers.
>
> This is an up tape, it makes me walk faster, keeps me at a distance from the people brushing past me. I like music. More than that, I love music but I'm definite in my tastes. (18-19)

A characteristic example of Ari's distancing and alienating himself from the external world is the fact that while he slips out of his brother's house and travels by bus to the city centre, he prefers to indulge in the musical journey rather than the actual one into the real world, with which he maintains a distance, as is witnessed below:

> The day is warm and the sun stabs hard at my eyes. I put the headphones on my ears, blink and turn the Walkman on.
>
> Riding on a bus always makes me horny, something to do with the sensation of moving while looking down into the world below. I sink behind a seat in the back and shift my tight cock.

The music enters my head and I rock back and forth a little to a pulsating, electric beat. (7)

We observe that the way he speaks of music and the influence it exerts on him is likened to that of drugs ("The music enters my head", like a drug in the bloodstream) and eventually he identifies himself with both music and drugs, as we realise in another instance when he talks about his most beloved cassette which listens to more than any other: "A tape I put together over several days. But it has become my soundtrack to happiness. A soundtrack that goes nicely with speed, with summer" (24).

However, although he obviously adores music more than drugs and sex – perhaps because in the final analysis it cannot harm him in any way – and despite the fact that it helps him escape, this escape remains deficient and incomplete because it is temporary. That is, it remains once again an illusion since his "story" does not really change, regardless of the "fire and passion" that a song like that of Greek Manos Loizos can have: *"The road has its own story, the story is written by the youth.* I listen to the song on the Walkman and think that it is better to leave, move away, exit, end the story. Better to leave than stay and become fat and inert" (86).

Eventually, towards the end of narrating his own story, Ari realises, implicitly but clearly, that music too is nothing but one more "drug" like the others he is addicted to and depends on to face up to the daily routine. He is aware of and admits that his dependence on these three addictions is neither recreation nor relief nor redemption but, conversely, an equally painful (physical and psychological) experience as the reality itself from which he would want to escape, since after having used them he feels a wreck. But although it is a vicious circle, he needs this addiction, if anything, so that he can "disappear" even temporarily from the martyrdom of his thoughts about the real world:

My body is still pumped from the drugs. My head is hurting, a tiny pinprick of pain somewhere close to my forehead, a pain that pushes back onto my skull and affects my whole nervous system. My jaw is clenched. My cock feels heavy on my groin, bruised from the sex. I put one foot forward and begin a slow walk towards home. There is the sound of trams, cars, the familiar voices of shopowners, the familiar landscape in which I have spent all my life. I'm beginning to hate this city, hate its fucking familiarity. I want to go away, get out of here. I put on the headphones, press play and the music pushes my thoughts way back to some space in my head where I can't hear them. In the voluptuous thunder and rhythms of the Walkman I disappear and I am out of here. (145)

Ari's confession is a way – perhaps a unique one – of admitting his weaknesses, his impasses, his anxieties, but above all his fears and, a means, perhaps, to hopefully overcome them. He is well aware of how timid and timorous a person he is and this, he realises, is the greatest obstacle to changing his life and himself, from which he constantly seeks to escape. This is the reason he always feels outraged and admires the brave, extreme fringe-dwellers like his transvestite friend Johnny, whom he considers his mentor, of whom he says – perhaps with some secret jealousy: "Johnny has Toula. His dresses and skirts are also battle fatigues. He can't remain silent. Silence would kill Johnny" (146). As he does not possess the courage to confront himself, other people and the world, he cannot help but think – certainly without confessing it – that the least he ought to do is to speak, like Johnny, so that he does not go mad or commit suicide. And that is exactly what he does: he confesses. It is the first and perhaps the most decisive step in his attempt to liberate himself from the unbearable bonds of oppressive reality. And although this act of confessing may not redeem him, it consoles him. It is in any case a brave deed, even though he doubts as to whether he will be making it to the real world, because he is not only timorous but also sluggish:

The sun is very harsh and the hill seems neverending. One foot moves sluggishly after the other. I think of Johnny, think of him calling me gutless in one of his drunken rages. I fantasise that when I get home, I'll yell at Mum and Dad that I am leaving, that I've found a man and I'm going to move in with him. I can feel myself smiling in the open street, dreaming of a little house by the sea with George and me in it. But I smell solvents and the fantasy evaporates under the hot sun's glare. I'm so slow from the come-down that I couldn't say a word to my parents. I couldn't make a sound.

I'm nearly home and maybe it is not glue on the street kids I'm smelling. Maybe I'm smelling the residue of chemicals on my own skin. Johnny tries to tell me things all the time, prepare me for the way the real world works. But I move too sluggishly to care about making it to the real world. Johnny is right but he has Toula.

Drugs keep me quiet. And relatively content. (146)

Eventually Ari's whole Weltanschauung reveals that he is an unconventional "anarchist" who detests the beaten track which most people are forced to adopt:

> Fast forward through more instructions. This is how you fuck, this is how you drink, this is how you take drugs, this is how you treat a girl, this is how you recycle your garbage, this is how you save the planet, this is how you can make a difference. Pause play. We are the world. Play. Play that funky music white boy. Fast forward. Failing school, signing up for the dole, uncles, friends, aunts, neighbours telling you about some shit job going in some shit store in some shit street in some shit suburb. Play. Say no thanks. Dole office sends you for an interview. Bald man, not looking at you, looking out the window, asks what you want to be. I say I don't know. Asks why you want to work in his store, in his factory, in his office. I shrug my shoulders, don't say the

truth that I don't want to work in his fucking store, his fucking factory, his fucking office. I say, don't know. Interview lasts ten minutes. Go back to the dole office. (148)

But above all Ari – at the end of his self-confession – accepts that he is a "runner" (obviously from the world but also from himself, without admitting it) because of the fact that he is poor and lazy and consequently he has no choices, as he says:

> There is no way out of this boring life unless you have lots of money. Unless you are born with lots of money it takes a lifetime to make lots of money. Hard work bores me. I ain't no worker.
>
> I'm ruled by my cock. I see someone I think is attractive and I want to be with them, taste them, put my cock in their face or up their arse or through their cunt. I can't imagine any of this ever changing. Marriage is out.
>
> I'm not Australian, I'm not Greek, I'm not anything. I'm not a worker, I'm not a student, I'm not an artist, I'm not a junkie, I'm not a conversationalist, I'm not an Australian, not a wog, not anything. I'm not left wing, right wing, centre, left of centre, right of Genghis Khan. I don't vote, I don't demonstrate, I don't do charity.
>
> What I am is a runner. Running away from a thousand and one things that people say you have to be or should want to be. They'll tell you God is dead but, man, they still want you to have a purpose. They'll point to a child and say there it is, that's purpose, that's meaning. That's bullshit. A child is a mass of cells and tissues and muscle that will grow up and will become Jack the Ripper or the president of the world. Maybe. More likely it will grow up and become a dole statistic. Worse, it will grow up and become an accountant. A child isn't a purpose, a child isn't meaning. A child is an accident that occurs when a piece of sperm bumps into an egg. (148-149)

But in essence he chooses to be a "runner" because he does not want to assume any responsibility in his life.

Antitheses and contradictions

As a character Ari is riddled with antitheses and contradictions. As far as racism is concerned, for example, while he is supposed to be anti-racist and to abhor the attitudes and behaviour of racist people (34) at the same time he has no qualms himself about behaving in a racist fashion when, for example, he does not approve of his sister's relationship with her boyfriend Charlie who is of Arabic background:

> Alex is breathing hard. Her brown eyes are dancing. She takes two cigarettes from the pack on my desk, lighting one for me as well. Do you like Charlie? she asks me.
> -I don't trust him, I say.
> -You don't trust Arabs. She's right. I don't trust Arab boys with my sister. Alex can do what she likes with boys, it's not my place to judge her, but she'd be stupid to fall for an Arab. (31-32)

This contradiction can also be witnessed elsewhere in the book as, for example, in the relevant dialogue between Ari and Janet:

> Janet asks Peter why I've got an image of Africa on my T-shirt. Mum, I say, how are you, I slept over at Panayioti's house. He's anti-racist I hear Peter say, not adding that it's an old T-shirt of his. Yeah, I'll come home soon, I tell Mum. No, I don't think he's coming up. Are you coming home? I ask Peter. I am home, he says. He's not coming up, Mum. I don't know, maybe he's busy. She asks me if Janet is there. I start talking in Greek, trying to be discreet. She wants to talk to Peter or Janet. I say goodbye and hand the phone to my brother. I'm all for racism, I tell Janet, moving slowly towards her, rolling my eyes and putting on a mean motherfucker sneer, dropping my voice very low. I think every whitey deserves to get it in the throat, I whisper in her

ear. How about you? she counters, moving away. You're white. I just look at her. I'm not white, I'm a wog. You're white, she insists. I say nothing because the conversation is boring. I'm just talking crap to get at her. I read the papers, I see the news, I talk to people; white, black, yellow, pink, they're all fucked. The T-shirt feels heavy on me. (4-5)

Let it be noted, however, that any 'racist' behaviour of his is not an end in itself, but a means to 'provocativeness' ('to get at her'). It is just another part of Ari's taking on everything and everyone.

"Greekness" as a centrifugal and centripetal element

Ari's antitheses, contradictions and discords can be witnessed more than anywhere else in his ambivalent attraction-repulsion relationship to his "Greekness". To begin with, it is no accident, obviously, that his eye and attention are captivated by the family photograph in the house of his brother Peter, from the very second introductory paragraph of the narration, as it shows the significance of the family in his life. The description of this photograph is quite telling:

> On the mantelpiece I notice an old family photo. I've forgotten this photo. My brother in a red shirt and black shorts has one arm around the old man and another around my mum. She looks like Elizabeth Taylor, or at least is trying to, and Dad is wearing a grey suit with a narrow black tie. He's trying to look like Mastroianni, or like Delon. The tie belongs to me now. I'm in the picture too. Sitting cross-legged on the grass, in a blue shirt, aiming a plastic gun at the camera. The colours in the photo are rich, bright. Colour photos don't do that any more. Technology makes things look too real. I turn away from the photograph and look at last night's mess strewn across the lounge room. It's not my place. (2)

The overall description of this family snapshot, apart from the fact that it brims over with a sense of nostalgia for the past of innocence – implying that it was not so deadlocked as the present – it also underlines, at the same time, the strong sentimental bond among the members of the Greek family, especially that between parents and children ("My brother [...] has one arm around the old man and another around my mum"), something which time and life have eroded. Hence the apparent, though suppressed, emotion and nostalgia that the narrator-hero feels. This photograph which Ari has almost forgotten is not just a decorative souvenir, a sentimental "heirloom" but something much more important: the only substantial point of reference both of Ari's external space (house) as well as his inner space (emotions). Because the chaotic situation which reigns in the room as well as in the whole house, preceding the description of the photograph ("I hear noises from throughout the house. A robotic voice is squealing over a bass-beat on the CD. [...] I walk past cobwebs, stains on the carpet, a biro on one step, a cigarette butt on another. [...] I turn away from the photograph and look at last night's mess strewn across the lounge room. It's not my place", 2) and following it, regarding Ari's psychosomatic condition ("My head hurts", 3) is counterbalanced by the security of the family home which, in this case, is symbolised by the photograph, hence his longing: "I wish I was home" (3).

This photograph, of course, is a symbolic announcement in advance of the future rebellious character of little Ari, as not only does he not express any emotion by having "one arm around" anybody as his brother has but, on the contrary, he is "aiming a plastic gun at the camera."

The bond of the narrator-hero's family is also indicated in the fact that: (i) Ari feels proud of his siblings and their looks (as he says: "I am proud of their beauty. It is as if it reflects glory back on me," 31); (ii) he associates and entertains with them ("-Poor baby, she smirks. Corrupted by his brother's friends", 3); (iii) they care for each other ("-You can make your own coffee too, blurts out Janet. Peter gives her half a dirty look. I catch it and feel immediately better. I'm his little brother. He's got to look after me" ibid.); (iv) Ari is concerned about his sister's affair with her Lebanese boyfriend, as we have seen before (31); but (v) the children themselves, notwithstanding their protests, quarrels and conflicts with their parents, are not cut off from them and are always concerned about them by keeping them informed as to their whereabouts, what time they will return home ("-Breakfast and coffee first. Then you have to ring Mum and then you can roll your own joint", 3), even when they take drugs in secret (31) and they do not reveal the truth about their lives. This family bond is also testified to by the dramatic way their mother confronts Peter's flight from home with which she never comes to terms:

> -I never see your brother any more. Not since that bitch took him away from us, I hear her yell loudly from the kitchen. [...] I'm not listening to Mum. She can go on about my brother having left home for ages. She broods, cries about it, holds her head low sometimes, sighing deeply, lamenting her boy's betrayal of her. Yet she nurses the betrayal, cultivates it, makes her pain ecstatic because it adds a sheen of tragedy to a boring life. I let her rave and watch the movie. (13-14)

We also realise how traumatic Peter's decision to leave home was and how guilty he feels about it:

> Ari, he whispered to me, taking one of my cigarettes, I'm going to move in with Janet. Sure, I answered, she seems nice. Mum and Dad will make a big fuss, mate, he told me, this might not be a pleasant house for a long time. I got up and turned off the television, sat down next to him. I put my arm around him. It's okay big brother, I can handle Mum and Dad. Peter started crying, a slow, quiet cry. We're not normal wogs are we, Ari? he said quietly. No, thank God for that, I answered. (75)

This centrifugal and centripetal situation which exists in the relationship between children and parents – where nobody is absolutely happy with the other side but no one can break free of the other – this almost masochistic situation on both sides erodes and destabilises the overall psychology of the children. But at the same time, it holds together their emotional world like a magnet, preventing them from going off on a tangent and disintegrating in the chaos of the abyss. In this respect, the ambivalent love-hate relationship, much as it may seem odd, is necessary if a relative psychological and emotional balance is to be secured between them and give some meaning to their joyless life (as, for example, when Ari observes about his mother's reaction to Peter's flight from home: "Yet she nurses the betrayal, cultivates it, makes her pain ecstatic because it adds a sheen of tragedy to a boring life", 14). It is not at all strange then that this ambivalent and formal parent-child relationship is presented by the narrator-hero like a tragi-comic game in which both sides participate willingly, being fully aware of the game's conventions – hypocritical behaviours, lies, etc.

A small sample of this game is the one where Ari's mother rings Janet's house and speaks with Ari to establish when they will be back home:

-A barrage of Greek hits me and I suddenly realise I'm stoned. Hi, Mum. I take a deep puff of the cigarette and listen. When she's finished I say slowly, making sure I'm not slurring my words, Mum, I'll see you in the afternoon. Another burst of yelling in Greek. They're not coming, I tell her, they're both studying this afternoon. Bullshit, she says loudly in English. She tells me to come straight home. I tell her I'll come when I want to and we hang up on each other. (6)

What is indeed interesting in this case is that the narrator is so conscious of the hypocritical dynamics and theatricality of these scenes, which he enjoys dramatizing by matching them and identifying them with those in the cinema. Thus, he compares art with real life, as we observe in the quote that follows – where Ari's mother, upset, asks him why his brother did not turn up for lunch at her place:

She looks at me, smiles a little. Is he at the library? she asks. Yes, I lie, he'll be there all day.

-You can tell me, she says, he's gone out with Janet, hasn't he? I just stare at the TV. He's studying, Mum. I finish on the food and she starts clearing away the mess. [...]

On screen an ugly bad guy has started a fight with Jimmy Stewart. A blonde woman in tight black suspenders and a white petticoat helps him out by smashing a bottle of spirits over the bad guy's head. She's got great legs and no talent. You can see her eyes wandering towards the camera. I'm not listening to Mum. She can go on about my brother having left home for ages. She broods, cries about it, holds her head low sometimes, sighing deeply, lamenting her boy's betrayal of her. Yet she nurses the betrayal, cultivates it, makes her pain ecstatic because it adds a sheen of tragedy to a boring life. I let her rave and watch the movie. Soon she gives up on me and weeps silently to herself in the kitchen, doing the dishes. (13-14)

However, whereas Ari is fully aware of this "game" between them, his mother apparently lives through it only subconsciously, if we are to judge from her son's comment: "Mum is part of the television generation as well, and she knows shit about anything except what the television and magazines tell her. Brain dead. For her the real world begins every day at seven in the morning with 'Good Morning Australia' " (14-15).

The same tactic is adopted by Ari later, when the family drama culminates in the house creating a rift between his brother and his parents, resulting in Peter's decision to leave home. In this case Ari does not use television exactly as he did the first time, that is just as a means of detaching himself from his mother's whingeing ("I'm not listening to Mum [...] I left her rave and watch the movie", 13-14) but as a channel both for escaping and participating in the drama ("I stayed in my room watching the television, watching the American news with the sound turned low so I could hear the screaming", 75). That is, although he has physically removed himself from the room where his mother is, he can still hear her screaming. This is something which confirms the centrifugal and centripetal role of the Greek family universe, as the latter provides the necessary inherent self-regulating mechanisms of balancing and preserving itself. Thus, even when this universe reaches its utmost limits (see 75-76) television works like a *deus ex machina* to save it in the last moment, as happens in Peter's case after his decision to defect from the family home. Here is how his brother Ari reacts: "I got up and turned off the television, sat down next to him. I put my arm around him. It's okay big brother. I can handle Mum and Dad. Peter started crying, a slow, quiet cry" (75). Despite the fact then that Ari's family has often in the past been led to extremes and the edge of the cliff (like other families who, as he says, "can detonate. Some families are torn apart forever by one small act, only solitary mistake", ibid.), eventually this family has not broken up but has managed to hold together, as if out of mutual necessity.

The suburbs

There are cities of reality and cities of the imagination. [...] Every city does not only function as a place of habitation and cohabitation, a place where social and cultural changes take place and produce the diachronic flow of History, as well as the synchronic flow of the present. The city is also the place where the function of memory occurs, since, without the specific place, time has nowhere to inhabit, nowhere to be experienced. The city functions as a reservoir of our recollections. "Lost time" is regained inside its spaces, since these spaces are full of the shadows and ghosts of the individual and collective past. The spaces of the city – streets, crossings, squares, houses –, as time passes through them and is embedded in them, acquire, for each individual, a separate polysemy. After a certain point in time, when memory appears, the spaces acquire a double face. They are those which are experienced as present and those which have been experienced as past and function refractively as images through memory. Then we have the creation of a dual relationship of reality – experiencing of the present – and its representation, through memory. This relationship leads to the creation of two cities, the real, the one that exists now around us, and the one that has been converted into a memory, that has passed into our subconscious, that has been filtered and transformed into a personal city, a city that reflects our face. (Elena Houzouri, *I Thessaloniki tou Giorgou Ioannou*, Patakis Publishers, Athens 1995, my translation)

In *Loaded* Melbourne, as a city, plays a very important part. To start with, it constitutes the central setting-framework in which the narrator-hero's personal drama unfolds. Moreover it is the city which has contributed greatly to shaping his psychological makeup and personality. As far as the narrator is concerned, this city and especially its suburbs, represented in the story by the four equivalent parts of the book, that is "East", "North", "South", "West", are not at all a typical geographical area. On the contrary, it is an urban area full of life in which he wanders and lives. In other words it is an interactive organism which he constantly interacts with, interrelates to and depends on, since it feeds his story non-stop. Besides, as Elena Houzouri adds,

> The spaces of the city, as time passes, do not only have a topo-geographical situation and utilitarian function but they also claim their personal voice, speak their own language, which is none other than the collective one (social, cultural, political). The spaces of the city, as they drag their footsteps through History, are encumbered with multiple signals, which subsequently they transmit. Thus, depending on the collective and personal experiences of each individual, a kind of conversation with the city is realised. The stronger the experience, the stronger this conversation is with the spaces of the city. That is, a retrogressive relationship is created. [...]
>
> This conversation, in its most creative form, suffices to transform the city and its spaces, to convert it into Myth. Then we

talk about cities of Myth. Because when the experience surpasses reality, it touches the borderline of Myth. And when the Myth is transcribed into sophisticated written expression, then we are in the domain of literature. Thus, the cities follow this route: Reality>Myth>Literature. They become cities of literature, cities of texts. They speak through the texts. Michel Butor ("La Ville comme texte", *Répertoire V*, Minuit, 1982) notes that "When I arrive in a foreign city, I'm accompanied by the relevant text. This text has spoken to me, I have already read about its subject in books and newspapers." (Elena Houzouri, ibid., my translation).

It would not be an exaggeration to claim that without the existence of this particular city Ari's story could hardly stand and develop, as it constitutes the canvass upon which it is woven. That is why the division of the book into the aforementioned four parts is not only for practical but – perhaps more so – for symbolic reasons. That is while we may assume that the four parts, which are named after the four points of the compass, constitute a means of orientation, as far as the life and activity of the narrator-hero are concerned, in fact it is the opposite: a compass which disorients, given that both the narrator-hero, as well as the reader, are lost in the labyrinth of the city and in the melting-pot of its suburbs, the same as "the city of Melbourne blurs into itself" (37).

More specifically: Although Ari frequently dashes out to the city, alone or with others, in order to unwind, to entertain his boredom and to escape from his depressing family environment, eventually these outings not only change the negative psychological state he is in but, almost always, make it worse. Here is a characteristic example from a typical outing of Ari and his sister Alex on their way to a party that their friend Joe gives in his place:

> Alex pulls at my T-shirt. The tram is running down a large road and apart from the street lights, on either side of the highway houses stretched for miles and miles in darkness. I pull the cord

and we get off at an intersection. There is a petrol station at each corner. The four of them are huge, all brightly lit, each with its own car park. The Shell, BP, Ampol and Caltex signs form a neon oasis at the centre of the dark flatlands reaching out from all sides of the intersection. I put a cigarette to my mouth, light it and offer one to Alex. She takes it and we cross the road, into the suburbs.

No one, of course, is on the streets. And every street around here looks like every other street, every stranger you meet walking along looks like the same stranger you passed blocks ago. The blocks are huge. Big brick buildings, one after another. This could be Balwyn, could be Burwood, could be Vermont. Could be Mitcham. Maybe if you grew up around here all the space might mean something to you. East, west, south, north, the city of Melbourne blurs into itself. Concrete on concrete, brick veneer on brick veneer, weatherboard on weatherboard. Walking through the suburbs, I feel like I'm in the ugliest place on the planet. (37-38)

We realise that this description by Ari is made up of only negative elements such as the following: (i) A depressing urban monotony and uniform boredom ("on either side of the highway houses stretch for miles and miles in darkness. [...] And every street around here looks like every other street [...] The blocks are huge. Big brick buildings, one after another. This could be Balwyn, could be Burwood, could be Vermont. Could be Mitcham", ibid.); (ii) an anti-aesthetic construction and ugliness ("Concrete on concrete, brick veneer on brick veneer, weather board on weatherboard. Walking through the suburbs, I feel like I'm in the ugliest place on the planet", ibid.); (iii) Desolation – a product of the inhuman urban design – which contributes to the anti-social behaviour and alienation of people ("No one, of course, is on the streets", ibid.). The only somewhat positive "oasis" in an otherwise grim scenery is the petrol stations which are all "brightly lit." However, this is just a parody since we have an "oasis" which is a product of "neon" ("The Shell, BP, Ampol and Caltex signs from a neon oasis at the centre of the dark flatlands reaching out from all sides of the intersection", 37).

The above is obviously not an objective but a subjective description of the city and its suburbs, as the narrator-hero's perspective is coloured strongly by the way he feels. In other words it constitutes an extension of his negative psychological and emotional state which the external environment-surroundings completes. It is therefore natural that Ari's negative feelings are reflected on the overall visualization of the external urban space. Two obvious reasons that the narrator-hero feels alienated from the environment he is wandering about are, firstly, that he has no memories to connect him to or to identify with the suburbs he mentions ("Maybe if you grew up around here all the space might mean something to you", ibid.) and, secondly that Ari's receptive clarity has been altered by the drugs he has taken ("I don't listen, I just keep walking a little ahead of her, letting the drugs wrap themselves around my head...", 38).

For the narrator-hero the various areas, the various places of the city in which he wanders signal, even semiotically and fragmentarily, the otherwise aimless existence of his – the same as his other addictions (drugs, sex, music) – by acting like its receptacles. Something like a *tabula rasa* upon which he aspires to leave a miniscule trace from the temporary passing of his existence, an existence which – as he knows too well – has no meaning whatsoever other than satisfying the senses. This need to give meaning to his life – even when he knows that it is yet another illusion which forces him to be self-deprecating as we will see further down – arises from the resounding failure of human communication. The absence of the latter is substituted by the various parts of the city (streets, parks, buildings, bridges, beaches, walls, etc) which from being inanimate and neutral, they are transformed, by the narrator, into passive receivers willing to respond – unlike humans – to a paradoxical fruitful interaction. The above points are reflected in the incident below where Ari, having been rejected by his fellow human beings – even when he attempts to help them – resorts to a wall with which he desperately attempts to be in touch, something which others have also tried to do, by leaving their fleeting mark on it:

> At St George's Road I stick out my finger and head towards the City. Cars fly past me. I hear occasional shouts and abuse but none of the cars stop. At the lights a young punk girl is vomiting against a wall. Are you okay?, I ask her and she tells me to fuck off. I lean against the lightpost and watch the yellow bile pulse out of her mouth. When she's finished she staggers off across the street, ignoring the traffic and enters a pub. I stay leaning against the post, listening to the acoustic hippie-shit music coming from the pub.
>
> The vomit seeps down the wall and runs in a little stream into the gutter. The wall is plastered with graffiti. Rap art and political graffiti. Act Up is sprayed in red. An anarchy symbol in black. Someone has scribbled Nelson Mandela Was Duped in blue. Underneath, in white, red and blue, a picture of the Madonna. A blank wall on which people want to leave their mark. Like dogs pissing on a shrub. I wish I had a texta on me, to write my name, and then underneath, to write; I'm not saying anything. (77)

The above naturalistic description reflects vividly the brutalization of the people in this city, whose behaviour is likened to that of animals ("A blank wall on which people want to leave their mark. Like dogs pissing on a shrub") since, when they don't get their inner feelings out on the wall (writing them with spray or marker) they imitate the dogs. The only difference being that instead of "pissing", they vomit ("a young punk girl is vomiting against the wall. [...] I lean against the lightpost and watch the yellow bile pulse out of her mouth. [...] The vomit seeps down the wall and runs in a little stream into the gutter"). In this respect the wall is a mirror, a mosaic which reflects not only Ari's personal situation but the overall human condition of which Ari now becomes an eyewitness. As for his remark ("I wish I had a texta on me, to write my name, and then underneath, to write; I'm not saying anything"), it is a self-ironic comment regarding his meaningless and aimless boring life. The reason he would write "I'm not saying anything" is, apparently, because this specific "fresco" alone can tell more than a thousand words.

The narrator-hero's relationship with all suburbs is one of repugnance and hate. In the sub-title "I detest the East" he begins his narration by saying: "I detest the East. The whole fucking mass of it: the highways, the suburbs, the hills [...] A backdrop of Seven Elevens, shopping malls, gigantic parking" (41). The reasons for this repugnance are not entirely clear despite the fact that his perspective seems to have class-conscious motives ("I detest [...] the rich cunts [...] The whitest part of my city, where you'll see the authentic white Australian, is in the eastern suburbs"). Here of course it is arguable – judging from his own experience – that his repugnance could also spring from the fact that the rich people of the eastern suburbs have the facility to enjoy sex much easier ("I was picked up by a guy once, he lived in this shithole suburb somewhere, Burwood or Balwyn or Bentleigh or Boronia and I woke up in this strange man's bed..."). Because, for all his hate for the rich and his inability to believe the enormous wealth existing in these suburbs, yet, he feels more comfortable inside his working-class shell ("... went into the front yard, looked down the street and thought oh-my-fucking-god-is-this-America? I didn't feel sane again until I reached the corrosive stenches of the city. Lead and carbon dioxide in my lungs to make me forget the Disneyland I had woken up to", 41).

Ari's erotic behaviour, however, is not restricted to and does not concern only the rich white Australians but also the *nouveau-riche* migrants (everybody, including the Greeks of course of whom he is being more vitriolic), as well as the poor migrants about whom he speaks with contempt and disgust. Indeed, he occasionally attacks the latter more aggressively and bitterly, apparently because the poor who manage to become *nouveau-riche* eventually prove to be more cruel and inhuman than those who are born rich:

For my Aunt Nikki, Alan and his family don't exist. And it is true, they don't exist. They are invisible to the rich wogs by the river. The wog community is a backstabbing, money-hungry, snobbish, self-righteous community. It has no time for losers or deviants. The peasant Greeks who have made their money working the milk bars, delis, markets and fish shops of Melbourne look down on the long-haired loutish Greek boy and the bleached-blonde sluttish Greek girl with disdain and denial. The denial is total. You are not me. We are not you. Fuck off. You don't exist.

Ethnicity is a scam, a bullshit, a piece of crock. The fortresses of the rich wogs on the hill are there not to keep the *Australezo* out, but to refuse entry to the uneducated-long-haired-bleached-blonde-no-money wog. No matter what the roots of the rich wogs, Greek, Italian, Chinese, Vietnamese, Lebanese, Arab, whatever, I'd like to get a gun and shoot them all. Bang bang. The East is hell. Designed by Americans. (43)

The reason he attacks the *nouveau-riche* migrants so violently is because they discriminate against their own folk, who were not lucky enough to become like them – to the extent that they write off their existence, especially those who were complete failures and fringe-dwellers: "It has no time for losers or deviants. [...] The denial is total. You are not me. We are not you. Fuck off. You don't exist" (43).

For Ari the suburbs gain some meaning, that is, his viewpoint becomes more positive, only when he associates them with his life and some of the childhood memories he retains of them. In that respect memory plays a relaxing, soothing, conciliatory role in relation to his environment: "I have managed to snatch some pleasure in the East. Long family drives when I was still a very young kid, driving up to the hills and we'd play amongst deep green trees, a rainforest so beautiful that it looked like it came out of some lush dream" (42).

Thus, Ari's "pleasure" from the East derives – as the first time in the beginning of the book – from the references to his happy family moments and, in this case, the outings to nature during his childhood years. These are two poles (childhood – nature) whose innocence and purity the all powerful time and the degeneration of life could not erode in his consciousness. His childhood is a dimension of his life – perhaps the only one – which has remained untouched, pure, chaste (to the extent that "the rainforest [was] so beautiful that it looked like it came out of some lush dream") apparently because, as he says, "I was still a very young kid." Yet we realise again that this bygone taste of his "lost paradise" was brief and ephemeral ("I have managed to snatch some pleasure") is his expression, which implies that he was lucky that he "snatched" even "some pleasure" from this forbidden, for his social class, fruit of happiness ("of the lush dream"), since people like him are children of a lesser God. Equally interesting is also the fact that his visual perception and feelings about the suburbs remain the same since his childhood years to his present age, that is, their inhuman urban formation, their boring uniformity and ugliness, in combination with his deep-seated fear that he would become a part of and lose himself in them:

> Later, there were long drives out of the city where we would cleave through the Eastern suburbs, drive down the long stretches of road. I would lie back on the passenger seat, music throbbing around me in whatever car we were, the continuous loop of brick-veneer houses forming a visual mantra. In a car where you can move through the suburbs but never walk out and be part of them, never to lose yourself in them, I feel safe. (42)

Finally, Ari's painful impression and repugnance for the suburbs could be summarised in the fact that they are cold and inhuman, like open prisons which mould the psychology of those they shelter. In short, they are places where human communication is absent as "Television rules. School, work, shopping, sex are distractions to the central activity of the Eastern suburbs: flicking the channels on the remote control" (42).

Ari says the same about an uncle of his who "lifts crates every day, and is bored out of his skull every night. He comes to visit my father every weekend to enter the old world of coffee shops and intimate dialogue. In the East, in the new world of suburbia there is no dialogue, no conversation, no places to go out: for there is no need, there is television" (43).

Another equally important sub-chapter where the narrator-hero continues to be preoccupied with the suburbs and the relationship and meaning they have in his life is the one entitled "Hit the North" (81). Here too his perspective, views and feelings about the northern suburbs are the same as before; the difference being that in this case there is not a single trace of a positive and optimistic note. It is characteristic that the very negative depiction of the northern suburbs is conducted, firstly, in reference to their anti-aesthetic urban planning and structure ("The Northern suburbs are unrelentingly flat with ugly little brick boxes where the labouring and unemployed classes roam circular streets; the roads to nowhere" (81); secondly, and most importantly, is the fact that the character of these suburbs has been shaped decisively by the strong migrant presence, to the point where the Australian presence – to which not a single reference is made – has been entirely eliminated. Besides, the following statement by the narrator is indicative of the above observations: "The North isn't Melbourne, it isn't Australia. It is a little village in the mountains of the Mediterranean transposed to the bottom of the southern hemisphere..." (81-82). This seems not only paradoxical but a bit of an oxymoron also, since, in this case, we have a peculiar kind of racism: that of the hero, who is of migrant heritage, not against white Australian but indiscriminately against all migrants who have settled in and dominated the northern suburbs. Ari's detestation, hate and contempt for the North are due not only to the anti-aesthetic look of these suburbs but also to the fact that they function as places-traps, as locations where migrants live, die and are "buried":

> The North, if you're a wog, will entrap you. Push, push, push against it. Little Arabic communities, little Greek communities, little Turkish and Italian communities. The Northern suburbs are full of the smells of goats cheese and olive oil, hashish and bitter

coffee. The Northern suburbs are unrelentingly flat with ugly little brick boxes where the labouring and unemployed classes roam circular streets; the roads to nowhere.

The North isn't Melbourne, it isn't Australia. It is a little village in the mountains of the Mediterranean transported to the bottom of the southern hemisphere; markets of little old ladies in black screeching in a Babel of languages. Harridans, fishwives, scum. The North is a growing, pulsating sore on the map of my city, the part of the city in which I, my family, my friends are meant to buy a house, grow a garden, shop, watch TV and be buried in. The North is where the wog is supposed to end up. And therefore I hate the North, I view it with as much contempt as possible. (81-82)

The hero's detestation is also due to the fact that the migrants tend to transplant their cultural traditions, their customs and habits and their old way of life in their new homeland, unaltered, under the illusion that they live in their old homeland from which either they were driven out or they were forced to leave. And this is exactly where the oxymoron lies: that in spite of all this – the reasons of their uprooting – they persist masochistically in their old attitudes and way of life. In this respect the notorious multicultural diversity, according to the narrator, does not enrich Melbourne – as so frequently the politicians and the media are trumpeting – but on the contrary it stagnates and makes the city regress since nothing new is born out of this "colonization." Much more so when the fate of these very migrants and their children is unlikely to change:

> I resist the North, the spaces in which Greeks, Italians, Vietnamese, and the rest of the one hundred and ninety other races of scum, refos and thieves hold on to old ways, old cultures, old rituals which no longer can or should mean anything. I hit the North, get off the bus and walk along the steaming asphalt streets and I want to scream to the fucking peasants on the sidewalk, Hey you, you aren't in Europe, aren't in Asia, aren't in Africa any more. Face

it, motherfuckers (and motherfucker is appropriate, the greatest obscenity: the matriarch reigns supreme in these wog houses. She may be kicked and beaten, exploited and hated, but it is she who maintains a rigid grip on the traditions that blighted her life and will blight the lives of her children). Face it motherfuckers, I want to scream, there isn't a home any more. This is the big city, the bright lights of the west, this is a wannabe-America and all the prayers to God or Allah or the Buddha can't save your children now. (82)

Here too, as in almost the whole book, we observe Ari reacting impulsively. In other words it is his impetuousness and not prudence that guides his "reasoning." Something which is natural, after all, given that nobody (not even himself) believes seriously that he wants to convince anybody. His aim is – mainly – to protest, to complain, to get indignant and angry. Hence his only satisfaction is that he is a spirit of contradiction, a thorn in the eye of society that detests, using and flaunting himself as an embodiment of his views, that is as a living denial of the migrants' unfulfilled dreams, as the following quote indicates tellingly: "I put on a scowl and roam the North in my dirtiest clothes, looking and feeling unwashed. I am the wog boy as nightmare" (82).

The last oxymoron but not paradoxical fact – as we are used to the narrator-hero's contradictions – is that for all his venting of spleen on the North, eventually Ari is forced to compromise with this suburb (seeing that his fate is essentially there) and also to find himself, as he confesses, as opposed to the other ones where he loses himself: "In the North I find myself, find shadows that recall my shadow. I roam the North so I can come face to face with the future that is being prepared for me. On my knees, with hate written on my face, I spit out bile, semen, saliva, phlegm, I spit it all out. I spit on the future that has been prepared for me" (83-84).

In the sub-chapter "The smell of the sea" – regarding the northern suburbs – the narrator-hero, taking as a starting point the present and the sea-side suburb of St Kilda, embarks on a nostalgic retrospection to the past, in order to reveal how this specific suburb and its "beach which for decades has been the home of junkies and whores, refugees and migrants" (131) together with his father's insults, influenced and "have forced me, they have nourished me" (132), as he claims, since "Under the piers, in toilets, in the back of discos, St Kilda offered me in my youth a smorgasbord of illicit pleasures. Cheap drugs, free sex. Getting drunk, getting stoned, getting high" (131). But the pleasures that this disreputable suburb of fringe-dwellers has offered Ari are not only sensual but at the same time spiritually uplifting, since its geographical position lent itself to day-dreaming and escaping into other worlds through the imagination. It is characteristic that the mediation of memory, as in the case of the North that was discussed before, does not simply transform the landscape-place-suburb but spiritually uplifts the psychological and emotional world of the narrator-hero – something that rarely happens in the book – lending to the description a nostalgic, emotional charge, an almost poetic tone, as we realise:

> Many nights I would take the tram and head down the beach, walk along the sand and sit on the end of the pier looking out to the darkness of the bay and dream of what I could find if I dived into the waves and swam away. Looking out to the horizon, I would dream of new places, new faces, new lives possible to live at the other side of the world. Never thoughts of ice, instead I thought of the North, the places my mother and father talked to me about. The arid soil and hot weather of the Mediterranean. (131-132)

Conversely, Ari's reference to the present and St Kilda's current state, reflects the negativism of his viewpoint, the coldness of his feelings, his psychological emptiness and the fearful feeling that – the way this suburb is shaping up, stripped off his personal memories – he is in danger of losing himself, as in the other suburbs: "The beach [...] now being redone, remodelled, restructured into a playground for the sophisticated professional. [...] Along the coastline of the city, the beaches open up to the chasm which is the end of the world. Below us there is ice. Nothing else. No human life, no villages, no towns, no cities" (131).

The reason why Ari is not alienated in this suburb but feels comfortable and can identify with it is because, as he observes, "To the South are the wogs who have been shunted out of their communities. Artists and junkies and faggots and whores, the sons and daughters no longer talked about, no longer admitted into the arms of family. In the South, in the flats and apartments smelling of mildew and mice, are all the wog rejects from the North, the East, the West. Flushed out towards the sea. When you look straight across the ocean you look into the face of your dream" (132).

Which means that Ari, who admires the "outcasts" and pariahs, when visiting and wandering in this suburb, has the (pseudo) illusion that he is being initiated into their world and way of life, something which allows him to be his authentic self and feel free of restrictions, constraints and compromises: "To be free, for me as a Greek, is to be a whore. To resist the path of marriage and convention, of tradition and obedience, I must make myself an object of derision and contempt. Only then am I able to move outside the suffocating obligations of family and loyalty" (ibid.).

In this suburb of St Kilda, Ari feels more at home than anywhere else because, as he alludes, he too thinks of himself as a living corpse, like those of the outcast migrants who "Flushed out towards the sea" (ibid.) given that the seaside constantly reminds him of it. For all this, it is as if the domination of the sea all over the geographical area, with its commanding and magic presence, assimilates, neutralises and abolishes the existing urban monstrosities of the damned, namely "the flats and apartments smelling of mildew and mice" (ibid.) because "When you look straight across the ocean you look into the face of your dreams" (ibid.). In other words, for the narrator-hero, even though he was born in Australia, the seaside has the magic ability to reflect the bygone paradise of his childhood, which reminded him of his Mediterranean origins ("The arid soil and hot weather of the Mediterranean", ibid.) but also his present hell ("The sea breeze of the southern ocean, the breeze that comes up from the end of the world, makes me strong, draws me to the whores and faggots and junkies. I am a sailor and a whore. I will be till the end of the world" (133).

In the last part of the book "West", although the narrator-hero refers to the western suburbs of Melbourne, at the same time he attempts to summarise his views about the big city of Melbourne, generally, under the sub-chapter "There is this urban myth" (142). To begin with, we observe that Ari's reference to the poor, downgraded and marginalised western suburbs, is done at a purely theoretical level – in order to strengthen his already known views about the suburbs and the life in them, as in a final account – and not at all at a practical and personal level. Thus, in spite of the fact that he uses arguments equally passionate as previously, he does it by keeping a strange distance from the western suburbs ("I don't belong to the West. The West of chemical-vomit skies", 143), with the exception of a general and indirect reference to the past with the use of the first person plural ("The noise of the factory was the soundtrack to our childhood", ibid.). Otherwise the narrator-hero does not walk, does not wander, does not relate personally to the West. The reason he distances himself now – physically – from the working class suburbs of the West is due, as he himself hints at, to the fact that his belonging to any social category – to the rich or poor minorities or Australians – would undermine the whole spirit of the book as well as his conclusions of this sub-chapter regarding the city and its residents, hence his neutral stance: "Us, them. I am neither. I don't belong to the West" (143). This stance of his – for all its contradiction with the one he has adopted previously for other suburbs – in this case is appropriate, in the sense that, at least on the face of it, it makes his positions more credible as if deriving from inside the view of an unbiased, objective observer-urban planner. Thus, initially we have the general division of the city into two, reminiscent of heaven and hell:

> There is a point in my city, underneath the Swanston Street Bridge where you can sit by the Yarra River and contemplate the

chasm that separates this town. Look down the river towards the East and there are green parks rolling down to the river, beautiful Victorian bridges sparkle against the blue sky. Face West and there is the smoke-scarred embankment leading towards the wharfs. The beauty and the beast. All cities, all cities depend on this chasm. (144)

The narrator-hero's comparison of the deceptive looks of the western suburbs to the illusory dreams of migrants and young people is remarkable and successful. Specifically, at night the West takes on the dreamy dimensions of "a shimmering valley of lights" (143) only to be invalidated at day time when its true nightmarish face is revealed in the form of an "industrial quilt":

The West at night, as you drive over the Westgate Bridge, is a shimmering valley of lights. In the day, under the harsh glare of the sun, the valley reveals itself as an industrial quilt of wharfs, factories, warehouses, silos and power plants. And the endless stretch of suburban housing estates. The West is a dumping ground; a sewer of refugees, the migrants, the poor, the insane, the unskilled and the uneducated. (143-144)

However, it does not suffice to demythologise only the *face* of the city but also the *dreams* of the "outcasts" who dream of living in such a city which eventually proves to be their leveller. At the same time, moving a step forward, the narrator-hero, having previously stripped his "city" of any recognizable feature of its identity which might make it stand out from other cities – as if motivated by a thirst for revenge – decides in turn to demolish completely the city itself, as he identifies it with "All cities" which he likens to "sewers" which host "international human refuse":

All cities, from Melbourne to Karachi, New York to Istanbul, Paris to Nairobi, include sewers for the international human refuse that keeps being churned out through war, famine, unemployment, poverty. The insane migrant will pack some bags and leave the shithole they were born in for the promise of better pay and a better life somewhere else.

There is no America. There is no New World. There is no future available to the refo and the wog any more. Nowhere to turn, like the song. They don't need factories any more, they have elegantly-sculptured machines powered by microchips. They don't need labour any more. Not now, now that they have the Internet. Nowhere to run, like the song. The sewers keep filling up, they are fucking overflowing and the refuse is choking up the atmosphere. From Singapore to Beijing, from Rio to Johannesburg.

There is a last, and very cherished, urban myth. That every new generation has it better than the one that came before it. Bullshit. I am surfing on the down-curve of capital. The generations after this are not going to build on the peasants' landholdings. There's no jobs, no work, no factories, no wage packet, no half-acre block. There is no more land. I am sliding towards the sewer, I'm not even struggling against the flow. I can smell the pungent aroma of shit, but I'm still breathing. (144)

Conclusion

Loaded has a rudimentary, almost non-existent plot, a few not particularly impressive characters – with, perhaps, the exception of transvestite Johnny – and a spontaneous, almost impulsive – not so masterly crafted – narration which is mingled with dialogue, because of the use of the dash instead of inverted commas. (This makes the text awkward, as the voice and thoughts of the narrator-hero cannot be distinguished from those of the other characters). In this narration the writer manages to cover a twenty-four hour period of orgy and debauchery of his hero within the space of 151 pages of dense, vibrant and unrelenting prose, regardless of the calibre of the novel's characters.

If we exclude the extreme naturalistic element, in the form of raw scenes of debauchery (a cocktail of binge drinking, promiscuous sex and drugs), in combination with the provocative, vulgar and, occasionally, shocking language used, we would say that there is little else remarkable or unusual in the novel. And yet, although Ari's low-key life and story are scarcely dramatic or eventful (given that action and happenings are minimal and the hero is faltering, despite his raging rant and deceptively rebellious pose) the novel is nevertheless pulsating with unusual fervour, dynamism and a radiant – almost bestial – vibrancy and energy which permeates every single page of it.

That is why, regardless of whether the reader feels attraction or repulsion, agrees, disagrees or remains indifferent to the hero and his views and rantings, what is eventually left as a memorable highlight in his mind, once the reading is over, is not some kind of "message" or "enlightenment" but a strong sense of frenzied *energy* which gushes profusely out of the pores of the book's pages, as if it were a living, vibrating body. And this is, I think, what fascinates and, at the same time, compensates the reader more than anything else for any shortcomings in this fictional debut of Tsiolkas: the irrepressible and irresistible *energy* radiated by a primal heart-rending howl of pain, through the anguished hedonistic spasm of writing.

2

THE JESUS MAN:

The curse of the (in)human condition

(Labouring with the loss of faith)

Introduction

The story of the second novel by Tsiolkas *The Jesus Man* (Vintage, 1999) is about three characters, the three brothers of the Stefano family – Dominic, Tommy and Louie – of Greek-Italian descent, a family which is allegedly haunted by an old curse. All four males of this family, including their father Artie, are dysfunctional characters, both as individuals as well as a family. In spite of the fact that their individual problems differ in range and magnitude, as is natural after all, most of them are nevertheless common to all four and could be summarised *grosso modo* as the following: (i) identity problems (cultural, religious, sexual); (ii) economic and socio-political problems (unemployment being the worst of all); (iii) relationship problems (with the family, the opposite sex, colleagues); (iv) psychological problems (with self-image, self-esteem, obsessions, guilt, metaphysics, superstition, depression, etc). Notwithstanding the fact that these four male characters are recounting, to various degrees, their own individual story each – so as to compose a mosaic of the history of working class suburban Melbourne in the late part of the 20th century – the novel essentially focuses on the life and times of the middle brother Tommy.

The novel begins with Tommy's childhood recollections of the notorious political event, the sacking of the Whitlam Labor Government in 1975, which enrages his family. Much more so when this event virtually signals the fading of the hopes and dreams of millions of working class Australians for a better life, making them now bewildered, disheartened and disempowered. The actual setting of the story, however, takes place at the beginning of the difficult nineties and their socio-political changes, with the conservative Liberal Party governments coming to power, thus exacerbating the already precarious situation of the low socio-economic classes. Hence Tommy's dismissal from work through redundancy – due to the economic climate and the restructuring at his work-place on account of the invasion of modern technology –, and of course his failure in finding another job, precipitate his complete collapse. Because by losing his job, he also loses control over his life.

Thus he gradually becomes introverted, indifferent, obsessive with his body image and hostile to himself. In order to escape from and entertain his impasses a little, by compensating for his psychological emptiness – as he is eventually cut off from everybody and lives in seclusion as a recluse – he turns to some forms of entertainment which prove to be self-destructive. Namely, pornography, alcohol, excessive masturbation and the obsessive watching of television programs with violent content, all of which lead him, gradually but steadily, to depression, insanity, murder and suicide. Because it does not take long for Tommy to crack, as he is sinking every day further and deeper into the dark paths of his existential abyss, by stubbornly avoiding seeking external help.

It is not at all by accident that the following facts contribute decisively to Tommy's downfall and eventual demise: Firstly, the decline of political life in Australia – with the appearance of the ultra right-wing racist politician Pauline Hanson (aptly nicknamed 'The Racist' in the novel) who is elected in Parliament in 1996, preceded by the climbing to power of the conservative Prime Minister of the Liberals, John Howard. Secondly, the relentless television bombardment of negative news bulletins, pessimistic and depressing shows and other programs and spectacles of atrocious violence – especially of a sexual nature. Thirdly, all the above culminate when there intervenes the accidental as well as fatal meeting – and indeed in the most inappropriate moment – between Tommy and a half-crazed born-again Christian, Neil. The latter preaches publicly the forthcoming doomsday and perseveres in convincing Tommy, too, that the Apocalypse in already *ante-portas*.

As there also intervene some additional historic incidents which Tommy deems as ominous (such as the fall of the Berlin Wall, the release of Nelson Mandela, the War in the Gulf, etc), it does not take much for Tommy to be convinced of Neil's predictions, given his vulnerable psychological state. Especially when he mistakes all these happenings as a forerunner for what will follow, as they are combined with and reflect his overall misfortune and decline, which are sealed catalytically by the stopping of his unemployment benefit and the forthcoming eviction from his rented flat. Thus, the last act of the drama is played out when Tommy ends up in the savage killing of Neil, whom he considers a serial sex killer of children, whereas, subsequently, he castrates himself in an inhumanely hideous manner.

This desperate deed leaves his family and beloved ones aghast, asking themselves, with untold sadness and despair, what has gone wrong and how and why this unspeakable evil has come about. At the same time, they are puzzled as to what extent this indescribable tragedy could be the result of a self-fulfilling "curse", which was rumoured to haunt their family for generations.

The second part of the novel deals with Lou, the youngest of the three brothers, who, in his attempt to come to terms with, understand and explain the tragic and irrational death of his brother, and at the same time to find his own way in the world, free from any future "curse", pain and unhappiness – paradoxically – chooses to follow an Epicurean way of life, where sex, alcohol and drugs are predominant.

The Role of the Preface

In all of Tsiolkas' novels, there is only one rather brief Preface which appears in *The Jesus Man*. Hence it may arguably be of particular interest, as the question arises: why is it needed and what is its role in this novel?

I think that in this Preface – which is, in a sense, not something separate but an integral part of the overall novel – the writer attempts to adumbrate the essence of his work, by predisposing the reader for what will follow, in regard to the thematic and manneristic treatment of the material. (This probably happens for the following reasons: Firstly, because the writer wants to somewhat prepare the reader psychologically and to stop him from being shocked. Secondly, because he wants to balance the grotesque, naturalistic and "anti-literary" element, with a professed real sense of mannerism. Thirdly, because mannerism, or what is called "literariness" (that is, the excessive displaying of sophisticated narrative techniques), is not one of his primary concerns. Hence he prefers either to ignore or parody it, by playing a purely personal, narratively uncommitted game that has no rules. I believe that all the above take place in this novel of Tsiolkas, with the latter – the element of parody and/or self-parody – being the most perceptible, as this ensues mainly in the Preface).

The Preface establishes most of the major themes which preoccupy the writer and are dominant in his novel, such as the following:

(i) The television obsession

> It was like there was me, the baby, there was Dom, the oldest and a man, and somewhere in between was Tommy. He was happiest watching TV, sitting close to the screen, the rest of the family behind him, not in view.
>
> Of course, I remember the television as well, that it was always on. But some of my earliest memories [...] are of being a small child and listening to the adults tell stories, their words competing with the TV. (5-6)

(ii) The obsessive preoccupation with the body: sex and pornography

> That night two things happened. I showered and slowly pulled

back my foreskin. It was tight and it hurt, hurt badly; it stung. But I pulled it back and started to lather up, spent five fucking minutes rubbing my cock raw till there wasn't a fleck of dried old scum on it. And the second thing? Later, in bed, Tommy still watching TV in the lounge, I tried masturbating by tugging for the first time. Before, what I did was to roll my cock between my palms. It felt different, it didn't feel as good, but it felt the right thing to do. This was how Dom did it, how boys were meant to do it. (5)

(iii) The religious element

I am an atheist but I once did experience the shock of a vision. [...] The terror I experienced is indescribable. All I can say of it is that I had stumbled across the mad order of nature: it was screaming out the riddle of God. (1)

(iv) The crows (as myth and reality)

This book is about a family, my family, which has been followed by the crow for generations. [...]

Later, around the fire, the children asleep in the tents, I started questioning Dominic about the crow. What did it mean? Why had it followed us all our lives? He was exasperated by my questions. Eva was smoking a joint, in and out of the conversation. (2)

(v) The curse as a self-fulfilling prophecy

As we emerged from the scrub and onto the beach, we saw a line of crows, a horizontal; dotting along the shoreline; they were pecking into the sand. The first bird we approached was tearing into a dark object, and it refused to move as our shadows fell across it. [...] The terror I experienced is indescribable. [...] Why did we feel fear? It was the insane symmetry, the *mathematical* symmetry of what I saw – the neat column of birds feeding on blood and flesh. I can understand why the crow appears again and again in folk superstition as the herald of death. I saw them hungry for meat, *famished*, their zeal murderous. (1-2)

Although in the Preface the theme of "guilt and self-punishment/suicide" is not explicitly mentioned, it is nevertheless alluded to in the "indescribable terror" the narrator felt in the presence of crows, the manifestation of "the riddle of God" (1).

But also manneristically, the writer outlines *a priori* the way in which he intends to go about in this particular fictional work. Specifically, referring to the, alleged, main theme of the novel, that is the *curse* which "follows" his family and is symbolised by the ever presence of the crow, he observes: "This book is about a family, my family, which has been followed by the crow for generations. This is a myth and, like all myths, atheists and skeptics will scorn it. I'm not sure that I myself can claim a faith in what I am about to tell you" (2).

At first we need to point out that here, in this Preface, as indeed in the overall novel, the narrator is Louie, the younger of the three Stefano family sons, who adopts the first person narration ("It was like there was me, the baby, there was Dom, the oldest and a man, and somewhere in between was Tommy", 5). But a closer reading reveals that this voice, under the "veil" of Louie, belongs more to the actual writer and less or not at all to the persona of Louie. This ensues from the fact that the narrator constantly contradicts and self-refutes himself, as we notice in the aforementioned quote. That is, whereas on the one hand he states confidently and categorically that "This is a myth" and that "I'm not sure that I myself can claim a faith in what I am about to tell you" (2), on the other hand he is full of doubts and uncertainties, compelled to ask his brother for explanations ("Later [...] I started questioning Dominic about the crow. What did it mean? Why had it followed us all our lives? He was exasperated by my questions", 2). Even from the very first introductory line of the novel, while he confesses affirmatively that "I am an atheist", he immediately hastens to accept the existence of the divine presence by adding: "... but I once did experience the shock of a vision. [...] I had stumbled across the mad order of nature: it was screaming out the riddle of God" (1).

However, the dividing line between the narrative voice of the writer (narrator) and that of the narrator (Louie) becomes absolutely clear in the following quote: "But some of my earliest memories – very early memories, those memories that reach back beyond when time became concrete, before time became clocked – are of being a small child and listening to the adults tell stories, their words competing with the TV" (6).

In the above quote, no matter how much the writer strives to hide behind Louie's voice, he betrays himself, for the very simple reason that in a very skilful way he touches upon matters of purely narrative interest. Specifically, whereas just a moment earlier Louie was conversing with almost childish naivety (even though he is a grown-up student) and questioning his brother (2), all of a sudden he speaks about whether the frontiers between memories and time can be established ("very early memories, those memories that reach back beyond when time became concrete, before time became clocked", 6) as well as the "competition" and the inferences he was exposed to the medium of the spoken word of his family and the medium of television ("some of my earliest memories [...] are of being a small child and listening to adults tell stories, their words competing with the TV", ibid.). In other words we are dealing with some essential elements of literature which can be of interest mainly to an experienced practitioner of fiction and perhaps less so to a young student such as Louie.

Subsequently, this narrative problematization is intensified and deepened to such a degree that there are very few doubts left in the reader that this alleged narrative voice of Louie is that of the writer. Initially the narrator makes an ostensible separation between the two stories – that of his family and that of his own ("I want to offer a history [...] in my own words", 6-7). With this professed naive comment, the component of the fictional process is obviously being parodied. In fact we are dealing here with a game of self-parody, as the boundaries between what is domestic and what is personal are in any case blurred and indiscernible in the narration, as equally indiscernible is the myth and reality of Louie's "family curse": "-It's a myth, Louie, he told me. Understand? It's part of our family, who we are. [...] –But myths aren't true, I insisted. [...] –That's university, he goaded me, you just want to question everything. –So myths are true? –Some are. [...] –Our family are a bit obsessed with myths, aren't they? [...] –The crow is nothing, Lou, all right? You don't need the crow to understand our family", 2-3).

This game of self-parody continues in the same mode and culminates with the narrator talking now about "honesty" in the narration of his story ("I'll try and be honest, tell you what I know", 7), only to refute it as soon as he utters it, by underlining the true nature of narrative practice, which is the myth: "But it is an interpretation; and I have to go back to beginnings and in the beginning I wasn't there. So it may be that some of what I say is bullshit, is speculation, lies and fabrications passed on. Myth. But in wishing to describe a family it would be ludicrous to deny it its myths" (7).

The refrain with which the writer closes his Preface, and which is reminiscent of an entry in a dictionary of narratology, confirms the self-reflective nature of the Preface, in which the voice of the narrator-writer stands out.

Finally, what is most inappropriate, contradictory and odd in the said Preface is the comic element, reflected in the funny story that the narrator remembers from his childhood, regarding the paedophile village priest in Greece, who was caught in the act by his wife. The insertion of such an unexpected event which is out of place both with the content of the Preface as well as with the rest of the novel, remains a mystery. A possible explanation could be that the presence of this comic element arising from a random memory counter-balances the tragic aspect which reigns everywhere in the novel (in the form of the "curse" and its consequences) with the infiltration of this incidental hilarious note. Besides, it may not be at all by accident that the Preface closes with the following addition: "Before I begin there is one thing I must insist on, that you must understand: we also shared laughter" (7) – even though this "laughter" is not to be found anywhere else in the novel.

The nightmare of unemployment and the psychopathology of the unemployed

The subject of unemployment has preoccupied Tsiolkas since his very first novel *Loaded* and in the case of his second one (*The Jesus Man*), not only does he continue to see it as a subject of pivotal importance but explores it even more thoroughly. (Indeed we are often under the impression that the story of Ari, sworn enemy of any effort – such as studying and working – continues and comes to a completion in the character of Tommy this time, as if he is taking over the torch from Ari).

It is a theme which the writer not only handles with great mastery, but also authentically and convincingly, given that, as a child of working class migrants he has first-hand experience of the spectre of unemployment in his immediate environment (family, relatives, friends). Indeed it happens in the same way as his hero Tommy (who also happens to be a child of Greek migrants) experiences it in all its dramatic and nightmarish splendour, even though he is a second generation migrant: for this is exactly the greatest irony or curse of being a migrant. Because although Tommy's parents migrated in order to escape from the curse of unemployment, not only did they meet with it in the euphemistically called "Lucky Country", but now their own children are also experiencing it to the core, perhaps under worse circumstances (according to Tommy's mother), as if it were a kind of original sin that hounds them. The relevant dialogue conducted in the Stefano family is quite revealing:

-How's work, Tommy?
-Fine, Dad.

-They still talking of selling up?

-Yep. Tommy didn't look at Soo-Ling.

-Well, you should keep your eye out for other jobs.

-It ain't that easy, Dad.

-It was easy for me. Maximum two days and I'd find me a new job. I'd knock at every factory door. And you've been to fucking college. You gotta get off your bum.

It isn't that fucking easy any more. Soo-Ling wanted to scream the words. [...]

-Arto, you're a malaka, an idiot. There's a recession on, it's not like when you and I started. (71)

Thus, although not stated explicitly but only implicitly, it is understood that an inseparable element of the legendary "curse" haunting Tommy's family, is also the unemployment problem which has contributed to Tommy's suicide.

It would be superfluous to point out here the importance of work, not only as a major source of income and livelihood for the vast majority of people but also as an essential factor of their dignity and self-respect. Thus, any restructuring in the workplace, with the invasion of modern technology, resulting in the dismissal of staff, naturally has a huge impact on the mental health and generally on the people's destiny. That is why one could assert that Tommy's overall misfortune (which is summarised in the expression "He was falling" (99) which led him to his tragic death, has as its starting point the imminent closure of the print shop in which he was working, as reflected in the following quote:

> The company was to shut down the print shop. That decision had already been made though it had not yet been communicated to staff. But the threat of closure had been a strong rumour for months and the unease and fear had begun to accentuate the petty differences among the staff. For a long time the print shop and the

mail room had been divided. [...] For the administrative staff and among the mail clerks – young, some straight out of school – the union did not exist.

Tommy had paid union dues from the day he started work. It had been a familial obligation. [...]

He was falling; he knew it. He was going to lose this job and he had no idea and no inclination for future work. (98-99)

The whole climate of uncertainty, with "the threat of closure [which] had been a strong rumour for months and the unease and fear" (98) intensifies his stress and anxiety by worsening Tommy's already problematic mental state and widening the crack inside him. ("He had been given a script for Serapax, to relieve his anxiety", 140. And elsewhere: "Rent, he recalled, frustrated, angry, rent was due", 89). Let it be noted that Tommy does not like nor is happy with his job. He rather sees it as a chore. But this does not necessarily mean that he would prefer to lose it either. Much as he dislikes it, it does not cease to be a crutch for him – not just an economic but also a psychological one, as it offers some purpose to his daily life, by "entertaining", so to speak, his boredom and taking his mind off his problems. In short, it is a kind of work-therapy for him since, if anything, it offers him a minimum of self-confidence and dignity, especially in terms of the fragile mental state he is in. In this respect, his job constitutes for him a kind of "life-jacket." That is why, just the prospect or rather the certainty of losing his job panicked his girl-friend Soo-Ling, to the point where she did not hesitate to confide her concerns to Eva ("-Eva, I'm scared what'll happen if Tommy loses his job", 112. And elsewhere: "The fear had no meaning. It was fear, pure, concrete. It touched her, engulfed her", 114). As for Tommy, it was the *coup de grace* as it removed "the life support system" which kept him alive. Hence his absolutely negative attitude, even before the decision of his dismissal was announced to him: "He was falling; he knew it. [...] he had no idea and no inclination for future work" (99) which essentially means that the end of his working life signals the beginning of the end of his biological existence.

Apart from the martyrdom of uncertainty that precedes his dismissal, equally painful is the official announcement of this bad news, as well as the overall atmosphere that prevails during the process of settling his work entitlements and his departure ceremony. All this emotionally charged atmosphere – with the typicality of mechanical, cruel bureaucracy, the gap between employer-employee and the lack of understanding, support and compassion being dominant – is portrayed with exceptional authenticity and vividness. A contributing factor to this is undoubtedly the second silent dialogue, reflecting of the thoughts and feelings of Tommy, which is conducted in a peculiar manner, that is parallel to the real (aloud) dialogue, so that we have a simultaneously dual representation of the external and internal reality which is experienced by the hero. This creates dramatic irony, since the reader becomes a witness of this two-dimensional reality, something which does not happen with Tommy's interlocutors:

> When Somers, coughing, not looking at him, told Tommy that he was to be retrenched, that the corporation was downsizing to reflect the realities of the current economic situation, Tommy's first thought was of Laika, a fuzzy black and white image of a sad dog in space (125) [who, as mentioned earlier, had been abandoned "Starving to death, in perpetual orbit", 115]. [...]
> -What am I entitled to?
> Susan coughed.
> -The company has offered you quite a generous package. [...].The company is a cunt. [...]
> -Anything else, Tom?
> Yes, can you get on the desk, can you spread your thighs? Do you want a big fat fuck, you frigid bitch?
> -No." (118-119)

How does Tommy react to this expected but nevertheless heavy blow of his imminent dismissal? Initially in a natural manner, as if nothing had happened:

> After the initial shock of being fired, Tommy had regained his composure. He told his family, he returned to work, and though conscious of the silences that began whenever he was near, he pretended relief at the opportunity for another future. [...]
>
> Even when he had finished work he continued the routine. He woke early, at seven-thirty, and walked to the shop for the morning paper. He would dress in neat clothes and visit the Commonwealth Employment Service; he would inquire for work. In the afternoon he was at the gym. (139)

After his dismissal he blames and pities himself for his failure which, unfortunately – and this is perhaps even more painful – he should announce to his family. A small sample of his feelings and reaction:

> Failure has the smell of sweat, but not the euphoric stench of physical exertion. Nothing of the erotic. Failure smells of decay, of stagnation. Tommy leant into the mirror, staring hard at his face. He pulled back. The fleshy cheeks, the beginning spread of a double chin. He swept a hand through his hair; the thickness waning. He pulled back and surveyed his body.
>
> –You're ugly, he said to the mirror. He could smell the ugliness with the failure.
>
> He packed his briefcase, put on his jacket and left. Swift goodbyes. Outside, the traffic screaming, he paused for breath. He was fighting an urge to giggle, to laugh, to skip. Beyond the moment lay a vast uncertainty. But within the moment he experienced a freedom. Tommy had never longed for liberation – freedom was terrifying not exciting. This moment, however, was an exception. [...]
>
> Inside, he groaned. He and Soo-Ling were supposed to go to a Grand Final barbecue at Dominic's. The cold pumped through his stomach.

I'm fired. How could he began to express those words? Again, he could smell the failure leaking through his skin. (119-121)

The overall time-consuming, soul-destroying and operatic procedure of finding work from home by checking newspaper ads and making telephone calls is depicted with particular vividness as Tommy is confronted with a wall of indifference, heartlessness and cynicism on the part of employers where the unemployed feels ridiculed. The overall procedure is substantiated authentically and successfully as the narrator adopts a stereotyped, automated language (with sharp, telegraphese words and expressions) comparable to the inhumanly cold treatment he is subjected to as an unemployed person). A characteristic sample:

He rang.

882 3456. Engaged.

543 2323. Engaged.

428 4076. Engaged.

652 6765. A woman's voice.

-Laser Write. Can I help you?

-I'm inquiring about the position advertised in today's paper. The sales position. Can I have a job description?

The woman took down his name and address and quickly put down the phone. [...]

-Quickprint. Can I help you?

-I'm inquiring about the position advertised in –

The woman cut him off.

-Sorry, sir, position filled.

428 4076. Engaged. (137-138)

Subsequently there is an equally graphic description of the overall ritual at the Commonwealth Employment Service (such as e.g. the queues, the exhausting waiting, the discomfort and friction among these children of a lesser God, so to speak, who are dealing with the heartless authority of bureaucracy, 156) and, much more so, there is a description depicting the very mindless mechanical interview of Tommy with the "red haired man" from the DSS. The writer parodies the commonplace, silly and ridiculous questions used at the interview which, apart from underestimating the unemployed person's intelligence (e.g."-How long have you been unemployed?" or "-What work are you looking for?", 158), interfere openly with his private life (e.g. "-You live on your own?" or "-Seeing anyone?", 158). But the same happens with some of the answers of the interviewee which are either given subconsciously as an impulsive reaction (e.g. to the question where was his last interview he attended, Tommy replies: "-Club X, the porn shop", 158), or as a silenced thought-reaction ("-Seeing anyone? None of your fucking business. –No" or "-Good luck. Suck my fat cock, you piece of poofter shit", 158-159). As mentioned previously, this exchange between external and internal dialogue-monologue intensifies the lampooning of the situation, by escalating the dramatic irony.

Tommy's difficulties and adventures with the Commonwealth Employment Service escalate when he visits it for the last time, one day before his eviction from the apartment he rents, due to rent in arrears ("He owed them one thousand two hundred and thirty-six dollars. He knew he could never afford to pay them back", 217). Given that Tommy has, apparently, decided to put an end to his life, this visit can only be seen as an act of revenge, much more so when, filling in his application, he answered that he had not tried to find work, without giving any reason, leaving the rest of the form incomplete. Consequently, the narrator's remark "He filled out the form" (218) constitutes an oxymoron, as he put only one little mark to the question whether he had tried to find work and for the rest "He left the spaces empty" [...] –He signed the form" (218). It is likely then that Tommy goes into this meaningless process, because he wants to get his piled up repressed emotions out of his system, by taking a sweet revenge, something he was unable nor did he have the courage to do earlier. The fact that this whole visit-"show" was premeditated by Tommy is obvious, firstly from the way he has groomed himself – something that had never happened previously, and which is reminiscent of the practice undertaken by the ancient Spartan warriors before embarking on a battle and confronting death – ("Tommy had washed this morning. [...] He washed, showered, even cleaned his teeth. He drank his coffee", 217) and, secondly, from the way he thinks and feels, when filling in the application ("*Have you sought work for the period 8/11/90 – 22/11/90?* He was happy, this time, not to go through the humiliation of looking through the yellow pages", 218). We observe that not only is Tommy not concerned about the consequences of his negative action (the stopping of his unemployment benefit) but, on the contrary, he feels "happy." Of course another seemingly logical counter-interpretation would be that Tommy's behaviour should not be seen as a revengeful reaction, but as an act of insanity. Some indicative signs are when, for example, the woman officer tells him that "-Mr Stefano, the form is not complete. He insisted that it was" (218). But a little later too, when he is being interviewed to establish what is happening, we observe a dialogue reminiscent of the theatre of the absurd, in relation to Tommy. A small example:

-Tommy, have you looked for work the last fortnight?

Tommy shook his head.

-Why is that?

-I have my work.

James looked up.

-What's that?

Tommy squirmed in his seat and said nothing.

-Tom, we can't make a payment to you. This is a contract. James pointed to the dole form. If you don't honour your side of the contract, which is to look for work, then we can't pay you.

-I don't need your money.

Your money is death. [...]

-Tom, I'm going to make an appointment for you to see one of our counsellors.

-I don't want to.

James sighed. Fuck this idiot, he thought to himself. He fingered his cigarette packet.

-Up to you, Tommy. But this means you're off the dole.

Tommy stood up. His task here was accomplished. He shook James's hand.

-Thank you.

As he was leaving he spun around in the doorway.

-I don't need you any more, I got Jesus, he said. (218-219)

In concluding, it is difficult to distinguish whether Tommy wanted to avenge (the system-bureaucracy, the authorities or society in general) or indeed he had gone insane. But couldn't suicide be considered the ultimate form of protest and revenge?

The television obsession

Before we discuss in some detail the subject of pornography, we need to stress its direct and decisive relationship with some of Tommy's other obsessions, such as television. The latter has marked his life from a very young age, up to the point where virtual television reality has substituted authentic life itself, transforming him into a "zombie":

> The television was a connection with a previous life and he immersed himself in it. His old friendships were now a bus and a train ride away. So they stopped. The kids in the new school were strange. Only a very few had mothers who spoke with an accent. A sea of blondes, and he had became a foreigner in his own country. When Tommy saw *The Stepford Wives*, he was mesmerised. Because, scared of the sudden smashing of his

world, he had only one desire. To not be hurt, picked on, accused. Tommy had decided to become a zombie. (48)

Thus, even if Tommy was somehow by nature disposed to becoming 'zombified', he did not become a "zombie" because he "had decided" it, but because television had contributed to shaping his character. A characteristic of this is the fact that, even when he is together with his girl-friend Soo-Ling, he cannot do without television, causing her to protest and justifiably so, since "The television did annoy her. It created a space between them, a white noise, a stranger separating them" (93). His pathological dependence on the small screen leads him eventually to a situation where he cannot live without it, to the point where he identifies with it completely before his self-destructive deplorable end, having previously replaced human communication and human relationships with the inanimate device, as the following quote reflects so tellingly: "[...] terrified of a world without light, without television. He had begun sleeping in front of the screen now, unable to deal with the wide expanse of the bedroom, all that space. He allowed the TV to play all hours, fell asleep to the shuddering light. [...] Tommy was talking to the television" (191-194).

The irony is that, even when Tommy does not watch television at home (for example during his and Soo-Ling's visit to friends like Nadia) he ends up again watching the latter's trip to Europe on video, – which in many respects is a miniature of *Dead Europe* (p. 168-171). When the video comes to its end, Tommy, being addicted to the screen, "reached for the remote control" but his girl-friend's reaction is instantaneous: "Soo-Ling stopped his hand. –No television now, Tommy. I couldn't bear it" (171).

Finally, the disastrous influence of television's magic power contributes to his being led to insanity and his first attempt to cut his so much despised body:

Tommy crouched on the floor, turned on the television, flickered furiously through the channels. Every image disturbed him. He left it on static, requiring the radiation, but jumped to his feet and searched a shelf. He kicked the porno, looked down, grabbed it and flung it against the wall.

Go to hell.

He switched on the radio, hustling through stations. Words made him sick. He found a song, an electronic shudder of noise. Only beats and snatched words. He poured the music through the flat, the decibels corrosive, and finally lay relaxed on the floor. The bass of the music massaged his body and a voice above him ordered: Beat dis, beat dis. His fingers searched the floor and curled around a pen. He pushed the ballpoint and started slaying at his arm. [...] The light from the television. Even with the music screaming he could hear the crackle of the screen. Keeping on slashing at his arm, he relaxed into sedation. (214)

This introduction was necessary in order to emphasise that Tommy's addiction to pornography did not ensue out of the blue but is likely ascribed to and is in step with his relationship with television. Its beginnings are to be traced to his childhood and teenage years, as was previously mentioned, in order to cover a psychological communication vacuum. Because Tommy's voyeuristic tendencies are manifested long before the more serious problems of his adult life (job uncertainty, coping with dismissal, etc.) emerge, even start, and their starting point is television, which, as will be seen subsequently, aggravates them. Thus we observe from the very beginning of the chapter "Thomas Stefano", that even a film of historical-religious content shown on television, regarding Christ's birth, assumes in Tommy's eyes a kind of voyeuristic, irreverent, almost blasphemous nuance, in the way the protagonists are portrayed:

Tommy was alone in the lounge room, watching the TV. The birth of Christ. Mary was blonde, an LA nymph. Joseph was soap opera handsome, young and smooth.

> Tommy was thinking, sipping at his beer, how cheap Mary looked, what a cheap American slag. There was dancing in Jerusalem, the young Mary had just spotted the pretty Joseph. The camera cut back and forth, back and forth, to the blonde Mary with the silicon breasts, to the bearded Joseph with the sculptured chest. Their eyes met. Commercial break. [...] Joseph was stripped to the waist, drawing water from the well. (39-40)

We may say that whatever the perspective of the film shown on television was, we effectively see Tommy's perspective and not that of the film itself. Besides, the specific title of the film is not given, as it happens on other occasions, so that we can check the credibility of what is being described. Of course one could counter-argue here that this perspective is a criticism by the writer against the cheap way American cinema exploits religious subjects for commercial and television rating reasons, but this is debatable. What is certain is that the introduction of the religious element is hardly coincidental, as it constitutes a crucial factor in Tommy's life and death, as we will realise further down.

Television violence

The role of the media (of the press but especially of television, with its negative news reports) influences and shapes decisively Tommy's psychology, as they constitute – television in particular – an integral part of his life. Thus in the novel, it is as if we observe the unfolding of two parallel realities: one being that of television (that of news reports, pictures of violence, wars, etc.) and one being real life (that of Tommy's misfortunes), where the two not only go hand in hand with each other, but where one (the former) influences and compliments negatively the other (the latter).

These two realities identify to such a degree with each other that, often, we have the feeling that one is imitating and copying the other, or as if one constitutes an integral part of the other. This is realised from the beginning, that is when the first problems at Tommy's workplace appear, as he is pressed to become computer-literate, whereas "He began to hate that word" (137). It is interesting how the narrator (or should we say Tommy himself, subconsciously) identifies his personal stress with the murder incident about which he reads in the newspaper and how the latter is juxtaposed to "The day was fine" and spoils it for him. As a result of this, instead of the newspaper reading relaxing him during his lunch break, it seems to aggravate his anxiety even more: (e.g."Inside, all the time, Tommy groaned. I just want to not think, I just want to stop. At lunchtime he bought a roll – salad and beef – got the paper and read in the park. The day was fine. A guy had murdered five children, blasted about thirty more, a place called Stockton in California. They seemed to be getting crazier over there", 53).

Thus it is no wonder that while the bad climate of his interpersonal relationships in the workplace is intensified, and having no other way of reacting to the insults he is subjected to, he resorts to fantasizing that it would be great if the murder, about which he read a moment earlier, could take place in his workplace, so that the people who make his life miserable are punished ("The Stockton guy, coming in, gun, shooting up and down the corridor. Shooting this prick, this sweaty ugly cunt. Shooting that snooty bitch in the buyers section, that up-herself blonde, fucking her, gun in her mouth, shooting", 55). Thus, prone as he is to the negative news reports of violence, and even more so to the magic the television screen exercises upon him, Tommy has embarked on an addiction which, in combination with his personal adversities, will lead him gradually and fatally to self-destruction, since violence (even on television), can only breed violence. Hence, the next repeated episodes of television violence which follow, could be entitled "Instructions for prospective murderers and suicides" as Tommy is not only prone to television violence but also to his dangerous fantasies.

Evidence of this is the fact that, in the next grim news item which is in relation to the disappearance of a girl student, Tommy participates mentally in her murder, following the sadistic acts and rape that have preceded it. We realise then that such sort of news reports find fertile soil in his disturbed psyche and morbid fantasies to grow, as he is stimulated sexually by them:

> The news is on the television. A story about the missing schoolgirl. Three weeks and still no sign of her. Fears that she may have been murdered. [...]
>
> Tommy thinks of the missing schoolgirl. She's eleven.
>
> Tommy thinks about what it would be like stealing a girl, how would he do it.
>
> He would pretend to be a tradesman, hire a station wagon. He would drive around the streets and maybe a schoolgirl would be walking home alone. And he'd pull up next to her and ask her if she knew the way to somewhere. And he'd pull out a road map and maybe she would come over and look at it with him. He would drug her, with ether. That's what they did on TV. And take her home. Then he would blindfold her and just keep her in a room, just for a few days. He would just get her to suck him off, slap her if she refused, he'd just fuck her, a few times. Just to see what it was like. A girl's cunt, hairless, smooth, tight.
>
> Tommy blew a jerk of thin semen. It fell on his groin, ran down his legs. (60)

This perverted fantasy that Tommy has of the murder-rape continues, as he hears the news item on the radio while working, followed by other brief but graphic descriptions of rapes and murders of women on television news which have preceded, such as that of "Six teenage black youths bashed her, raped her, tore her apart. Left her barely breathing" (75), as well as about "The young girl, the eleven year old, the girl gone missing" whose "body was found, raped and slaughtered" (77). The difference being that, now that the young girl's murder is a *fait accompli*, one cannot distinguish the borderlines between the "tragic and perverted" and what exactly touches Tommy more – the girl's atrocious murder, the heart-broken pain of her parents, or sodomization hinted at in the newspapers by which he is sexually stimulated. A very significant role in this perversion should be attributed to the media and the way they present it on the news, with the aim of achieving maximum ratings:

> They'd found the girl's body in a stretch of bush in Pakenham. The body was poorly concealed under scattered branches and torn shrubs. Her face had appeared on newsprint, on television screens, had made the glossy pages of the magazines. Eleven, dark, pretty; and her distraught weeping parents. [...]
>
> She had been missing for four months; her tortures were referred to obliquely and therefore seemed even more tantalising. Was her corpse sodomised? The torture is unimaginable, thought Tommy. His eyes were moist, her suffering was tragic. But it was also perverse. His eyes were moist, he was conscious of his cock. (80)

The media then, which interfere with and invade as intruders at any time into peoples' lives and activities, are partly responsible for the shaping of their psychological and mental states, to a degree that not only do they upset the daily routine of susceptible people like Tommy, but also quite normal people like his girl-friend Soo-Ling. Quite interesting and characteristic of how television violence intervenes in people's daily routine and how what is described in the news is identified symbolically (e.g. the premeditated cold murder of the girl, with the methodical way Soo-Ling "sliced the chicken fillets") with any successive activity, is the following scene, in relation to the aforementioned news item of the young girl's murder:

> They kept flashing her picture throughout the night, in between every program break. Soo-Ling pointed the remote at the screen and the little girl's face jerked, flashed and disappeared into darkness. Soo-Ling jumped up and walked into the kitchen, grabbing food and saucepans, but she could not forget the face. It was not that she was particularly shocked by the rape and murder.

Nothing new there. It was the vulnerable youth of the victim that hurt. Soo-Ling sliced the chicken fillets methodically, neatly. The violence of the murderer struck her as absurd, a madness in men which she had no wish to understand. [...]

I wish I hadn't watched the fucking television. (89-90)

This sequence of Tommy's internal turmoil and the impasse he experiences as "he could smell the failure leaking through his skin" (121) is, apparently, in step with and coexists in perfect harmony with the external turmoil and adventures of the world, as these are reflected in the negative news reports of violence ("An article, venomous in its anger, was directed towards the bleeding hearts asking for clemency for the Aboriginal man on America's death row. A tiny black and white photo, badly reproduced, smudged. A man alone", 121). In the same parallel motif we observe the alternation of domestic (Australian) news reports with their international counterparts. The frequency and intensity of these overseas news reports of violence are of such texture that it is as if we observe their metastasis and transformation into obsessive ideas in the mind of Tommy, who is fantasizing that he would like to experience these scenes as if he were the protagonist himself. The snapshot with the prostitute in the following quote is revealing:

> The day came in. Work, Pathis. The Aboriginal man rapes and kills a blonde woman.
>
> He closed his eyes and drifted far into the fantasy, imagining himself black and violent, the woman on her knees before him someone he could kill. It would be so easy, she was so young, so soft. [...] He imagined the Aboriginal man above the bleeding body of the blonde, her face bruised, her lips fat, her cunt raw, shitting herself. Fucking her from behind. Fucking her so hard she was bleeding. (126)

A common feature to almost all similar mental episodes which Tommy likes to indulge in, is that there is always the precedence of a despondent state which Tommy seeks to eliminate and/or counterbalance by juxtaposing a sweet vindictive act in which he participates in his imagination – in the same way he resorts to pornography every time he is under stress. Hence, following the joyless and repulsive process of finding work over the phone, Tommy resorts to reading the newspaper news in order to relax rather than be informed:

> Tommy put down the phone and picked up the newspaper. Another schoolgirl had gone missing; she had disappeared after school, walking home. [...] The girl's distraught mother was crying on the front page. A small shot. The main picture, the top half of the tabloid page, was of a smiling freckled pigtailed young girl in blue and white checked school uniform. [...]
>
> Fourteen women shot at a Canadian University. Another thirteen wounded. A male student had taken a rifle to a seminar and proceeded to murder. Pictures of crying students. An editorial. Violence, against girls, against women. Stiffer penalties for sex offenders.
>
> Tommy shut the paper and turned on the television. Noni Hazlehurst on 'Play School'. He thought of fucking her in the mouth. He twisted in anger, furious, as he came on his pyjamas, his eyes closed, Noni Hazlehurst replaced by the little schoolgirl. (138-139)

Tommy's habituation with raw television violence ("A bomb in Jerusalem [...] Tommy watched the television, blood and limbs, hysterics and prayer", 216), the rapes of which he hears and fantasises so frequently about ("Tommy fantasised the rape. He fell asleep on the couch, the television on", 162) is such that he eventually suffers a kind of callousness which results in leaving him emotionless, as the following reaction of his reveals: "On the news there were two photographs, two young men. In Holland. Killed by a bomb. They were Australian and one of them looked Greek. The photo grabbed Soo-Ling's attention. –That's so bad. No, it isn't. Tommy didn't feel sad at all. His indifference was complete" (163).

The culmination of his morbid relationship and complete obsession with television occurs when Tommy, having cut off all lines of communication with the external world (parents, family and girl-friend, 176-177) and having become prey to the virtual reality of television, realises that he has now transcended into another state – from apathy to joy. That is, he realises, even in the realm of his fantasies, that he is not different, that "He no longer felt separated from anyone" (177), as he thought all these years, but that he is an integral part of the "crumbling world" and "he rejoiced" since he could now completely identify himself with it as his alienation was absolute. Hence he "realised that for Neil the Apocalypse was a wish, a desire. He was suddenly aware that he too wanted this cataclysmic shower, he too wanted a deluge" (184) and looks forward happily to the prospect of a universal disaster because, consciously or subconsciously, he has started flirting with the idea of suicide, if we take into account the following allusions: "Tommy turned from the mirror. And thought of nothing more but ecstasy of excising his body from the world" (87). And elsewhere: "One night he took a knife and traced a path across his stomach. He would cut here and there, he would cut away at the flab. Then his legs, carve his calves and thighs, the round paste of his arms. He threw the knife in the sink" (192).

We realise then that, firstly, as far as he himself is concerned (and especially his body) Tommy perceives reality through the reflection in the *mirror* ("The mirror taunted him", 192) and, secondly, as far as others and the external world are concerned, Tommy perceives reality only through the reflection and filtering of *television*. It is striking that the latter, although it broadcasts exclusively cases of "rape and murder, adultery and thievery, of betrayal and falsehood" (177) – or Tommy chooses to watch only these subjects – for him the inanimate device replaces the absence of genuine human contact. Thus, alienated from society, the world, even from his close environment ("It had been a month since he had visited his parents", 142. See also 193), he looks for communication, consolation and affection in the company of the television screen ("The emanation of the screen kept him warm", 164). Hence television seems to play a solacing role for Tommy, as it is personified by the narrator ("He did not leave the house and was nursed by the confessions from the television", 177).

But even in the rare cases where television reports broadcast happy events, such as for example, "Mandela's walk out of the prison", oddly enough, it does not change anything of the grim picture Tommy has about himself and life. On the contrary, this comparative juxtaposition of "Mandela's walk out of the prison, televised on a billion screens, only served to deepen Tommy's despair. The world was celebrating. The Wall had fallen, apartheid was ending, and the future was free of nuclear menace. But Tommy was still unemployed" (154).

This domination then of his life by television is so absolute and oppressive to the point that made him "sick", since, cut off from real life communication, he experiences the television version of it:

> Tommy was talking to the television. The Americans kept coming in, discussing sex and love, marriage and failure, deviance and truth. Daughters were raped and sons were bashed, women slept with their fathers and fathers slept with their sons. Tales punctured by commercials and flashes from the Persian Gulf.
>
> War. Tommy so desperately wanted war.
>
> He was made sick by the force of his need to communicate with the figures on the television. Watching a woman berate her daughter, live in front of a studio audience, the daughter sullen and overweight, watching the mother yell at the daughter for her laziness, her refusal to respect her parents, Tommy wanted to reach inside the television and place his hands around the older woman's throat, to destroy her. Destroy her. He was talking back to the television. (194)

Notwithstanding this and although from early on Tommy's mother had warned her sons about the "deceits of television" (especially after the traumatic censorship incident she had to endure, 305-308) which, as Louie says, "changed my mother's attitude to the media forever", this did not change the situation for Tommy and his brothers, according to the narrator: "She warned all of us against the deceits of the television but her three sons refused to listen; we found much solace there" (306).

The obsessive preoccupation with the body: sex and pornography

In *The Jesus Man*, there is only a fragmented and not a complete picture of Tommy's personality, therefore we cannot have a clear understanding of the real causes that shaped him into a problematic individual. (It is doubtful that the "family curse" can be taken seriously into consideration, since if anything, it constitutes an object of parody). What is certain is that a huge gap divides Tommy from his parents, due to the absence of mutual understanding, as well as discord in the family life which is attributed to his parents, as the narrator notes: "Tommy was still hurting. He was scared by how much he did not understand of his parents. He had spent his childhood listening to arguments, shouting and bickering, but also to the breathless fucking from across the thin walls of the Clifton hill house. He had been happy that when they moved out into the suburbs he was given the back bedroom. He was spared the sounds of his parents loving each other" (43-44).

Another serious reason for Tommy's problematic character later on is the way he was seen since he was little and the ideas his family had of him, as their attitude and comments made him feel "the weight of his white collar" (43), as well the rest of society, "everybody", as the narrator points out tellingly: "His mother thought of him soft because he did not believe enough, his father thought him soft because his body and his work was, and Dominic thought him soft because that's what everyone thought of Tommy. Except Lou maybe" (44).

Generally speaking we realise that family gatherings, even on special, festive occasions such as Christmas, where one was supposed to enjoy an atmosphere of joy, merriment and feasting, for Tommy they are nothing but a typical, boring and necessary chore that made him suffocate in silence:

> Tommy counted down the remainder of the day, counted down the drinks. Wine, with fruit. Wine, with dessert. A short whisky with the coffee. Now he could go home.
> -Stay, pleaded Maria, your uncles are coming, later. Stay the night.
> -No, Mum.
> Stop it, stop it, let me go. [...]
> When he turned the corner, when he knew he was left to himself, alone, in the car, it was a supreme joy. He put on the radio loud, travelled the roads, took the long way. The breeze. He had been holding in his body for hours. (45-46)

Furthermore, apart from the suffocating, overprotective environment, we realise that Tommy, since a very young age, had a peculiar relationship with the world around him, with time, and the way he was experiencing or would like to experience reality: "This had been Tommy's fantasy ever since he'd been very young. He would fantasise about stopping time, but only for humans. And never for himself. He could then wander the world and do whatever he liked. Then finally, tired or bored, he would snap his fingers and everything would return to normal" (49).

It was naturally expected then that Tommy would have liked to change the reality which he was living in and which he resented – as it was not in harmony with what he was thinking and feeling – finding a way to escape from it. This he achieved through three accessible outlets, as he had no other choices like Dominic (49): (i) isolation; (ii) the virtual reality of television and (iii) the exploration of his body, mainly through masturbation ("When they moved to the new suburbs, he began to close himself in his room, wank, watch a small black and white television.

He began to stop time and within that eternity he could be anyone he wanted", 49).

It was obvious that Tommy's pre-existing problems (with his parents) and *time* deteriorate with the change of *place* "When they moved into the suburbs" (44). Thus, whatever external changes happen in his life have an equivalent serious impact on the changes taking place in his internal world. Let it also be noted that his reactions to whatever changes happen in his life are expressed mainly through *passivity* and rarely through other forms or re-*actions*. (The aforementioned three outlets, e.g. as a child, are all passive, hence the exhortation-reprimand: "-Why don't you do something, mate, his father would say, waste some energy, get some of that fat off you. But Tommy preferred to masturbate" (49). But also later on, as an adult, he is characterised by "lack of ambition" (101) and refuses to be in step with the new technology, much more so when "his competence alone was no longer enough" (50) by becoming computer literate, so that when he loses his job he refuses to find another one, and as a result he is led into an impasse. In this respect Tommy has always felt like an exile, both as a child, something that forced him to "close himself in his room" (49), as well as an adult, when he was dismissed from his work – especially then he felt to the core that "The city screamed his exile" (122).

But even before this event, Tommy was yearning for solitude, the overall idea of being "a stranger", as he contemplates, following Soo-Ling's suggestion to travel together overseas ("I want to see the world on my own, thought Tommy, no-one there with me. Then I could be a stranger, do anything I wanted and no-one would know, no-one would see me, no-one could tell on me", 94). And later too, after his dismissal, his misanthropy, distant and uncanny behaviour, create problems for others (his girl-friend in particular), as we realise in the striking dinner scene at Nadia's place ("Conversation stumbled between Soo-Ling and Nadia. They both, at separate moments in the evening, shared the same thought: I wish Tommy was not here. He desperately attempted conversation but beyond the television and the food there was nothing he could talk about", 166). Finally, his introspection, antisocial behaviour and alienation from the rest of the world are absolutely confirmed by his complete compulsive dependence on the virtual reality of pornography, as his visit to the porn shop indicates ("Tommy stood there, engulfed by the mechanics of sex; the hunger to scout the room, to immerse himself in the given call of mute genitalia. At Nadia's he had watched the video with increasing horror, the gulf between himself and the world was immense. He *needed* to walk the shelves of video and magazines, to find equilibrium", 173).

Generally speaking then, we are dealing with a loner who prefers his solitude to any company and pursues it by all means. Thus, when he pretends to his mother, for example, that he would "Go out with friends" (46), he is lying. He simply wants to free himself from the uncomfortable company of others and be on his own, enjoying his solitude, as we have seen (ibid.). His differentiation is marked by a *passivity*, by the desire "to not think... to stop" (53) which is manifested in a tendency to abstain from a conversation because, as he says, "I don't want to talk about fucking work" (41). It is indicative that to his girl-friend's question "-How is work Tommy?" he reacts as follows: "Tommy crashed, Tommy closed his eyes. Tommy was close to screaming" (76). Much more so when he is sacked, whatever reminds him of or makes him conscious of being unemployed, causes him a traumatic "humiliation" ("He wondered if he should take the train home, [...] but realising [...] the train would be filling with workers rushing home from work, he decided against that humiliation", 130). For him, the question "What do you do?" is perhaps more painful, humiliating and tormenting that his actual dismissal. Even more telling is his physical, allergic reaction to the above question posed by Alanah, one of Soo-Ling's colleagues, at the Christmas party:

-What do you do? [...]
He could not put words together. He looked around the room. [...] Suddenly the noise was everywhere. The noise was a dizzy buzzing, a discord and a ferocious thrashing. He had to cough.

His mouth was dry. Alanah was looking at him strangely.

What do you do?

Tommy, without apology, got up and walked slowly to the toilets. [...] The woman's question was not new. It was unavoidable. Previously he had answered it with the past or concocted a future. The answer always implied a continuum. I am. I will be. But tonight the present was the past and was the future and in this present there was no answer he could give. [...]

There was one answer, the only possible answer.

Nothing.

What do you do?

Nothing.

The full force of the word hurt Tommy so much that he began to shake, a sweat, uncontrollable, gathered on his brow. (153)

However, it is not only work that Tommy avoids talking about, but anything whatsoever, as Soo-Ling reproaches him: "You don't want to argue about anything" (75). See also 113). Essentially he was a man of silence, something which "disturbed" his girl-friend (92). It was natural that this stance of his would soon lead him gradually to a situation where "His indifference was complete" (163).

What is ironic in this case is that what preceded Tommy's aforementioned psychological state and escalated its deterioration rapidly, until it led him to his demise, was his obsessive preoccupation with the external appearance of his body. This obsession appears from early on, long before his work problems emerged, his dismissal and its consequences, that is before he introduced his Chinese girl-friend to his family. Hence at the Christmas family gathering, the following scene is depicted: "In the bathroom he pulled up his shirt, looked at his belly. The fine black hair, the stretch of fat. He clutched at the flab, shook it, wished he could tear it off" (40). This obsession with what he considers to be his repulsive body, escalates when he compares his body with that of his brother Dominic:

> Few people guessed, on first meeting, that Dominic and Tommy were brothers. They shared dark skin, their mother's delicate mouth, but that was all.
>
> Dominic took off his T-shirt. His skin was olive, tanned by the sun. His chest and belly an explosion of fine blond hair. He's not fat, he's bulky, thought Tommy, and again he wished he could rip through his skin, get to the meat, to the flab, to the excess. Rip it up and start again. (41)

The same happens when he compares his body with that of his colleagues; his disappointment is equally great when he realises that his physical dissimilarity (which seems to be perceptible only to him and not to anybody else) is due to the indifference or, better still, to the fact that "his only joy was in the restful calm of his inertia" (180) which was previously mentioned: "Somers was brown. Tommy couldn't work out how. Somers had taken only the days between Christmas and New Year off. Tommy was dark only on his face and hands. He knew that beneath his lab coat, beneath his shirt and pants, his skin was a distinct pale. The beach seemed an effort and his own holidays had not gone on long enough. What had he done? Reclined, not thought, just dreamt" (51).

What is odd in this case is that although he feels a repulsion and disgust for his body, this is not the case with his girl-friend Soo-Ling who is sexually attracted to this same body that he hates, as the following quote reveals: "His body, which when clothed had appeared clumsy, assumed a potent grandeur when naked. Tommy's body, in its softness and its solidity, was the first body in which Soo-Ling allowed herself to disappear. His smells, his touch, the roughness of his hands, the swell of his cock inside her, the taste of his mouth. His lips praised every part of her body" (92).

However, his girl-friend's view-point about him does not appease the negative idea and low self-respect he has about himself (except in the cases when they made love since "only in sex with her was he not ugly", 92) and that he does not deserve to have such a wonderful woman as a girl-friend ("He was so fucking lucky to have Soo-Ling", 86). Much more so, it does not abate the frequency and intensity of his self-destructive obsessions about the ugliness of his body, as the following quotes suggest:

> "His fat gut, his rolling gut, the obscene flesh" (60). "He felt sick, his stomach was bloated" (72). "... Tommy was conscious of his weight. He sucked in his stomach" (76). "Fat. [...] He banged his fist into the hideous softness of his body" (84-85). "His fat was shaking as he pedalled" (86). "His tits hung, just a slight podge, but he could only see a hideous limp bulk. The heavy lead of his stomach. [...] Tommy turned from the mirror. And thought of nothing more but the ecstasy of excising his body from the world" (87). "Tommy leant into the mirror, staring hard at his face. He pulled back. The fleshy cheeks, the beginning spread of a double chin" (119-120). "In the afternoons he was at the gym. Losing his fat, becoming trim, this became his obsession. [...] His workout would last an hour and a half and he would sweat furiously, working off the fat. He began to look in mirrors again. But his weight refused to descend at a rate that made him happy" (140). "He had become lazy with the gym and lazy with his diet. Now, after a shower, the room steaming, he refused to look in the mirror. If he glanced at the folds of his belly, his day was shattered. His self-hatred would be so staggering that he'd be incapable of action" (161). "He had learnt to control his hunger, rarely eating now, but he was still ashamed of the flesh on his body. He was still pinching at his flab, wishing it to disappear" (181). "He clenched his stomach, feeling the fat, feeling the excess" (185). "He pulled at skin. He tugged at his T-shirt, wishing to go beyond to the fat, to escape the obscenity of his obesity" (213).

Finally, Tommy is divorced from reality as he fantasises about his image in a delusory manner ("Tommy was not ugly but this too was not known to him. The mirror reflected back the asymmetry of his weight", 87). The scene inside the bus is also characteristic: "All through the journey Tommy was aware of Neil's bulk, the looks he received from the strangers on the bus. Did he hear a small child say, Look at those two fat guys? He turned around. The child was silent, next to its mother, drawing circles in the window dust" (183). His compulsive ideas about his body are largely attributed to a false image he has created and not his real self. That is confirmed by the narrator's remark, even when Tommy has lost a lot of weight: "The man who was a mirror had frightened him. He compared his own body to the apparition's. His own fat body, his weak ugly body" (177).

Tommy's overpowering obsessions with his body (regarding weight, looks, etc.) and his undiminished compulsive preoccupation with it, as well as his overall psychological condition (emotional distance with his family, lack of motives/ambition, low self-respect, introspection, isolation, etc.) lead him, unmistakably, to another obsessive preoccupation – that of pornography. Again, it is an act which involves the voyeuristic, this time, viewing of naked bodies, except that, firstly, they take part in sex acts and, secondly, that Tommy's attention is distracted and transposed from his own body to those of strangers which, however, are anything but attractive, that is why "the ugliness of the jerking figures on the screen disgusted him" (160).

Tommy's seemingly innocent visits to Club X porn-shops are initially paid in order for him to let go of the oppressive, faceless and inhuman working environment of "the discordant moans of machines and the wicked clacking of computer keys" (119) which overwhelms him, as it takes on Kafkaesque dimensions: "The afternoon was spent circumnavigating the guts of the organisation. He walked through distracted shoppers, busy office staff, through rooms and corridors he had not known existed. He followed a map. The buyers, boys in designer suits, girls in fashion, no-one looked at him" (54-55). A proof of this is that before his first visit to the video-shop Club X "Tommy looked at the clock so he wouldn't look at Pathis. If he looked at Pathis, he felt the poison flood his guts, soar into his blood" (55). Thus, although he has a fantastic girl-friend and lover, he often refuses to be with her because he is "exhausted" (56), preferring the passive – and not inexpensive – entertainment of voyeurism and masturbation. Tommy is fully aware of his foolishness in spending good money on this useless and soul-destroying activity instead of saving it, especially when his job is at risk. Neither is this activity painless, given that, apart from money he also pays the price for the following guilts:

(i) That he spends his money foolishly, reprimanding himself for it ("You fucking idiot, you fucking idiot. Save. His father said. Save. Soo-Ling said. Save. Save. He kept promising himself, one day, he would save", 58). (ii) That he is under the impression that he does something bad while being watched and feels ashamed of it ("Tommy wandered the flat, checking every room, the video in its brown bag under his arm. It was a superstition, he never could shake the feeling: someone was watching him", ibid.). (iii) That he feels detestation and disgust about this activity of his – voyeurism and masturbation ("He is disgusted. [...] He takes off his shirt, cleans himself up. He hates the look, the smell of semen, it makes him sick. [...] He goes to the bathroom. He washes his hands, wipes his chest and stomach with a towel. [...] He washes his hands, scrubs, rinses, scrubs, rinses", 59-60). (iv) That he feels the need of repentance and atonement ("Tommy gets into bed, fully clothed, looks up at the Madonna and Child on the wall. His hands move to prayer. His prayer is an apology", 60).

The question that arises is, why does Tommy – who is fully conscious of the fact that the results of his activity are negative – not stop it but continues and indeed with greater frequency and intensity? Given what we know about Tommy's personality, some possible reasons could be the following: Firstly, because the voyeuristic entertainment suits his temperament (addicted as he is to television), his introvert, lonely and anti-social character and the fact that, initially at least, he might have seen this activity as a superficial but nevertheless harmless habit. Secondly, because, as he is used to watching television from a very young age, he considers it quite natural to experience, even temporarily, the illusion of a hedonistic pleasure of a parallel virtual universe, especially when in his real life (such as, for example, in his workplace "Work had gone bad", 50) and things are getting worse. Under the stress of such conditions, for a passive character like Tommy (by nature prone to inactivity, pessimism and with no 'initiative", ibid.) who is incapable of managing his problems, let alone finding solutions, the only visible and feasible outlet to his impasse is the resorting to the mechanical world of pornography which offers him immediate satisfaction and instant relief, by filling in a psychological vacuum. Thirdly, by initially embracing the innocent television entertainment and later on the superfluous activity of voyeurism, it is likely that he never imagined the possibility of this activity developing into a self-destructive vicious circle. Being an addictive and compulsive personality, it may have never crossed his mind that his engagement with pornography (helped by the sequence of violent scenes on television) would aggravate the impasse of his situation from which only as a dead person would be able to escape. Fourthly, Tommy's erratic, confused and impulsive character constitutes fertile soil in which the roots of a habit like pornography – which addresses the baser instincts of man and rarely his reason – can grow.

Something then which begins as an innocent curiosity or entertainment (such as prostitution and pornography) develops into an addictive practice, usually preceded by a cause which has triggered it. Thus, we observe, for example, that following Tommy's dismissal and departure from his workplace, he feels a compulsive, bulimic need to eat junk food like a beast. (Notice: whenever this happens, he always feels guilty and reproaches himself for it, 46, 56, 84, 123, 140). So he ends up at McDonald's (123) whereas, subsequently, "He was now aware of only one thing: he wanted sex with a stranger. The thought of disappearing in sex was so delicious he shivered as he handed over the money" (125). It is possible that here is the "key" to interpreting Tommy's relationship or obsession with sex and pornography. That is, the hedonistic pleasure of sex is not so much a bodily need but its epicentre is in his mind and thoughts. For the simple reason that "Entering the brothel was a humiliation: the terror that his mother, Soo-Ling, that *someone* was watching; even if it was only God, that was still someone bearing witness. [...] He had to be led by alcohol, he had to be smashed to go. What alcohol did was to carve away the voices. Alcohol dismissed them all. What remained was only the appetite for lust" (125). As for this "lust", it would not be possible without having "sank the alcohol" (122) which numbs thoughts and feelings ("Soo-Ling crossed his mind and he quickly set her aside, set her far back into consciousness", 125), puts the body on an auto-pilot, so that any pleasure is artificial ("The sensation was delightful [...] but the technique and its effect were mechanical", p. 126, or "He jumped into her, a machine...", 127) by dehumanising the individual ("He closed his eyes and drifted far into the fantasy, imagining himself black and violent, the woman on her knees before him someone he could kill', 126). No wonder then that Tommy was fascinated for the first time, at the age of fourteen, by the movie *The Stepford wives*. Not because "the ladies in Stepford [...] are all zombies" (48) like him, but because "the men of Stepford are replacing their wives with machines" (ibid.) Therefore it is not altogether odd that he fantasises that he could "steal" a young girl-student and rape her, as if she were an inanimate doll, because "that's what they did on TV" (60). That is why sex constitutes an instinctive and "overwhelming urge" (120), an impulsive or rudimentary pleasure which lasts only a moment, as Tommy is against prostitution, feeling shame, disgust and guilt, especially when he comes back to his senses. Something which, once again, shows that for him sex is a way of escaping from harsh reality:

> Prostitution had soon lost its dread. The anxiety of Tommy's first time, having to decipher the economic and moral codes which bound the brothel, was never to be repeated. But even once the

costs and procedures were explained and made sense of, there still remained the shame. [...]
He roamed the streets, his tie loose, his shirt not tucked in. The briefcase in his hand ridiculous. Footscray was unfamiliar but in the daylight, everything grey in the drizzle, it was also pragmatically suburban. [...] Only minutes had passed but already the disgust had again been replaced by a hunger. He walked on. (125-127)

However, despite Tommy's negative experience in the brothel, his vicious circle of dealings with the corruptive world of pornography (visits to porn shops, 129) continues; this time triggered by the guilty feelings of his sinfulness which are aggravated by an incidental event (the locked church door) which Tommy, being superstitious, perceives as an indication that "God did not want him either" (ibid.).

Thus, Tommy's compulsive behaviour, addiction to pornography and his subsequent guilt have attributed to being cut off from society and the people he loved, since "He wanted nothing more than to shed the stain of family" (See 152, 133), looking for consolation and refuge in these faceless places (as well as the gym) where he could experience the pleasure of sex in his imagination, without any commitments:

He thought of her blood and was sickened. He wanted to drive straight to the porn shop, become immersed in the comfort of sterile vaginas, to be among women who didn't talk, who didn't bleed, who didn't answer back. He wanted Soo-Ling far away from him. (152).

The simplest comfort remained the gym. [...] There was one more sanctuary. His visits to the porn shop. After gym he would wander in and take his time walking along the shelves, picking up videos, putting them back, glancing at the covers and the backs of magazines. [...] No fuss was made if Tommy remained in the shop for hours. [...] Once, sometimes twice a week, always on the

Thursday when the benefits got paid, Tommy would enter one of the booths and masturbate. [...] The dole office, the gymnasium, the porn shop. The routine. (140-141)

Now, as "Tommy recognised that he was spiralling out of control, that a big bang was approaching" (177) and having overcome any feelings of guilt, feels the need to remove the icon from the wall and hide it, so that nobody could watch him or, rather, he has the illusion that he is not being watched by anyone. That is why "He had taken the icon off his bedroom wall, had wrapped it in cloth and stored it carefully in his trunk, separated from the videos and magazines by sheets and blankets" (141).

Finally, it should be stressed that for Tommy pornography is a vicious circle. That is, whereas as was pointed out previously, Tommy's preoccupation with pornography has its roots in the "innocent" television, in the process the obscene pornographic spectacles function mainly as a temporary antidote to his anxiety – as afterwards he is plagued by guilt – caused by the painful blow of unemployment, rather than a genuinely hedonistic pleasure. Much more so when this voyeuristic activity almost always bores and disgusts him ("... the ugliness of the jerking figures on the screen disgusted him. [...] The fucking bored him and Tommy left the booth", 160). So his resorting to these joints could be interpreted as a compulsive reaction to his bottled up, repressed emotions. That is why every time he feels choleric, for example when he departs from the dole office, he resorts to visiting these places – which he otherwise abhors – to try to unwind (159). Effectively though, the visits, far from easing his anxieties, do exacerbate his condition since they become part of and not a solution to his problems, perpetuating thus this vicious circle. As a result of this, Tommy is alienated gradually from society, the world, even his close environment, seeking communication and warmth in the radiation of television, as the visit to Nadia shows tellingly: "Without waiting for a reply, Tommy flashed on the screen. He had taken a pill to steady his anxiety. [...] The pill had begun its work and he settled into the couch. The world compacted into the distance between himself and the screen, the bobbing miniatures of actors. Outside his vision, Nadia and Soo-Ling disappeared. The emanation of the screen kept him warm" (164).

Thus, pornography ceases, gradually, to be an entertaining, anxiolytic activity for Tommy, ending up becoming a meaningless mechanical act, an impulsive habit, as the narrator confirms: "He did not leave the house and was nursed by the confessions from the television" (177).

The religious element

The religious element in this novel is equally important as the pornographic one. For Tommy, oddly enough and blasphemous as it may sound, as far as religion is concerned, it functions equally impulsively as sex does. It is indicative that, following the announcement that "he was to be retrenched" (116) he reacts as follows: "His next thought was that he wanted to find a church and to pray. And then – fuck prayer – his thoughts turned to sex" (ibid.). The same happens after his departure from the brothel which he visited when he left his workplace for the last time: "He was not looking for a church but on coming across one he was violently happy. Protestant; simple, that did not matter. That it had the cross was enough. He tried the door. It would not budge and stepped back, first shocked and then accepting. He hadn't the courage to knock. He prayed on the steps, a simple chanting. The repetition of apology" (127-128).

Before proceeding to discuss the subject of religion, we need to point out that Tommy's stance and behaviour towards religion is not any different to that which he adopts towards any other aspect of his life (work, family, girl-friend, society, the world), that is erratic. We should mention here, *inter alia*, that Tommy is unpredictable and in fact does not know what he wants. Whereas, for example, his girl-friend Soo-Ling is a fantastic girl and loves him a lot, Tommy is unjustifiably annoyed by "Soo-Ling's presence" (152). This does not apply only to his girl-friend but also to his family and everybody around him. After all, this is natural for Tommy, because given that he cannot put up with himself, how could he put up with others? An indicative quote: "He would ask her to marry him when he found another job. [...] She was planning the future. [...] Tommy clenched his stomach tight. The thought of not being alone, of living with Soo-Ling, every day, every moment, filled him with a vertiginous nausea that was close to disgust. But so did the thought of losing her" (141-142).

Consequently it is not at all odd that Tommy feels so confused that he is incapable of understanding the past, the present and what happens to him generally, in the world and life around him ("Tommy was also spending a lot of time dwelling on the past, on everything he could remember of youth. And he was shocked at how little made sense, or rather, that he had so little memory of time. Everything was all jumbled up and he had no idea how life had happened", 177). The more his condition deteriorates the more baffled he is with his thoughts and, as a result, he has no clue about how to interpret his life and what he should do: "Failing. Had he always been a failure, he wondered. He didn't even want to think of that. [...] He thought of finding a job and he thought of killing himself. [...] He thought of childhood, he thought of adulthood. He thought himself unlucky and he thought himself a fool. He couldn't stop thinking. That's where the Serapax helped" (178).

This erratic behaviour, to the point of insanity now, culminates when Tommy, having mauled Neil, seeks refuge in Soo-Ling's residence, regardless of the fact that he had previously announced to her their separation over the phone. Subsequently he makes violent love to her. Afterwards, despite her pleading with him to stay, Tommy leaves her for good (189). Finally, although he hates himself (161) and feels "desperately unhappy" (166), he considers his situation as ambivalent – that is not only as a curse but as a blessing too: "Sometimes he was so delighted by not having to deal with the confines of office life that he thought himself lucky, blessed. [...] This was not a life without moments of joy. [...] But he also knew he was spiralling and he knew he was incapable of decisions, let alone action. So he had started praying again, for he needed a miracle" (179).

Given all the aforementioned, it is natural that his, so to speak "religious life", moves more or less on the same wave length. For a start, due to his family background (his father is Catholic and his mother Greek Orthodox), Tommy tends to feel, from a very young age, divided and in limbo as far as religion is concerned, that is "Neither Catholic nor Orthodox but both" (p. 128). Much more so when his mother Maria "had refused to allow her children to sit in on religious instruction at school", since "These classes at the local primary school in Clifton Hill were taken by volunteer officers from the Salvation Army and Maria would not allow her children to be indoctrinated by Protestants" (175). Apart from this, his mother is generally characterised by an ambivalence and contradiction in relation to faith and religion, according to Louie's assertion: "My mother believes firmly in God. She's not going to give up on that, otherwise her life is a waste. [...] But she doesn't believe in heaven or in hell. That's just make-believe she tells me, this is it. The world and nothing beyond it." (289). Consequently, the issue of religion assumes an equally contradictory and nebulous, almost fairy-tale dimension in young Tommy's mind ("The Bible was Easter and Christmas, the biblical stories glimpses of fables in storybooks", 175). Thus, his flirtation and association with the Baptist Church "when he was fifteen" (ibid.) without his family's knowledge, was not done out of any thirst for faith or conversion but mainly out of curiosity and as an extension to exploring his teenage sexuality and as some atonement for feeling guilty because of his masturbation ("Tommy began attending the Baptist church because he badly wanted to fuck Helen Thompson. Nights were furious thrashings, a silent, self-conscious masturbation interrupted by sleep or the sudden intrusion of a human sound", 175). Failing to find any response to his teenage "love adventure", Tommy "stopped going to church" (176). It needs to be stressed here that whatever "faith" Tommy has in God, springs out of his constant impression that "he was always watched" – an obvious symptom of his guilt – and his unspecified fear of the unknown ("But he did not stop believing in God. This faith had its basis in one feeling, a sensation he carried with him all of his life: that he was watched. Even though he would have preferred not to believe, to be atheist, he experienced God through this fear. [...] It being unknown was what terrified him", 176).

Thus, as Tommy cannot distinguish between "good and evil" in the metaphysical presence ("It did not matter to Tommy whether this presence was good or evil", 176), he equally cannot distinguish superstition from religion and superstition from rationalism. This is evident when, after his departure from the brothel he felt the need to pray but found the door of the Protestant church locked, he mistook it as a sign of rejection, a refusal of God to accept him ("Coincidence, a rationalist and a secularist would say, is the root of all superstition. A door locked is not at all improbable, let alone a miracle. But for Tommy, drunk, desiring to sedate all his hungers, it was a sign. God did not want him either", 129).

Thus, retrogressing and wavering among his doubts and ambivalences and not knowing what exactly he wants and should do, even when the priest unlocks the church for him to pray, he changes his mind at the last minute (and instead of the church he ends up in the porn-shop) with the following superficial excuse, in relation to the priest: "Tommy disliked him, his normalcy. The cheap grey jumper struck him as an absurdity, ill befitting his role. He waved, limply, turned and walked away" (128-129).

Another element which is directly related to that of religion is that of guilty feelings. Tommy is riddled with heaps of guilty feelings. Except that, he is so confused intellectually and emotionally, it is not so easy for us to distinguish the real source of his guilt, or that Tommy is in fact deeply aware of "evil" and his sinfulness. Which means that, regardless of whether he realises it or not, Tommy, up to a point, is possessed by some religious sense.

Consequently, Tommy's guilty feelings do not derive so much from the fact that he mindlessly spends money on pornographic material and then reprimands himself (58), as from the fact that, because "It was a superstition, he never could shake the feeling: someone was watching him" (ibid.). That is why, once he masturbates after having watched porn videos, subsequently there follows something like a temporary ritualistic process of repentance and atonement, that is a ritual of purification of body and soul from shame and sin:

> He takes out the video. He forces it into its case, he grabs a key, goes to the bedroom, opens the lid to the trunk, throws the video in there. He doesn't look into the trunk. He closes it up.
> He goes to the bathroom. [...] He washes his hands, scrubs, rinses, scrubs, rinses. [...]
> Tommy gets into bed, fully clothed, looks up at the Madonna and Child on the wall. His hands move to prayer. His prayer is an apology. (60)

A starting point of his guilt is obviously his first visit to a brothel, where he felt that "After his first visit to a whore Tommy was convinced that the encounter had soiled him forever" (79). Hence he followed the same ritual: "Tommy washed and washed when he got home, washed the whore off his skin. He scrubbed and washed, to get rid of the sickness" (78).

Tommy feels guilty, even when he is "dreaming" (76) various scenes from porn videos during his love-making sessions with his girl-friend Soo-Ling (and afterwards "detested his dreaming", ibid.). These guilty feelings are intensified and multiplied because, although he is "aware of the damage" (132), that is his involvement in the vicious circle of pornography, which he considers to be a "sickness" (79), manifesting itself occasionally with "crying that... was shocking, he was howling" (132) and despite his good intentions and the oaths he takes both with himself and the "icon" to reform, he eventually fails to keep his word and relapses ("He, drunk, went into his room and kicked the briefcase under the bed. He stood before the icon of the Virgin and Child and said sorry, softly. He promised tomorrow he would burn the contents of the case, burn the trunk. Tomorrow he would begin again", 132).

That is why when he realises that it is beyond his power to overcome this morbid obsession of his, which has become an integral part of his life, "He had taken the icon off his bedroom wall, had wrapped it in cloth and stored it carefully in his trunk, separated from the videos and magazines by sheets and blankets" (141).

Finally, the overall atmosphere of guilt is rendered authentically and vividly when Tommy meets accidentally at the porn-shop this unknown till then, but fatal for him person, Neil, as both are products-victims of the dole office and their problematic relationships with religion, but not just that. What is characteristic here is how the external ugliness (embodied in the physical unattractiveness of Neil) is identified with the internal disgust of shame and guilt that Tommy feels – qualities which in both cases pertain and refer to animal conditions. At the same time they specify allusively the atrocious murders-suicides which will follow:

> The man who had emerged from the cell had disgusted him. He was fat, grossly overweight, rolls of flab. He was sweating. His thinning hair, his double chin. He was fat and ugly and obscene. He was familiar too. The dole office? Yes, probably, that was his world too. The dole office. This filthy frightened man, caught out by Tommy, scurrying away, an animal in flight. The eyes that could not look ahead, could only look down, look away. His eyes." (173-174)

The crows (as myth and reality)

A constant motif which runs through the whole novel and which, allegedly, constitutes the core of its storyline is that of the "curse" which is professed to have marked the Stefano family and which is embodied in the continuous appearance of the crows. "Family curse", of course, is a well known motif in literature, which we first encounter in ancient Greek drama (e.g. the curse on the house of Atreus) which has never ceased to appeal to writers of our age such as Tsiolkas. Indeed, for the latter it is such a popular motif that his preoccupation with it is not restricted only to

The Jesus Man but extends to subsequent works like *Dead Europe*. The "curse-crows" is an interesting and fascinating motif which nevertheless functions in the main stereotypically (that is as a link in the chain of the individual stories and the broader story of the novel) and to a lesser degree organically. I mean that, as we will see in the process, the image (real or fictitious) of "crows" is pre-eminently poetic (and not just because it is reminiscent of Poe's famous poem "The Crow") and to a lesser degree prosaic. This is because the "crows" are sometimes used as reality, sometimes as myth (fairy-tale, ghost, joke) and sometimes as an object of parody. In the best case, the only thing these birds manage to do is to identify with: (i) the "evil" that has happened (such as e.g. the death of Nona's brother, as Artie saw "A crow danced in the air above him", 236. Also when Artie finds out that his grandfather killed his Aboriginal wife, "The sun burnt his eyes, there was a diving flash of black and the flash became the crow", 245); (ii) the evil which is about to happen (such as, e.g. the murder of the missing eleven year old girl: "-So you fear crows, Tom? [...] At seven o'clock the alarm was the radio. [...] Her body was found, raped and slaughtered", 77); or the evil which is already happening to the lives of the Stefano family members (such as e.g. the abortion that Dominic's Aussie girl-friend had: "A crow danced in the air above him. That's my baby, thought Dominic, and for one brief moment he was sad", 35). Through this identification, a rudimentary narrative coherence is retained in an otherwise structurally fragmented novel.

More specifically, the fact that "crows" are used as a stereotypic motif (image-idea-belief) is realised from their frequent cliché-like reminders which emerge, sometimes out of the blue, like a glimmer in the stream of consciousness. Some examples:

"In the blackening sky, a crow had swooped" (regarding Artie's relationship to Maria, 232). "In the shadows of the trees, a crow is circling" (Louie contemplating in an internal monologue, 329). "The crows are watching me" (Louie meditating at the cemetery – identification of crows with death, 339). "The sky is black with crows" (Louie's silent thought-response to Soo-Ling rejecting his love, 396). "A crow flies low, and above us the seagulls scatter" (a remark by Louie at the sea-shore together with his little niece Betty, 400).

Thus, to the question "what's the crow", we have a variety of view-points and interpretations, usually contradictory, occasionally entertaining, even when these birds are supposed to symbolise "evil" and tragedy. The first of the following representative examples is how people who do not belong to the Stefano family but are related to it by marriage see and interpret this issue. It is a dialogue conducted by Soo-Ling and Eva (wife of Dominic, Tommy's elder brother):

-Eva, what's the crow? [...]

-A story and a joke. Some bullshit. She touched, softly, Soo-Ling's hair. The crow is a Stefano obsession. Dom reckons that when there's something bad about to happen, he'll always see a crow. It can terrify him. Stupid, isn't it?

-Do you believe it? [...]

-What's Tommy say? [...]

-He says it's bullshit.

-Then he's probably right. Eva raised her glass. Let's drink to the smartest Stefano brother. (113)

Effectively, however, these birds have not only become an obsession, so that for Tommy "everywhere there was the crow" (178), but he comes to a point where he personifies them by pleading with them to speak to him! Thus, following his bitter disappointment with the locked church, his visit to the porn-shop and subsequently his visit to and exit from the pub, we have his following reaction: "Up in the sky he could see a crow flying. Speak to me, he wished. He would court madness for that experience. The crow dived, disappeared behind a Victorian facade" (130). Something respective also happens with Lou (the youngest of the Stefano brothers and narrator of the novel) when he states: "The crow I see it all the time. The old wog grandma and the old black crone, flying together. But maybe that too is bullshit" (292). This ambivalent stance by Lou can, in turn, be considered equivalent to and also be identified with his bisexuality since, straight after the aforementioned statement, he confesses: "I'm stopping myself loving but I'm falling in love all the time. I'm in love with Soo-Ling, in love with Sean, even in love with Saverio Rocca. That makes me a slut, I guess, but an emotional slut because I don't have lots of sex" (292). The same ambiguous stance is adopted by the mother of the Stefano family. Whereas initially she thinks of the "crows" issue as a funny "fairy tale" ("Mum laughs at the crows, says they are a fairy tale", 308), in the end – after Tommy's suicide and the crows' appearance at his funeral – she ends up believing in them:

> On the day of Tommy's funeral, a tall slowly weeping elm at the cemetery had been studded with the thick black shadows of the crow. The birds had observed the burial. All the Stefano men had noticed. [...]
>
> Maria too had noticed the crows and for the first time she too experienced a terror. She mentioned it, later, sitting crying in her chair, her face a darkness beneath the veil.
>
> -The crows, did you see them?
>
> The men shuffled uneasily. She looked straight at her husband.
>
> -See them? she insisted.
>
> Artie nodded.
>
> Maria groaned and fell to more loud crying. [...]
>
> Lou realised that his father had been as shaken by Maria's despair at the funeral as he had. His father spoke, and it was true, they were sharing the same thought. It scares me that she was babbling on about the crow bullshit, today. She's always laughed at it before. (254-255)

Another quality the members of the Stefano family attribute to the "crow" is that of the *ghost*. This transformation is, from a fictional aspect, not only interesting but natural too, since apart from the fact that it breaks the narrative monotony of the same image, by personifying the crow into a feminine entity ("That's what makes me think she's the crow now, watching me, wanting me to be better", says Artie to his son Louie, 256), it lends greater verisimilitude to its role and presence in the life and fate of the Stefano family ("He [Artie] had always thought of the bird as female. His Nonna had always spoken of a young woman's ghost", 232). And elsewhere, at the end of the novel, in the dialogue conducted between Louie and his little niece Betty, we read: "-Do you believe in ghosts? She goes quiet. -Yes, I answer, above me, around me, the crow. I believe in ghosts. Again, she's skipping. -Good, she says. So do I" (402). However any apparent verisimilitude is being denied in the process, given that the Stefano family members are wavering constantly between the myth and reality of the "crows"-story and whatever these birds suggest, symbolise and represent. Thus, the "family curse", for example, follows the family through the oral narration ("he had been told", 229) but also through the visual observation ("he noticed the birds", ibid). Another characteristic feature is that the crows do not appear only to signal and portend some forthcoming evil (e.g. Neil's murder, hence "The night sky was a blanket of crows", 188 or "In the treetops the crows were waiting", 220) or to seal with their presence Tommy's funeral (253), but sometimes (though rarely in the novel, 229 and 232) appear in order to mar moments of joy and happiness as, for example, on Artie's wedding day:

> A black crow had followed Artie Stephens for all his life. It had been there at his birth, he had been told, as it had been there at the birth of his brothers and his sisters. It was there on the day of his marriage, a shining liquid sky and the gentlest of breeze. Showered with confetti, holding Maria's hand, he noticed the birds keeping a vigil on the stone fence of the Orthodox Church. He stared straight into one bird's opium yellow eye and shivered,

wished to raise his arm to Catholic prayer. Instead he tightened his grip on his wife's hand and wrist, silently mouthed a promise to her. I will protect you."(229)

Louie's confession here is telling:

I know the crow is behind me, I've known it for a long time, but I'm not scared of it. This is not merely bravado. [...] The crow was something we all heard of from very young, but being the youngest, and by such a loud passage of time, I was protected by my mother's scepticism. I'd be playing at her feet, lost in the trance of shapes and colour, and above me she'd laugh.

-The crow, the fucking crow. *That*'s their excuse. (289)

Indeed, one would say that this "family curse", which is substantiated and expressed through the presence of crows, has been constructed only to be disputed and also to be parodied by the Stefano family members. It is as if they are getting a hedonistic satisfaction out of narrating it and wavering between its myth and reality. The following example (a snapshot from a family gathering in the Stefano household) is indicative of this ambivalence:

Soo-Ling had been quiet throughout, angry for Tommy. She waved to him and pointed across the garden.

-Look, Tom, there's a crow.

Everyone followed her finger.

Dominic laughed.

-She's looking at you, Tommy Boy.

-Bullshit!

Soo-Ling at a loss to understand the hilarity her innocent observation had caused.

Eva leant close to her and whispered.

-It's a family lunacy.

Maria was laughing hardest. (73)

The curse as a self-fulfilling prophecy

As mentioned earlier, Tommy is the epicentre of this novel around whose life all the other characters and happenings revolve. Without his sufferings and imminent pitiable end – whose suicide seals it, as a self-fulfilling prophecy of the legendary "family curse" (as Louie initially tends to think: "-Maybe that's why Tommy died, I whisper. I think there was a curse", 338) – the novel would be rather deficient.

Let it be noted that he is the only character in the Stefano family upon whom the alleged "curse" is fulfilled, whereas the others – in spite of the fears, the superstitions and their disputing the "curse" – conduct a more or less normal life. And the question which arises here is: why did this evil befall only upon Tommy, the most quiet and passive of all the members of the family; to what extent was this fateful and inevitable to happen, or to what extent was it something that he, consciously or subconsciously, brought upon himself? To this question however – as to whether there is indeed a "curse" and, if yes, what does it consist of – there is no answer. On the contrary, everything remains fluid, confused and disputable. To the point, indeed, that having read the novel, the reader questions himself whether the writer was indeed seeking to explore the above question or he simply wanted to send up this somehow or other controversial meaning of the "curse" by parodying it. Almost all elements of the novel converge on the second interpretation. (It is indicative that to Louie's interpretation, which attributes Tommy's suicide to the fact that "there was a curse", Tia Sophia replies with the following more pragmatic outlook: "-No, she whispers. No, there is no curse, Louie. Or if there is, it is simply the curse of life. That's all", 338).

Because one finds it hard to come to terms with the fact that, regardless of how eccentric, problematic and psychopathological a person Tommy was, he was led, either by internal impulses (obsessions with his fatness, low self-respect, guilt, etc.) or by external events (loss of his job, obsession with pornography, television violence, etc.) to Neil's murder and eventually to his own demise. Besides, Tommy was not a prey of fate.

Nor was he all by himself, with no help at all, like Neil who had nobody (and according to his brother Darren "Neil, he don't have many friends. No-one. [...] He's just lonely. [...] What you saw the other night, he's lonely", 197). Tommy had people around him who cared about him, loved and supported him – his family and his girl-friend. It was simply his own choice to cut himself off from everybody, to isolate himself and be led to a deadlock. As was mentioned previously, in fact Tommy did not know what exactly he wanted out of life and in this undecided and idle state he let himself be led to self-destruction as the only way out, especially after Neil's hideous murder (222). The latter he killed when he discovered inside a file, in Neil's house, the incriminating material (newspaper cuttings, photos) confirming his involvement in the "abductions, the rapes and the murders" (198).

This is why, after Tommy's horrid and tragic suicide, no one from his beloved family could understand what forced him to take that desperate step and understandably they keep asking themselves, as Lou does:

> Why did he do it? Soo-Ling never asks me this question, neither does Dad. Mum does, so does Dom. I think we all ask it of ourselves. I'm nervous about the day Betty asks it. It's going to come soon.
>
> -Why did Daddy die?
>
> Fuck knows. And that isn't an evasion. Fuck knows is the truth."(269)

But they can only delve into speculation (his younger brother Lou in particular) which range from superficial (that he "gave up music") to ridiculous (such as e.g. the alleged innocent homosexual-incestuous incidental event that happened between Tommy and Lou in their childhood years). The narrator realises fully the superficiality of the first theory by stating: "I have a theory, just a small one, probably worth shit, but I think Tommy lost some of his soul when he gave up music" (270). But this does not stop him from making assumptions with many question marks, correlating them directly with the hypersensitive personality of his brother:

> Did it happen suddenly? Did he decide one day that music was no longer valuable or precious to him? Did it remind him of home? Did someone he liked, because Tommy was easily shamed, did someone scoff at his tastes? Possibly. I realised early that was how to get Tommy to do something for me that he didn't particularly want to do. Just call him lazy, stupid, tell him his taste sucked. He never had faith in his own opinions. Maybe once the music escaped from his room, once it got tainted by other people, maybe it stopped being part of him. (271)

In the novel, of course, there is not the slightest indication that this might have been a remote reason for Tommy's suicide. They are simply unfounded causes that Lou likes to construct in his mind. The second theory (concerning the homosexual-incestuous incident) is more serious and could have some credibility if, firstly, the narrator Louie did not present the incident as an innocent infantile game ("Tommy never hurt me. Never. He put his cock in my mouth, when I was five, and that's it", 296-297), a family memory among so many others, where "Tommy's dick in my mouth is just one more family snapshot" (ibid.) and nothing more. Consequently it cannot be considered as a serious cause of Tommy's suicide. The only reason he mentions it is, obviously, to shed light on the shaping of his own homosexuality. Notwithstanding this, however, it was a painful and traumatic event which, although it did not create any homosexual hang-ups for Tommy (who was heterosexual, attracted to the opposite sex, e.g. 50), it nevertheless caused him so many ill feelings towards his parents and his family in general that he was never able to overcome them. His inclinations towards voyeurism of pornography and violence in his adulthood, as well as his endless feelings of guilt, are likely – as the narrator is alluding – to have their roots in this physically and mentally painful event for Tommy, which had been a traumatic violation of his childhood:

What hurt was seeing what they did to Tommy. And I blamed myself, for screaming, for getting scared. Tommy had sipped up, was crying by the time Dom smashed into the room, but I was still howling and semen was still a visible white trail across my face. Dad came in after Dom, and by then Dom was already knocking Tommy's head against the floor. Mum followed and when she saw me she went hysterical. She laid into Tommy, pushed Dom aside and she was fists and kicks. I had never seen this before and I never wish to see it again. The moment was a madness, a grand folly. Dad and Don were holding Tommy down, by now the boy was silent, and Mum continued to beat him, to curse him, to destroy him. I was now only silent terror. I thought he was dead. And the voice, just yelling, I think it was Dom: You animal, you don't do that to your brother. Then, I see Tommy's face twitch, he's crying, and his nose is broken. He yelps like an animal and I start hoeing into Mum and Dad and Dom. This is what I remember most clearly, I want to kill them for what they are doing to Tommy. The fear is now just an instinct to punish. (297-298)

Conclusion

In conclusion then, based on the specific aspects of this novel we have examined, we would say that the writer mainly explores and detects (like a mine-sweeper) unknown and dangerous paths of human existence, posing – directly or indirectly but always consciously – more questions than he is interested in answering such as the following:

(i) Why does life in the last decade of the millennium, where the novel is set, for a great number of people continue to be either hell or plagued by a psychological emptiness? (ii) Why have human values and compassion been displaced in peoples' lives and replaced by economic rationalization and utilitarianism? (iii) Why has man – notwithstanding millennia of knowledge and experience since his presence on earth, as well as the legacy of wisdom, religious, ethical and other commands and codes of conduct he has at his disposal – failed to become a wiser or better person? Because not only is he incapable of preventing "evil", by reacting timely and effectively to any forthcoming calamity, but he cannot even take control of his own life, rising to the occasion, as it happens in Tommy's case, by simply using common sense. (iv) Is there such a thing as "human fate" or even "curse" as far as the individual or humankind are concerned and, if yes, what exactly is their nature and how manageable or controllable are they? (v) Finally, is the prevalence of "good" or "evil" in life a result of human choices and actions or is there a metaphysical dimension to them?

To all the above and other similar questions the writer of this novel does not give any firm answers. Even when, occasionally, he seems to be doing so allusively, the way he goes about handling it is so awkward, obscure, contradictory and ambiguous that he confuses rather than illuminates these matters. But this is natural, as the writer is still in an experimental stage of his writing career, as this is his second novel. Because this somehow defective fictional performance is something of which the writer clearly has full knowledge. Hence these fictional defects are ingeniously exploited by him both at the beginning of the novel (in the "Preface") as well as at the end of it (with Louie in the role of a thesis writer) in order to either justify or parody them.

As I pointed out at the beginning of this chapter, the writer, among other things, makes it clear in his Preface that "literariness" (that is, the excessive displaying of sophisticated narrative techniques) is not one of his primary concerns in this novel. Therefore he prefers either to overlook – if not ignore it completely – or to parody it, by playing a purely personal, narratively uncommitted game that has few rules. Something which becomes obvious, after all, in the overall treatment of narrative material and the way the novel has been organised and structured. Thus, various shortcomings become easily perceptible, such as, for example, the following: Narrative gaps in the flow of the story, imbalances in the way the fictional material has been distributed, unequal division of chapters – it is questionable whether some chapters were indeed necessary, given that the novel is centred on Tommy's life and fortunes – ad nauseam pornographic scenes of constant voyeurism, masturbation, sexual activity, rape, violence, as well as verbal extremities, without any respite or any other compensatory offset. The same is true of most characters who are inexplicably one-dimensional, uncongenial and boring. They are constantly angry with themselves and disgusted with the world, do not like anything or anybody, and are in a permanent state of self-pity. As they are incapable of finding any solution to their problems and generally feel helpless and useless, they are content with making impromptu and superficial remarks by maliciously criticizing everybody and everything, just to let steam off and make themselves feel better.

All the above indicative shortcomings give the impression that the novel is somewhat fluid and faltering, as if operating impulsively on some mysterious automatic pilot mechanism. It is not at all strange then that, in many respects, the overall fictional construct seems to form an extension of the writer's previous novel *Loaded* – especially as far as Tommy is concerned, who, one would think, is an embodiment of Ari. Much more so when Tommy could very well be identified with the writer himself, as both of them eventually lose control over things – the former over life and the latter over the novel itself. But with an essential difference: that Tommy is, most likely, not aware of this "loss of control" – something which is not true of the writer.

At the end of the novel, through the persona of his narrator (Louie) and *his* role as a thesis writer, the writer (Tsiolkas) employs a similar stratagem to the one he used in the "Preface": he provides explanations by clarifying his position. Although the latter are being served in a narratively clever device (with the narrator allegedly talking about his thesis, whereas in fact he is referring to the overall approach and outcome of the fictional work by Tsiolkas) they are not and should not be considered an apology or an excuse for any of his authorial shortcomings. On the contrary, they should be seen as a sincere and honest stance as to how the writer (Tsiolkas) sees and faces up to the act of writing, as well as his role as a devoted practitioner of it, with whatever doubts, positives or negatives this entails. At the same time he does not cease to declare his modesty, his love of writing, the candidness of his writing and the trust in his capabilities. Finally, he underlines his tendency to "ask questions", to be "open to a variety of readings" and his aversion to "anything being settled too comfortably" – that is his tactics which are reflected in his novel:

> They'll probably fail my thesis. It sure the fuck isn't classical, it sure the fuck isn't writing, reading or arithmetic. I'm not quite sure myself what I'm doing, but I'm trying hard to write something accessible and honest and which is worth spending a year of my life doing. [...] But I'm asking questions and making connections and hoping the connections spark more questions. [...]
>
> I should explain it, explain how it works, explain why it is. There is only one thing I know that I can do, and I don't even know if I can do it well. I can write. Somehow, I've got to trust it, somehow writing has to give me direction. [...]
>
> The ending is open to a variety of readings. I like that. I don't like anything being settled too comfortably. (311-312)

3

DEAD EUROPE:

A road map to self-knowledge through Hell*us*

Death in Dead Europe *is triple. It is the death of Communism, the death of the rural class, a class which was crucially Christian, Muslim and Jewish – another reminder that the current "problems" of Western Europe with non-Christians are not a new phenomenon but a fact of European structure for over a thousand years. The final death is a death that comes from war, racism and intolerance. Generally, this "death" is symbolised more cruelly and shockingly in the Holocaust of the Second World War. But every country and every land has its own version of this "death." In Greece, after the war, there came the civil war.*

(Christos Tsiolkas, excerpt from an interview to "Locandiera", http://www.locandiera.gr, 13.09.2011)

Introduction

The hero of the novel *Dead Europe* (Vintage Books, 2005) is an Australian of Greek descent, that is, he has a dual ethnic background and therefore a hybrid cultural identity. On the occasion of a photographic exhibition in Athens, for which he has received an invitation from the Greek Ministry of Arts to participate, Isaac grabs the opportunity to get to know in person his parents' homeland – which, up to a point he considers his own too. He has heard so much about it from his family, that he now wishes to explore and verify his understanding of it by attempting to separate myth from reality. As an extension of his journey to Greece, he decides to explore the rest of Europe, which he had idealised in his mind (through his family, school, history, books) by bestowing on it a cultural superiority and a glamour of mythic dimensions. Thus, whereas this journey to the Old Continent is supposed to have been a professional one, during its course it develops into a trip of self-discovery, where the hero seeks to confirm or refute expectations and stereotypes which he had fabricated in his mind, due to the tyranny of geographic and temporal distance.

Because of his dual identity (Greek-Australian) and family descent (poor, proletariat migrants) Isaac feels, if not divided, then surely insecure as a person, with an inferiority complex, where the fact of being an homosexual as well as a "failed artist" (according to his perception of himself) has played an important role. This means that there is, obviously, a problematic situation he has to face in his life, hence the need for this trip of self-discovery to Europe. It should, however, be clarified here that Isaac does not idealise his birthplace (Australia). On the contrary he considers it responsible for all his family's sufferings (both his parents were heroin users and his father actually died from an overdose), his partner's sufferings (Colin was a skinhead who used to be a thief and a vandal of Jewish graves, 251), as well as his own insecurities. He also knows equally well that, though Australia's history may not be so turbulent as that of Europe, that does not mean that this, otherwise, virgin land is free of the blood of innocent people and brutality towards them. Except that, because Australia is not as old as Europe, it has not accumulated and inherited quite so many crimes and guilt from its sinful past as Europe has. Or, if it has, these crimes are dexterously folded into the foil of democratic and other similar (deceptive) principles and values, in order to hide or silence the real motives behind such crimes (hypocrisy, racism, hatred, intolerance, wars). Thus Australia, not just historically but objectively speaking, is less infected than Europe, something which makes the hero identify (and not just because of his young age) more with it:

> I want to be home, in pure, vast Australia where the air is clean, young. I was not fooling myself. There was blood there, in the ground, in the soil, on the water, above the earth. I am not going to pretend that there is not callous history there. Everywhere the smell of the earth is ruthless but I want to be looking up into a vigorous, juvenile sky. The sky above me now is cramped and petty. I can't see the stars, I can't see the edges of any universe. The dome of London reflects back on itself. Europe is endless Europe. No promise of anything else. (375)

The novel *Dead Europe* is intersected by two different stories-narratives, that is it is two books housed under one, and whose narratives alternate.

One of the stories traces back to Rebecca (mother of the narrator-hero Isaac) and her family history and once it covers, with huge time gaps, quite a few decades, it reaches up to more recent times. Although this story is supposed to be true (due to the historical references, events and factual evidence provided), at the same time it gives a sense of myth. This happens because of: (i) the third-person narrative in the form of a fairy-tale; (ii) the focus on decisive human deeds, as well as on popular superstitions and beliefs; (iii) the prevailing metaphysical, demonic element, in the form of the haunted soul of the unjustly murdered Jewish youth. (Once the latter had been used as a sexual object by Rebecca's mother Lucia Panagis, he was subsequently robbed and murdered by her family who had promised and agreed to save him from the Germans during the German Occupation in Greece, in exchange for a big treasure).

The other story, in contrast to the previous one, is given in a first-person narration and mostly in a modern, trendy, youthful idiom, reminiscent of the novels of the Beat Generation such as, for example, Kerouac's *On the road* and the fiction of William S. Burroughs. Comparable to the latter is the narrator-hero's discerning glance on Europe, as well as on the faces of the photographs, as these are reflected in the description of the erotic scenes. On the occasion of a photographic exhibition in which he has been invited to participate, the young hero and artistic photographer Isaac commences his long journey from Oceania, with first stop-over his parent's homeland Greece (and specifically Athens and afterwards Agrinion, his mother's birthplace) in order to subsequently visit other European cities with obvious semeiotic significance, such as the following: Venice, Prague, Paris, Berlin, Amsterdam, Cambridge and London. This road trip to the above capitals does not have any tourist motives but is essentially a journey of self-discovery. Thus, the descriptive narration of the cities and generally of the European continent, even though rich and vivid, is far from one of a tourist nature, such as offered by travel literature. On the contrary, it is used and functions as a setting in order to highlight and study a rich heterogeneous gamut of characters (from the world of *emigrés*, artists, intellectuals, proletariats, as well as fringe-dwellers) but also human situations which arise out of these and within these capital cities. Most importantly: this journey facilitates a retrospective realization of the other "mythical" journey into history and time which the young hero had only experienced as a child through his parents' narrations. In this respect, one could assert that the (real) journey is an extension and completion of the other (mythical one) where both function retrogressively. Basic connecting links between the two alternating stories-journeys are some predominant motifs in the novel such as, for example, (i) the "photographs", (ii) the Jewish element, (iii) topography, (iv) sex, (v) the personas. Let's discuss briefly each one of them.

(i) *The photographs*: The art of photography is a major motif in this novel for the following reasons: (i) It is not just the basic vocational activity of the young hero Isaac, but also the basic object of his artistic interests. (ii) It is the cause and starting point of his journey to Athens (where he has been invited by the Greek Ministry of Culture to display his work in a photographic exhibition) and Europe at large. (iii) It contributes greatly to this road trip exploration of the (ethnic, cultural, religious, political) identity of the hero through the depictive-graphic description/narration of the photographs. (iv) The story of the photographs constitutes a third parallel narration, equally important as the two aforementioned ones which run through the novel, as it is not just a connecting link of the other two main stories but, at the same time, it feeds and fertilises them constantly. (v) The "photographic narration" has a dual quality: that of self-referential role and speech. That is, it functions as a regulatory factor in the novel as it provides a commentary upon both its story (that is the two parallel stories) but also their narration through its own presence (with the story and narration of the photographs). Because the photographs in the novel do not only reflect the story of the two parallel stories-narratives but also their own autonomous story which, essentially, is none other than that of the adventure of art in general. For all the above reasons we will devote the whole of this chapter discussing in detail, further down, the role of the "photographs" in this novel.

(ii) *The Jewish element*: According to Vivi Zographou Ponse,

> [...] another political idea in the novel [*Dead Europe*] concerns prejudices against the Jews. In his journey to Europe the protagonist seems to seek out the Jews of the diaspora. In every single country he visits he meets a Jew. The violence and hatred against the Jews concerns the narration throughout its unfolding. The narrator, already from the outset of the story, mentions mockingly the old story Greeks used to tell their children in order to scare them, that the Jews are supposed

to kill children and drink their blood. In the narration there are often mentions, in the past tense, of hostile racist acts against the Jews, during the German Occupation in Greece, in Australia, in clashes amongst gangs, whereas in a couple who live in exile in Italy, they had cut out the Jewish man's tongue and gouged out his Arab wife's eyes. But the Jews too, whom he [Isaac] meets in his journey are not victims any more. They hold key-positions in some dark business of the fringe ("A controversial meta-political novel", *Avgi*, 10.10.2010).

This (Jewish) is a strong and dominant element in the two parallel stories-narratives, both as *present* (with the presence of Jews in most European cities and their encounter and association with the hero) and as *past* (with the unjustly murdered Jewish boy who subsequently haunts the family and becomes the "curse" that follows the hero's mother and her family) functioning as a reference point in regard to the guilty conscience of Europe. In the sense that the Holocaust of the Jews has been the foundation upon which modern Europe was built.

The controversial issue of the Jewish tragedy is culminated and represented with masterful suspense in the accidental encounter of Isaac with the half-mad old Jew and Holocaust survivor in Venice. This unexpected bizarre encounter creates for Isaac mixed feelings (curiosity, empathy, suspicion, fear, repulsion) as he is perplexed and this results in confronting him with the ambiguous reaction-insult: "-Give me back my camera, you fucking Jew" (154). Perhaps it is the only recourse left to Isaac, to come to terms with (if not to free himself from) an unjust "guilt" for which he was not responsible but which he has inherited from his family and carries with him as some sort of original sin.

(iii) ***Topography***:

The city as a "literary genre", according to Michel Butor ("La Ville comme texte", *Repertoire* V, Minuit, 1982) appears effectively since the beginning of the 19th century, Paris, in the texts of Balzac, Hugo, Baudelaire, the London of Dickens and Edgar Allan Poe, the New York of John Dos Passos, the American cities of Kerouac, the Lima of Mario Bargas Llosa, the Alexandria of Cavafy and Forster, have entered the realm of Myth and imagination, the realm of texts. When Michel Butor anoints the city as "literary genre," he is referring to the texts which "imitate" the city; the texts which represent the images and the language of the city. The writer "names" the city with the only tools available, words. However, even when a text becomes autonomous from its creator, even when – in the most brilliant of cases – it is recognised every time and in any era as new by each of its reader, by giving him room to rewrite or to complement it in his imagination, with silences and pauses, even in these cases the text retains the inspiration of its creator. Words do not move on their own. Nor can the knowledge of technique and narrative rules always produce literature. Apart from technical knowledge, there is also sensibility, the creator's ability to experience and to internalise this experience, to surpass it and to transform it according to the power of his imagination. If he is an inspired creator, he will discover those words, their combinations and secrets, which can contain the world of his experiences and imagination.

The same also applies to cities in literature. And, of course, in the texts where the city appears to function either as a backdrop or as a protagonist, what is first required is how this (protagonist) is depicted through the words and narrative structures, how its "imitation" is achieved. But, the one who moves the strings of this imitation, of this representation, is the writer. He is the one who sees the images of the city and treasures them up in his memory, he is the one who "hears" its language and converts it into the language of the text, he is the one, finally, who experiences the city in its diachronic and synchronic dimension, that is, experiences the personal and collective adventure within the city. We can, therefore, speak of the cities of literature, cities that belong to the texts which refer to them. These texts, however, belong to the writers and, of course, to the readers. If this encounter proves to be a happy one, then literary cities belong to the history of literature, to the history of human intellect. (Elena Houzouri, *I Thessaloniki tou Giorgou Ioannou*, Patakis Publishers, Athens 1995, my translation)

As in his other novels (especially in *Loaded* which we have already discussed) the external spaces, as places and points of reference of history (in general) and of the novel's stories (in particular), form the backbone of the writer's narrative stratagems, because they entail the possibility of functioning on many parallel and opposing levels. That is, these places (the cities of Europe) are not just the cradles of civilization, the cities of a glorious past, with a long historical and cultural tradition, but the decadent and downgraded cities of decay and corruption, of capitalist degeneration, in which compassion and human relations are lost, of bankrupt ideologies, of racism, unemployment and fringe-dwelling, of exploitation, slave-trafficking, prostitution and drugs. Hence the hero-traveller prefers to "photograph" and highlight this dark side of the above cities which are absent from the tourist maps, glossy advertising magazines and postcards, as he tellingly confesses:

> In my time in Venice I did not watch the sunset from Harry's Bar, I did not visit the Guggenheim, I did not have tea at a palazzo or take a ferry to the Lido. I did not feed the pigeons at San Marco's Square, nor did I travel on a gondola. I did not eat seafood in a restaurant overlooking the Grand Canal, I did not step inside any basilicas or cathedrals. I saw no great paintings by Titian and Tiepolo. Instead I visited the ghetto and I drank coffee at the Café Beirut. I saw swastikas washed by the rain. And I looked

into the wretched face of a despairing man, and saw the ceaseless misery in his eyes, and yes, an external exhausting vengeance. The hatred in his eyes was fierce and passionate. They demanded something of me and they promised no forgiveness. I wanted to forget those eyes, to never ever look into such eyes again. For one deranged, terrified moment – I promise, only a moment; it passed, I willed it away immediately – I wished that not one Jew had ever walked on the face of this earth. (158)

(iv) *Sex*: In this novel, the hero's obsession with (especially homosexual) sex in general, leads him gradually to out of control beastly, perverse and extreme forms of sexual practices, to a point where he enjoys it as a vampire. The various strong naturalistic scenes which unfold are consistent with the disorganization, decay and decomposition which the writer intends to represent both at a world (universal) and personal level. Through the almost barbaric rawness of hedonistic sexual perversion, the writer conveys more convincingly and effectively his protest which comes out as a painful desperate cry: "I'm ashamed that I'm a person!" Here, homosexuality, as a vehicle, facilitates the writer's objectives, because it works retrogressively: both as a curse of the individual (absolute humiliation and dehumanization) and as a bliss (absolute freedom from social conventions) for an authentically "free" but faithful love, as the hero's father jealously professes, when he finds out about his son's homosexuality: "-I envy you. Freedom, no family to think of. You can do anything – remember that, you can do anything you like" (142).

(v) *The personas*: The hero's relatives, friends, acquaintances or those of his family, mainly from Australia, are an important component in the novel, as on the one hand they bridge the vast space-time distance, as well as the various (family, genealogical, emotional, idiosyncratic) gaps which divide the two worlds: the old (Greece and Europe) and the new (Australia).

* * *

To begin with, regarding the important role of the "photographs" in this novel which we have already mentioned, the narrator-hero gives in advance the mark of his cultural insecurities (and his identity crisis) when he realises that his photographic creations were incongruous and could not fit with the Greek environment, prejudging in this way that he felt like a "foreign body" in the country of his parents' origin or his "other" homeland as he confesses: "I was unsure how I fitted into this large, foreign metropolis. I doubted that my work belonged here at all." (32). It may not be at all incidental that Isaac's identity is determined here by his capacity as an artist and not in the least by other factors such as, for example, origin, birthplace, etc. In other words, he identifies himself exclusively with his artistic work and nothing else, hence his strong reaction and protest "-Just because I am homosexual doesn't mean my work is homosexual" (33).

His initial instinct-realization about the incongruous and irreconcilable character of his work in Greece is confirmed by the failure of his exhibition, as far as poor attendance is concerned ("Only a dozen people turned up for my opening and five of them were staffers from the Ministry of Culture who had paid for my ticket to Europe", 36). Indicative also of the gap between Isaac and his Greek folk is also the fact that he did not even dare to invite his own relatives to the exhibition, because he was certain in advance that they would neither understand nor appreciate or approve of his work, due to the sexual nature of his photographs (38). But this failure is mainly marked by the organisers' indifference both to Isaac's work as well as his actual presence as a "foreigner" and whatever outdated and insipid things, according to them, he had to say:

> As I spoke of migration, the history of the Greeks in Australia, as I watched the happily nodding faces, I realised that nothing I said was of interest to them, that what they were seeing was some nervous young foreigner mangling their language and pretending to speak with commitment on a subject that had long ago become ossified. They were not interested in my return. I

was not interested. I dribbled out in English, quoting Cavafy's 'Ithaka'. The applause was slight and polite. (36-37)

It is interesting here that this "lack of interest" is mutual. This is explained by the fact that the photographic exhibition is a product of a faceless, cold bureaucratic government machinery (the Greek Ministry of Culture) whose motives, while noble as they may seem (hence the "*activities celebrating the artistic achievements of the Greek diaspora*", according to the invitation Isaac received from Athens, 46), in reality are nothing more than mere public relations exercises with hidden expediencies. Evidence of the confusion, contradiction and hypocrisy of the Greek authorities is that, while they have invited Isaac as a "Diaspora Greek", they see and confront him as "some nervous young foreigner" (36). Whereas they have invited him to these cultural activities in Greece by paying for his "trip to Athens" (46) in essence, as he says, "They were not interested in my return" (36-37). While they allegedly invited him in order to honour and celebrate "the artistic achievements of the Greek diaspora" (46), the irony is that, firstly, the officials of the Ministry of Culture had no idea of either his true cultural identity (e.g. that Isaac felt and was an Australian rather than Greek, as they believed) or of his artistic identity – especially how hopeless he felt himself as an artist, to the point that he had given up ("As fortune would have it, just as I stopped my work, stopped believing in myself, the email arrived from Athens", 46). Secondly, apart from the aforementioned, they subverted the aim of the exhibition itself since they viewed the whole procedure as a cheap insipid show, a boring chore which they were all obliged to dispatch with (36). Thirdly, the overall venture of inviting Isaac to the photographic exhibition eventually ends up resembling a farce, if one takes into account the cheap and miserable, full of "grime and squalor" (41) hotel room they had booked for him, as well as the rude, offensive way he was treated by the reception staff (40).

But equally interesting is also the fact that Isaac acts and behaves accordingly. One could claim that this is done impulsively, so that he can give them some of their own medicine back. But this is not so. Because if we accept that there was some hidden agenda behind Isaac's invitation by the Greek Ministry of Culture (other than to honour his work), the same can be said of Isaac too, in relation to accepting their invitation. That is, Isaac saw the invitation like a god-sent gift and accepted it – knowing that he was not a Greek of the diaspora (as they either mistakenly or deliberately thought for their own reasons) but a "foreigner" (Australian) and knowing also his failure as an artist (46) – not out of some sentimental motive or duty to his "other" homeland Greece (besides he states it clearly: "They were not interested in my return. I was not interested" (36-37), but in order to take advantage of this unexpected opportunity for a (prepaid) trip of self-discovery.

It is not at all by accident that this trip comes up, like a *deus ex machina*, at a crucial crossroads of Isaac's life – when he thinks, that is, that he has no talent, that he is finished as an artist, and that for him everything is over. Therefore this unexpected honorary invitation comes to rekindle his extinct artistic dreams and his hopes for a new beginning. Let it be noted that this is not the first time that Isaac is visiting Greece – he had visited it some years earlier when he was younger. Except that the first time he had visited the country as an ordinary tourist, whereas now he is visiting it as an artist, and indeed as an "established" one.

Here then we have the following paradox: that is, whereas he himself has ceased to believe in himself and his artistic abilities, others (his partner Colin and the Greek Ministry of Culture) happen to believe in him. Whereas he states in hindsight that he is not interested in his (artistic) "return" to Greece, he looks forward to the prospect of this road trip of self-discovery which opens up for him and he is ready to duly make use of it, as he "dribbled out in English, quoting Cavafy's 'Ithaka' (37) – something of an oxymoron in this case. Nevertheless this symbolic act has its own logic: it shows the uncompromising character of a conscientious, provocative artist – especially against authority – who does not belong anywhere and is free from any (linguistic, cultural or other) commitments. (And English, as a lingua franca, confirms it, because apart from the fact that English was Cavafy's second language, apart from the fact that the poet was a Diaspora Greek, notwithstanding that he wrote in Greek, he is considered now a universal poet). It is with the verses of this poet then, which are not mentioned explicitly, that the hero of the novel chooses to sketch out the outline of the trip of self-disvovery he intends to take. Specifically: "When you start on your journey to Ithaca, / then pray that the road is long, / full of adventure, full of knowledge. / [...] You will never meet the Lestrygonians, / the Cyclopes and the fierce Poseidon, / if you do not carry them within your soul, / if your soul does not raise them up before you." ("Ithaca", *The Complete Poems of Cavafy*, translated by Rae Dalvea, Harvest/HBJ Book, 1976).

Talking about the magnitude and importance of the photographic art in the novel, it is worth mentioning in advance the reference that the hero thinks useful of making in the narration of the overall story, in relation to: Firstly, the experiential impasses of the artist and the guilt these entail, especially when he depends on somebody else, as he says, about his partner Colin: "I was guilty that I was leaving him back home while I was heading off overseas, I was guilty that I was looking forward to the pleasure of time alone. I was guilty that I was travelling, adventuring, when the last six months it had been his money paying the bills" (45-46); secondly, the artistic impasses which impede even more the already difficult and problematic work of the creator, especially when the latter is conscious of his inadequacies. It is characteristic that Isaac resorts to this personal confession in an intensely apologetic and critical tone, not only to express his remorse but also to emphasise that, despite his arduous efforts, the result was not what he had anticipated: "I swear that I attempted to work. I would take the camera, I would walk streets [...] I'd attempt to shoot [...] I would walk into the darkroom that Colin had built for me. I would emerge stinking of chemicals, exhausted and empty. And that was the problem with the photographs that would emerge. They were lifeless" (46). Thus, although he sacrifices the vigour of his youth, the result was to have "Dead photographs. [...] The eyes that stared back at me from my photos were dead. The streets and asphalt streets, dead. All my subjects were muted and still" (46).

However, despite the poor opinion he has about the quality of his work, as we already mentioned, others believe in it and support him (Colin and the Greek Ministry of Culture) and of course the person in charge of the Athenian gallery, Anastasia, who tells him approvingly: "-You are very talented" (33). Taking this as an amiable compliment, when Isaac asks her what she thinks about his photographs, she goes on to praise unequivocally his peculiarity as an artist, especially when she compares him with other Greek-Australians she has met, by saying:

> -It is inevitable, living here in Athens, she continued, that we meet so many Greeks from Australia. I cannot bear most of them. They are vulgar, ignorant and *très* materialistic. They are what we fear we are becoming. She looked down at her dress, her leather shoes. Eurotrash, she muttered and smiled ruefully. Then there are some Australians who are innocents. Young girls still worried about their virginity, young men who still practise their Orthodoxy as though the twentieth century had never occurred. Them, I like. But I do not understand them. It is as if they have not left the village. We laugh at them but they remind us of the past. And then there are a few who are not like Greeks here, and who are not like the French or the Germans or the English. And, thank God, nothing like the Americans. They are of their own world. Your work reminds me of those Australians. She looked around the gallery, taking in my work. (33-34)

In the eyes of a third party – and indeed of an expert like Anastasia – Isaac's work stands out, something that refutes his own convictions, by changing at the same time his overall mood ("My hangover was cured, my eyes ablaze, I was elated", 34). This, of course, is a good omen, a favourable starting point to begin his trip of self-discovery. All the above is nothing more than a commentary about the ups and downs (uncertainties, challenges, trials, disappointments, joys, sorrows and surprises) which the great adventure of art – and not just the photographic art but of art in general entails. By extension I believe that it is also a referential allusion not only to the "peculiarity" of Issac's photographic art but, at the same time, to the narrative peculiarity of the novel, since the young hero does not operate only in the capacity of a photographer but of a narrator-hero too.

Isaac's rekindling of interest in the art of photography also stems from his realization of how useful and necessary a tool the camera is for him. Although he considered it superfluous to take it with him on his trip to Europe ("I put down my camera", 46) and was eventually forced to take it when his partner urged him ("-Take it, you fucking selfish idiot", ibid.) when "Colin thrust the camera against my chest I put it away, folded it in my favourite dark blue linen jacket, buried it deep in my backpack" (ibid.). Isaac, now that he is in Athens, realises that this tool is not at all a mere tourist accessory but something much more important: an integral part, an extension of himself. Hence without his camera (as he "had not unpacked it" yet, ibid.) he feels like an invalid, incapable of "capturing", and immortalizing snapshots of both reality and his desires, by transforming them from fluid states and "memory" into something "tangible... solid", as he says, something which only art has the magic power to do:

> But now I wanted the camera in my hand, I wanted to capture, to make concrete an image. [...] I wanted to frame the older youth, the boy I had paid for nights before, I wanted him shirtless, his golden face against a bare white wall. I wanted him not smiling, not giving anything away. I wanted him resentful and suspicious, I wanted to capture that moment when he looked silently at me, rejecting me, his gaze demanding me to leave. It was that stare I wanted to capture. I wanted to make my memory of him tangible – so solid I would never forget the boy's brutal tenderness. (47)

In this respect, and whereas previously, just before departing from Australia, the narrator-hero had almost denounced the photographic art ("as I stopped my work, stopped believing in my myself", 46), now, as if by epiphany, and due to the absence of the camera (which he has not taken with him) he realises that this tool is doubly valuable and irreplaceable: firstly, as a recorder of images and events of reality and, secondly, as another medium of recounting this reality (external and internal) since, as we mentioned previously, the photographs do not only narrate their own story, but regulate and complement the other two parallel stories of the novel. Hence his decision to duly exploit it.

Thus, subsequently, we see that Isaac's passion for photography is aroused again and accentuated to such a degree that he comes to the point of being absorbed and enchanted by some cheap porno-photographs which "presumably one of the boys, had clumsily tacked [...] on the back of the bathroom door [...] from magazines and newspapers" (49-50) for voyeuristic purposes. These photographs depicted "The arrogant sneer of Eminem. A lascivious blonde with the largest silicon tits I had ever seen was stroking her shaved cunt. A black and white portrait of the calm messianic face of Osama bin Laden. The photographs were wrinkled from the humidity in the bathroom" (50).

Obviously it is not the beauty or the quality of these cheap photographs that enrapture Isaac but their content: art (Eminem), sex (porno-photos of the blonde) and politics-religion (Osama bin Laden) which (content) identifies with and reflects directly Isaac's interests – not just the photographic ones but, mainly, the stories the photographs narrate. That is why he is excited by the photographs themselves, as objects that narrate stories, that is, by the very photographing itself as an artistic (depictive-narrative) act. Hence his exaltation is accentuated when, he immediately asks the impoverished, fringe-dwelling foreign migrants, if he could take a photo of them. This request of him sounds absurd, to say the least, to the ears of these "foreigners", firstly because he does not carry a camera with him and, secondly, because, due to their situation (poverty, wretchedness, etc) they do not think they are ideal objects for photography. That is why they refuse politely ("Elena laughed and shook her head", 50). Despite all this, in an almost feverish state, Isaac departs hastily from their apartment to go and fetch his camera and come back to immortalise them. He does that, but in the end he does not find them because he cannot remember their correct address. This incomprehensible and absurd obsession of his, if anything, shows that the best – if not the only – way for Isaac to communicate with his environment (let it be noted that he communicated with these foreign migrants through gestures and mimicry) and enact the reality of modern Greece in this trip was through the universal language of the photograph. Something which other people are unable to understand and, often, see the camera suspiciously and at times inimically, as an intruder which intervenes into their personal lives, as we will see further down.

Subsequently, departing from Athens, Isaac visits his mother's birthplace Agrinion, not exactly as a typical tourist but, as he maintains, "I held my camera tight in my hand and willed myself to see Greece, her home through her eyes" (75). This is both absurd and contradictory and sounds more like wishful thinking, like a challenge or experiment rather than an achievable venture, for the following reasons:

Not to mention that it is utopian for anybody – and indeed a photographer – to see a country through the eyes of another person, what is surprising here is the fact that Isaac is aware of this utopia when he asserts that:

> Even as I pressed my finger on the shutter I was aware that the places I was framing through my viewfinder had changed unceasingly since my mother was born. I knew as I heard the click of the camera that my mother's hazy memories of this place she left when she was still a girl could not compete with the crisp colours and matt tones of the photographs I was now taking. I didn't care. I wanted her to have something more solid of memory than words. (75-76)

Thus, we may conclude that what really comes first for Isaac is not exactly to satisfy his mother, by asking her, as he claims "Do you remember this? Does it still look the same?" (75) as she retains only "hazy memories" (ibid.) of the place, being so many years since she had left her homeland, but to satisfy an innermost curiosity of his own, that is, to cross-check the stories she was telling him as a child ("I was a child, lying next to her in bed [...] I was wearing blue and white checked pyjamas and I was asking her about Greece", 75) – which is the parallel story of her family given in the third-person – with today's reality. Besides, that is why he has essentially visited Greece. This is precisely the reason that, as he says, "I [...] willed myself to see Greece [...] through her eyes" (ibid.) Besides, he states it unequivocally: "I took shot after shot [...] to ensure that the film would capture the houses, the fields, the narrow lanes, the faces, *as I wished to preserve them.*" (my italics, 76). It is obviously, a desperate attempt by the narrator-hero to distinguish truth (facts) from lies (myth) by comparing his mother's stories (that is the fluidity of oral speech-myth) with the stories of the photographs (that is, the tangible documented stories).

It is obvious that Isaac does not particularly trust "speech" as a medium of "documentation", despite the fact that he has been raised by the former, hence his statement: "I wanted her to have something more solid of memory than words" (76). It is nothing but an experiment which, although deep down he knows it to be just another deceit (since it is art, that is, an illusion of reality) this does not discourage him from wanting to experience its adventure. How does he know? From the fact that, whereas on the one hand he confesses that "This place [...] was where I came from" (75), on the other he admits that: "I knew [...] that my mother's hazy memories of this place [...] could not compete with the crisp colours and matt tones of the photographs I was now taking [...] As this was a foreign light [...] I took shot after shot of the same scene, altering the exposure that the film would capture to ensure that the film would capture the houses, the fields, the narrow lanes, the faces, as I wished to preserve them. I altered the aperture and attempted to capture the soul of the town" (75-76).

Something which is impossible, of course, given that – as emphasised numerous times in the novel – he was a "foreigner"; that is why "The old men of Karpenisi stared suspiciously at my camera" (76). But not just because of that. I do believe that here there is, at the same time, an allusion made about the suspicion, as well as, perhaps, the superstitions of simple peasants towards modern technology and, by extension, towards the superiority of oral culture (narration) against modern photographic narration. That is why, I think, this constitutes a preface (prolepsis) as to where and how this story-narration with the photographs will proceed.

Subsequently the narrator-hero introduces the "ghosts" motif which will dominate almost obsessively the rest of the novel, with his visit to the Jewish History Museum of Thessalokini where, despite the prohibition, Isaac manages to take a photograph, which acts as a preface to what will follow, by saying: "The photograph hangs above my computer, on the study wall. In the left corner the man's grey jacket is blurred, it dominates the bottom of the frame. But the smiling resistance fighters are clearly visible, their grins sharp and joyous. Ghosts. Blood and land and ghosts" (90).

It is characteristic here that with the last epigrammatic sentence, the narrator-hero presents allusively the great historical adventure of the Greek nation (with the epoch and tribulations of the Resistance) as insolubly connected to his mother's family adventure and the "curse" myth which follows it. Thus, we observe that the "ghosts" are inextricably connected to the "Blood and land" (ibid.) but, at the same time, to the two parallel narratives-stories too – the oral and the photographic, which intersect. That is, they co-exist, cross, complement and feed each other. This is evident from the fact that, whereas Isaac's female cousin asks the elderly peasant men at the village coffee-shop whether they know Rebecca Panagis (Isaac's mother) he, drowning in agony, instead of waiting to hear their answer, avoids it at the most critical moment of the meeting, by walking suddenly out of doors to take photographs, as if seeking an answer through his own photographic documents. Subsequently, we realise that despite the fact that for Isaac the whole landscape emits strongly a sense of being haunted ("I walked alongside heavy squat cottages and again I thought I could hear whispers following me. Shadows danced and twitched all around me, but every time I stopped, the silence would descend", 106), the "ghosts" appear and are substantiated through the photographic process, that is, when Isaac "began to take pictures" (106). It was then, as he says, that the following incident happened:

> I turned around and a young boy, his face dirty and his feet bare, was laughing behind the gate. His ragged clothes were thin and filthy and I wondered if he was a gypsy. I looked up at the sky, judging the light, then fiddled with my lens, and raised my camera to take a shot of the boy.
>
> But he had disappeared. [...] The cemetery was perched on the cliff's edge. I drew back and looked behind me but the gypsy child had disappeared completely. And then for the first time in years, as I walked out of the church grounds I found my hand had flown to my forehead and to my heart. I had made the sign of the Cross. And again I heard laughter. (107)

It is, of course, the ghost of the unjustly murdered Jewish boy (Elia) who was murdered by Isaac's grandfather (Michaelis Panagis), even though he had pledged to save him from the German conquerors, urged by his grandmother (Lucia Panagis), because she thought he was a cursed Jew. This "family curse" rumour is verified and sealed by Isaac's female cousin, at the end of the chapter, by announcing to him what he did not want to hear: "-My darling Isaac, my darling cousin, did you know your mother's family is cursed?" (108). That is, we have here a double confirmation-verification: an oral testimony (by others) and an experiential photographic testimony (of his own).

Afterwards, upon his arrival in Venice, Isaac tries to understand and make some sense of the "ghosts" reflected in the photographs he had taken at his mother's countryside: "It was usual for me, when examining my own photographs, to concentrate first on perspective, then tone, rejecting immediately the shots which struck me as clumsy or cluttered. But it wasn't anything technical I first noticed when I studied the photographs spread before me. What I first noticed were the ghosts" (132).

Here the narrator-hero attempts to provide explanations, to reconcile the rational with the irrational, the natural with the unnatural, the tangible reality with superstition. What is ironic, however, is that although he belongs to the "rational world" ("Cursed? What the fuck did that mean? That wasn't in my language, that wasn't part of my world. [...] Not my world, not my clean rational world", 134) yet the supernatural element is what dominates in the photographs ("What I first noticed were the ghosts", ibid.). But what is even more paradoxical for Isaac is his realization that, whereas the real persons have disappeared and are entirely absent (or as his cousin observes "There is no one remaining [...] Everyone in your mother's family has disappeared. The old men say that it is as if they were never in the village", 133), the ghosts are ever present ("What I first noticed were the ghosts", ibid.). Or, it is as if the former have been replaced by the latter. Finally, Isaac's desperate "determination" to give verisimilitude to this phenomenon by attempting to explain it, as he thinks "determined to bring this place to clear rational modern life with my flash and camera, through film and chemicals" (134) proves to be a bluff or yet another illusion, due to the contradictory and self-subversive argument he uses as if it were a rational one: "The boy's face was there as well. I shivered, ice fingers down my spine. Then I let out a slow, relieved laugh. Not a curse, not magic: a technical error. Superimposed. They fucked up my bloody film. *They fucked up my mother's memories. I'd got somebody else's memories superimposed on my film.* [...] This was a technical, scientific world. There was no evil eye. I was not cursed" (134, my italics).

The professed logical explanation (in italics) is nothing more than a delusion which is juxtaposed and clashes with the rational "technical, scientific world" (ibid.). Thus, the "memories" (myth) is inextricably interwoven with the "photo-document" (which is supposed to be the representational reality) where the one intersects with the other. Although the impression is given of a juxtaposition between the two, in fact there is no divergence but convergence, because the one caters for and complements the other, that is, the overall story itself. In this respect, the above quote constitutes a clear self-referential comment on the overall narrative development of the story in the novel, especially if we take into consideration the metaphorical mention that the narrator-hero makes when he refers, allusively, to the word "perspective": "when examining my own photographs, to concentrate first on perspective..." (132).

The aforementioned self-referential, self-ironic comment is consolidated and completed more effectively when, at the end of the chapter "Mister Old Talk", Isaac, repeating the same procedure of examining the photographs as previously, realises that: Firstly, the existing personas of his cousin Giulia and her boy-friend Andreas are equally diffused and equated, photographically, with that of the boy-ghost, in the photographs he shot at his mother's village ("But his shadow matched those of my cousin and of Andreas perfectly", 158). Secondly and most importantly: that the boy-ghost is as if he comments upon and parodies the whole situation, as "The pale thin face of the boy was still laughing behind them, his thin, poisonous face mocking and malevolent" (157).

Subsequently there is a change of scenery where Isaac's problematization is interpolated, as in an interlude, and is expressed in the theoretical discussion that follows between himself and his old mate and colleague photographer in Prague, Sal Mineo, as to whether the artist should prostitute his art in order to survive. Sal Mineo, unable to earn a living as a professional artistic photographer, is forced to work as a porn-photographer, something which makes Isaac indignant. Hence his friend's reaction: "-This is just what I do for money, mate, alright? This is how I make a living. Every guy I shoot, every single one of them, I take other photographs. Not porn. Real photographs. I make them real and I make them beautiful. I still do my job, I'm still an artist, does that make sense?" (197).

And since Isaac does not seem to accept and be convinced of the fact that his mate betrays his beliefs and art so easily, Sal Mineo is forced to emphasise his argumentation by comparing Australia with Europe as follows:

> -Look, Isaac. This isn't Australia. I couldn't even get fucking social security in Italy, let alone here. It's been tough. I've begged, you know that? I've begged on the streets of Naples. King Kike pays me in American dollars so don't fucking get moralistic on me. [...]
>
> I lit a cigarette. The coke high was subsiding but I was back in Sal Mineo's apartment looking down at his photographs. His real photographs, the photos he is not paid to take. There is clarity.
>
> -Then why are you still taking your photographs, Sal? Why do you care to make them beautiful and real? What are you hoping to redeem? Their souls?
>
> In a dingy dark bar in Prague, Sal Mineo punched me. (201-203)

Here the narrator-hero continues, by extending the discussion that started – just before he accepted the invitation for the photographic exhibition in Athens – in relation to the adversities of photography and his decision to give it up. Now (due to his friend's deviation) he probes into the same discussion by focusing on the relevance, necessity and importance of art in everyday life. What is ironic in this case is the following: The two friends realise and admit the professional impasses which the art of photography involves ("-Jesus, Sal, we never expected to make money out of our art, did we?", 202); as for Isaac, even though he criticises his friend, he is not in a better situation either ("-I still work part-time, sure. That's how I finance my photography. [...] I was ashamed to be thirty-five and to not be making a decent living" he says, 202). Notwithstanding however that both of them, indirectly but clearly, admit the marginal role of art and their own role in society and in an inhuman tough world that art cannot easily change, yet they (Isaac in particular) continue to be possessed by innocent, romantic ideas about purity, aesthetics and morality, forcing his mate to protest as follows: "-Look around you, Isaac. Look where you are. Do you know what contempt these blokes have for you, with your headstart in capitalism and you're still fucking mouthing off about silly ideas you learnt at college. Beauty and art and fucking politics. They'd sell their fucking children for a buck. And you want to talk about fucking aesthetics and ethics" (203).

As the hero's photographic travelogue reaches its end, we observe that although Isaac the photographer gives the impression that the focus of his photographs is coincidental (that is, he photographs objects which attract his attention and interest and excite his curiosity) this is deceptive. Because in fact, and specifically in the case of Paris, for example, two kinds of snapshots are immortalised and juxtaposed: the everyday, hard and decadent life and reality in the City of Light (what an irony!) with the (religious, cultural, monumental, historical) myth of the city, where the one snapshot intersects with and is diffused into the other, so that the two cannot be distinguished from each other but both of them form a unified totality, as the following quote shows:

> I take my photographs of Paris. I take a photograph of a boarded-up old butcher shop, of two African drag queens outside a bar, of a girl selling illegal cds to customers at an open-air cafe. The intense euphoria I experienced in the old Hebrew's truck is waning but I am still happy and fearless as I trudge the streets. I take a photograph of two Arab men smoking cigarettes in a Halal pizza shop. There is no God but Allah and his Prophet is Mohammed. I shoot the luminous spires of Notre Dame. Jesus Christ was the Son of God crucified and Resurrected on the third day in order to redeem us from sin. I capture the Hebrew lettering on the windows of a bakery in an alley off the Bastille. There is one God and the Jews are his Chosen People. The savage mythologies of ignorant, obsolete tribes. I am not tired, I am still elated. I am of this world,

only in and of this world. Revelation. Every photograph I take is an act of defiance against God. (301-302)

It is characteristic that, in contrast to the Chinese saying "a picture is worth a thousand words", in this case the photographer, uncertain as to whether these photos can stand as autonomous and self-explanatory entities, feels the need to frame them with various comments which function not so much as captions but mainly as stereotypic slogans that express how he feels and reacts towards them: "There is no God but Allah and his Prophet is Mohammed. [...] Jesus Christ was the Son of God crucified and Resurrected on the third day in order to redeem us from sin. [...] There is one God and the Jews are his Chosen People. The savage mythologies of ignorant, obsolete tribes" (ibid.)

Which means that Isaac, here, is not just a transmitter (photographer) but a receiver (spectator-commentator) as well. He does not recount events only photographically but also narratively, using speech. In this case the juxtaposition of the physical (modern Paris) with the metaphysical (religious) element underlines and explains, obviously, the incompatibility of the two. Much more so when the one (the decline of modern Europeans) is a result of the other (the fanatical religious convictions of the Europeans), hence the provocatively blasphemous statement-refrain by the hero: "Every photograph I take is an act of defiance against God" (302). This, after all, is natural since Isaac has been transformed into a kind of a vampire, due to the "family curse", on his mother's side.

The transformation of both Isaac and his photographs – as the two are identified with each other – culminates when his old friend Sam, who offers him hospitality in Cambridge England, is dumbfounded when he returns home and realises the paradoxical content of Isaac's photos which have just been printed. To his friend's question ("-What the fuck are these, Isaac?") the latter, as if answering to himself or to the reader, reacts as follows: "There were the cities of modern Europe. The modern streets of Europe: Alexanderplatz, Rue d' Alsace, Kalverstraat. The streets were modern and sleek but their bodies in these cityscapes seemed ancient and damaged and broken. In print after print, there appeared the same reptilian face. The dark, ghoulish boy, his face sometimes leering, sometimes grinning, always emaciated, always hungry, always reaching out grimly towards my gaze" (336).

Here, too, the same juxtaposition of a Europe that, on the face of it, has the lustre of modernity but which nevertheless contains within it and is inhabited by living "ghosts" ("bodies... damaged and broken", ibid.) that move about and ghosts from the adventures of history and myth (the boy), is reminiscent of a verse from St. Matthews Gospel, according to Matthew, where Jesus says: "Woe to you, Scribes and Pharisees, hypocrites! Because you are like whited sepulchres, which outwardly appear to men beautiful, but within are full of dead men's bones and of all uncleanness." As for Isaac, he is also so shocked himself by the content of the photographs so that, when questioned by his friend Sam, he denies that he is the one who shot them ("-I really don't know. Believe me. These were not the shots I took. I promise you", 337) only to change his mind a bit later and admit contemplatively that "I took those shots, those images, they belong to me. They're my photographs" (338).

In the second last quote, in relation to the "photographs" motif of the novel, there is one more attempt by Isaac to reciprocate to his friend's curiosity ("He had wanted to ask me endless questions about my photographs", 361) by explaining the paradox of his photographs. Of particular interest is the first epigrammatic answer he gives him ("I told him curtly that they were a response to Europe", 361) in which he summarises comprehensively the view expressed by the photographs, thus conveying the character and quintessence of the overall novel, in a clearly self-referential way. Because the one who answers, in this case, is not so much Isaac the photographer, as Isaac the narrator-hero. Much more so when this answer of his is not at all clear but allegorical, vague and ambiguous. Because, what was exactly the initial question, and which is Isaac's specific answer about Europe? Moreover, the other question which is in doubt, is: to what extent the representative art of photography can actually answer questions. The writer, obviously, knows this perfectly well and this is evident from the fact that he, subsequently, attempts a further bluffing in order to deceive his interlocutor (who, as his former lecturer, is a specialist in photography) asserting and justifying himself that his photographs are a product of some trick and "montage" of "digital photography": "I pretended that the bodies were grafted from pornography, and the vileness of the internet, and this explanation seemed to satisfy him. Of course, he exclaimed, they're montage" (361).

All this professed rationalised argumentation by Isaac, about the technique of photography, is nothing else than a self-referential parody to the art of fiction in particular, as well as of art, in general. Because the more inventive and convincing the arguments he uses are, the more the solution is subverted and the more the fictional game is parodied, instead of resolving the "mystery" of the photographs, which is already the objective that preoccupies both men. Something which is manifested in and culminates with Isaac's mocking remark: "You ignorant sad old fuck, I was screaming inside, it's film, it's real, this is not digital. [...] I was convincing myself as I spoke" (361).

Through these comments, the fictional conventions are underlined and flaunted, which – because they do not offer solutions to the mysteries and do not answer questions – in themselves become objects of intrigue and suspense, due to their "disturbing evil... and their ability to move", as the narrator-hero observes by self-parodying himself once again: "The inert fear that had taken hold of me, when I first glimpsed the photographs had now left me. Instead, I was delighted with them, aware of their disturbing evil, excited by their ability to move and confuse people. I was proud of them" (361).

The last quote at the end of the novel, which refers to Isaac's photographic travelogue, is given for the first time in a third-person narration (that is, distanced from the hero's point of view) through the eyes of Isaac's mother Rebecca and his partner Colin, who have come to fetch him, seriously ill, from the hospital in England and bring him back to Australia. In the dialogue that follows between these two persons, whom Isaac loves the most, there is an attempt to resolve conclusively the "mystery" of the photographs, that is, to separate myth from reality, and reach a final verdict through the objective glance of a third party. This, of course, is not at all easy given that: (i) These two individuals are dear to Isaac and, because of their closeness with him, it is natural that they function subconsciously and tendentiously, influenced by his own perspective. (ii) They are two dissimilar people in sex, age and cultural background, with entirely different experiences, education, perceptual capacity and philosophy, and it is natural that they cannot see the reality of the photographs in the same way. As a result, their interpretations differ markedly, as we observe in their dialogue:

> Colin was shocked by the obscene, ugly reality of the photographs: the landscapes awash as if in blood; the misery on the cadaverous faces of the figures. [...]
> -What do you think of those photographs? He was gazing down at the world below.
> -I think they are true.
> -And what truth is that? [...]
> -The truth of Europe.
> -That's not Europe in those photographs, his words rushed out. Those photographs are Hell. What Hell did Isaac see? What Hell is he in?
> -Europe has suffered Hell.
> -Fuck Europe. What Hell do they know? The truth of Europe is money. I fucking hate Europe. (403-404)

In the above dialogue we realise that, whereas Colin is "shocked" by the "ugly reality of the photographs" in relation to Europe, Rebecca sees the matter stoically and considers it natural. This is attributed to the fact that, as she says, "-You're Australian, you don't understand Europe" (404) whereas, conversely, she had lived to the core all the trials and tribulations of the Old Continent ("They had never gone hungry, never experienced war or exile...", 404). Their disagreement is not only attributed to their difference in age and experiences ("-What do you know of Europe? You're children. You're bloody children here and you're bloody children there", 404) but mainly to the way they recognise and interpret the photographic depiction of "The truth of Europe." That is, whereas for Rebecca the photographs reflect "The truth of Europe", which is "Hell", because as she says "-Europe has suffered Hell" (404) and she can testify to it because she has lived this Hell diachronically, for Colin (who is a foreigner to Europe), the photographs depict only Hell. The difference is that, by ignoring the cultural background and the background of Europe's "curse", as well as Rebecca's "curse", Colin is unable to distinguish the kind and dimension of this Hell, hence his query: "What Hell did Isaac see? What Hell is he in?" (404), something which creates a sense of an oxymoron. This question, of course, contains the seed of doubt and contradiction: that is, the photos do not reflect the horror of Hell that Isaac saw and experienced, but only part of it, and by extension, art's inability to capture and express reality fully.

Finally, the divergence in the perspective and interpretation of these two interlocutors in relation to Europe, is intensified, aggravated but also resolved eventually, after their confrontation regarding the status quo of Europe. On the one hand Colin thinks that "The truth of Europe is money" (404) and considers Europeans fortunate for their superiority ("-They're the fucking lucky ones. [...] They're the ones at the centre of the world. They're the ones with everything, they're the ones making all the decisions", 404-405). On the other hand, Rebecca believes that this worship of materialism and the haughtiness of the Europeans is their present misfortune but will also be the likely cause of even worse future tribulations. And she is astonished that Colin cannot see this unvarnished "truth", much more so that he does not distinguish the most important thing of all: that "Isaac had not photographed the past, he had captured the future." Hence her concluding Jeremiad:

> -They will suffer again. She said this quietly. And as soon as she said it, she knew it to be true. Could he not see it? In just three days she had seen it. The beggars on the streets, the Slav girls who cleaned the toilets in the hotel, the train stations plastered with warnings of terror. Their fear, their anxiety, it suffused the city. Could Colin not see the truth of the photographs? Isaac had not photographed the past, he had captured the future. (405)

If anything, this prophetic novel by Tsiolkas has no doubt confirmed once more (as in the case of Kafka and other great writers) that literature, not infrequently, can function as a self-fulfilling prophecy...

Conclusion

The photographs: The art of photography in this novel functions retrogressively. On the one hand it is used – through the hero's participation in the photographic exhibition in Athens – in order to make his artistic endeavour known to the Greek public, so that the latter can understand and appreciate the life of Greeks abroad, as well as that of Australians in the distant continent. On the other hand it is used as a means for the narrator-hero to understand both the urban and regional landscape, as well as the life at large, of today's Greek reality. In Isaac's wanderings and exploration, however, it is characteristic that he does not resort to a one-sided but a two-sided use of the art of photography. That is, he does not only use the photographic lens but also the "lens" of his own eyes to "see", capture and comprehend this reality – sometimes alternatively and sometimes in a combination of the two.

For a start, it seems natural that the hero resorts to the camera as Isaac is a professional photographer. This means that photography is not only his profession but also that the camera could be considered as a complementary "glance" or an extension to his physical eyes. I said "seems" because things are not exactly so. In fact it is about a sophisticated "optical illusion", equivalent to a magician conjuring tricks.

Let it be noted that Isaac is not a typical tourist who takes photos as souvenirs. Besides, although few "relics" are left from the once great European civilization, these have now been transformed into objects of exploitation by the tourist industry. He visits Greece as an invited artist-photographer to exhibit his work. Subsequently he utilises the opportunity of this trip to explore both his ancestral homeland as well as the rest of Europe. The reason he takes photographs is not to enrich his souvenir collection nor to give them as a gift to his mother, as he claims ("I wanted her to have something more solid of memory than words", by asking her "Do you remember this? Does it still look the same", 75-76) as she retains only "hazy memories" of the place (ibid.) but, as discussed earlier in this chapter, to verify for himself – through his own comparison – what corresponds to the reality and what he was told and had learnt as a child about Greece (75).

This means that the art of photography is used as a valid and authentic medium for the verification and interpretation of reality through the alleged irrefutable photographic document. Except that this perception – that the photograph reflects reality faithfully and irrefutably – is deceptive, since the human glance can never be impartial and objective. This is because every time a person "sees" something, reality changes – something which is supported by science too. Consequently there is no such thing as an objective "glance"' or an objective "reality" – external or internal – but only subjective (biased) fluid situations. Much more so when, in Isaac's case, the question is who exactly is he, that is with whose eyes does he "see" through the view-finder and what does he want to see, imprint and reveal? Because he also "sees" with other people's eyes such as, for example, mainly his mother's and various others, Greek and non-Greek as well. Furthermore, the situation becomes more difficult when the hero's photographic lens (camera) not only forms an extension of his own subjective (human) glance, as previously mentioned, but it is also an artistic device – that is, it has the inherent quality interfering with reality and transforming it. Thus, it cannot by any means guarantee a "faithful" recording of reality. Conversely – as is proven in Isaac's case – it eventually distorts reality both photographically (with the appearance of the ghosts) as well as narratively (with the expressionistically distorted world it depicts). Quite naturally so, since the hero's focus is primarily internal and to a lesser degree external, confirming thus the timely and diachronic remark by Cavafy, that: "You will never meet such as these on your path, / if your thoughts remain lofty, if a fine / emotion touches your body and your spirit. / You will never meet the Lestrygonians, / the Cyclopes and the fierce Poseidon, / if you do not carry them within your soul, / if your soul does not raise them up before you" ("Ithaca", op. cit.) It is not by accident either that this symbolic poem is recited by the hero at the launch of his photographic exhibition in Athens.

The identities: The "identity" issue – homosexual, Jewish, marginal or any other kind that is considered a "red rag" by society – constitutes a permanent backdrop in the story of the novel and feeds its narration constantly. The problematic identity of the Greek-Australian hero (due to his homosexuality, his dual and uncertain cultural identity, his mysterious family background, his insecure artistic status, etc) is entangled and aggravated even further by his negative contact with the Greek element. Especially through the suspicious and sometimes hostile way with which he is treated in Athens, but also in rural Greece, in his mother's village. For example, talking with an old peasant at the coffee-shop, the gap between native and expatriate Greeks becomes obvious when the question-censure is posed as to whether Greeks abroad have forgotten their motherland or vice-versa. This results in Isaac confronting now more acutely some of his pre-existing troublesome issues such as: who he is really, what he is and where he does belong in relation to his ethnic, cultural, ideological or even imaginative identity.

The odyssey: The above issues naturally make the hero realise, gradually, that his visit to his parents' homeland (which is a decisive entry point for what will follow during his wanderings in Europe) constitutes a miniature odyssey. But it is not an odyssey of external adventures, a search for some unknown golden fleece, but an odyssey mainly of an inner adventure and search for a metaphorical Ariadne's thread. The latter – through the opaque labyrinth of his family's past (which he has inherited as an ancestral curse or sin), the rough paths of various dark historical periods of Greece (being also responsible for his parents' migration to the Antipodes), as well as the unknown and dangerous regions of conscious or unconscious existence – will eventually lead him to the redemptive oasis of recovery and self-discovery.

This final resolution is mainly a result of intermingling of elements in the sophisticated synthesis of the overall narrative structure, as the writer has absorbed and married various *genres* of oral-popular narration (from his parents – fairytales, legends, mythology, history, religion, folklore, beliefs, superstitions, ghost-stories, etc) and written-erudite narration (from the Bible, historical, literary and other text and non-text books) which he moulds in his own practice into ghost-stories, thriller, fantasy, etc. These elements are incorporated harmoniously within the rhythms of the novel's flow which, as it comes to a climax, manages to dispel the "family curse (ghost)", bringing about redemption for the hero but also, at the same time, a fictional catharsis – intellectual and emotional – for the reader.

The hero's live contact with the Greek and, subsequently, the European reality of today constitutes a bitter disappointment to his embellished, unrealistic expectations. The latter had been cultivated imaginatively and emotionally since a very young age by his family environment and their homesickness – as previously mentioned – the school, the books (of history and literature) he had read and, at a later stage, by some of his adult European friend-lovers. The disappointment ensues from the fact that, in Greece, the hero encounters many of the decadent elements of modern western civilization such as: irrepressible consumerism (in the form of a superficially swanky and thus vulgar lifestyle), the love of anything foreign, but also racism, the decline of moral values, the hypocrisy of human relationships, the degeneration of tradition through an artificial folklore created for tourist consumption, etc. These negative phenomena are reflected not only in the realm of fringe-dwellers (e.g. in the poverty-stricken migrants) but also in that of middle-class young people – as this is portrayed, for example, in the superficial characters of the lady in charge of the Athens gallery, who acts like a cosmopolitan person, having previously sold her grandfather's farms in the village in order to study in Europe, as well as Isaac's conceited female cousin who has managed to get a job in a private television channel through contacts, etc.

In Europe the situation is even worse, as the various emblematic capital-cities – in which the hero had once sauntered mentally, through the novels of Stendhal, Flaubert and other classic writers and their stories about nobles and aristocrats – and especially the historic commercial centres of these cities, are now the embodiment of decline with their ugliness and vulgarity. This is because they have been transformed into a kind of meta-historic, meta-cultural, meta-ideological Augean stables, where evil governs in all its abhorrent manifestations: hatred, violence, drugs, prostitution, delinquency, illegal immigration, exile, religious fundamentalism, unemployment, sordid poverty, as well as various modern forms of slavery and exploitation – work-related, sexual, racial, etc. In these inhuman, dirty and monstrous mega-cities where the anonymous pulp-like masses live parasitically, the professed "citizens" (that is, individuals with no dignity and personality) are spent in their everyday struggle for survival by any means and at any cost. Thus, from once being a producer of civilization and humanism, Europe has now been transformed into a producer and procurer of a neo-barbarism of the worst kind.

However, although Europe is pronounced "dead" by the writer of the novel, preceded by "the end of its history" or its historic and cultural death, its "dead" history has been replaced by the metaphysical presence of ghosts which haunt it – such as that of the murdered Jewish boy Elia and other minor characters. Notwithstanding the above, as Vivi Zographou-

Ponse observes in her notable book-review, "this metaphysical presence of history however does not remain for long metaphysical. It is incorporated realistically within the narration, through the avenue of magic realism" (op. cit.)

Dead Europe is an ambitious and multidimensional novel and it is not surprising that it exhibits some grey, controversial and ambiguous areas which, occasionally, seem contradictory or even self-defeating. On the one hand, for example, it is clear that this novel is a political commentary about a decadent Europe which, if not dead yet, as the title of the novel explicitly suggests, nevertheless "is dying slowly, tied by the shackles of capitalism" (ibid.) On the other hand, this political commentary does not seem to correspond to the nihilistic "delirium of an homosexual" (ibid.) – something equivalent to that of the hero in *Loaded* – who indulges in sex-tourism in the Old Continent. Besides, the epigrammatic way in which Isaac expresses his position to his partner in Australia over the phone is revealing: "-Religion's fucked. –And capitalism? –Fucked. – Communism. –Fucked. –Australia? –Very fucked. –Europe? –Doubly fucked. –America? – Arse-bleedingly fucked" (349).

Thus, whereas the novel deals with a number of ideological-political, social, philosophic-theological and other issues, this discussion remains in mid-air, fragmentary and incomplete, without a clear stance on the part of the writer, most likely because, as the aforementioned reviewer points out, "in a novel with an extremely lustful narration, it is very difficult for anybody to locate and substantiate its political ideas" (ibid.). Much more so when these (political and erotic) elements disorient, confuse and puzzle the reader, so that the latter does not know exactly where to focus his attention and how these two elements are actually interrelated. Because, often, the hero functions and communicates – according to Vivi Zographou-Ponse – more as

> [...] a sexual and not a political subject. His relationship with [the world] is based on the arousal of the senses and his preoccupation with photography supports this relationship. [...]

If *Dead Europe* is primarily a political novel, we are obliged to see the unbridled eroticism of the hero from an approach that considers the erotic as political. The Europe of exploitation, then, can find its illustrated co-ordinate in the cannibalistic sense of the violent homoerotic sex act. Subsequently, the hero's transformation into a kind of vampire, who literally feeds on blood and loses his appetite for food, comes as a natural consequence of this political cannibalism that the traveller has experienced in Europe... [...]

Another idea in the novel concerns the end of ideologies. In a conversation the hero expresses his view on the September 11, but then he comes back to his personal burning desire for his lover, believing that the discussion leads nowhere. [...] Politics then continues to concern the protagonists but it does not create devoted supporters who would give their lives for it. Politics is simply a subject for conversation and indeed a conversation accompanied by alcohol or cocaine, as if it were a painful subject and can only be discussed when one is "stoned." [...]

The novel, then, poses various political issues, about which it does not seem to express a clear political view. The writing is balanced so that it does not weigh down on either side. The fragmentary reference to these issues, among the journey's adventures, does not allow us to substantiate a clear picture either. The writer probably was fascinated by the tradition of Cavafy, where the poet's eroticism was entwined with the decadence of Alexandria. He [Tsiolkas] has attempted to create a great narrative for Europe, which he presents as a violent, hostile and sordid continent. However, the political ideas with which he has partly engaged have been left incomplete, because they have been used as emotionally driven means to the creation of an aesthetic expression (my translation, op. cit.).

4

THE SLAP:
The bitter apple of (Greek-Australian) discord

Introduction

The singular form of the title *The Slap* (Allen & Unwin, 2011) could actually be considered misleading, given that in the novel there is not one but *two* different "slaps": an introductory one (that which Harry gives to Hugo) and a concluding one (that which Richie gets from his mother), regardless of the fact that the interest of the novel is monopolised by the former and hardly by the latter.

But let's deal with one thing at a time. At a family barbecue, held at the house of Greek-Australian Hector and his Indian wife Aisha, everything becomes topsy-turvy when Hector's cousin Harry slaps an unruly and spoiled four-year old boy, Hugo (son of Rosie, who is Aishas's best friend), just when Hugo is about to hit Harry's son Rocco with whom he has been fighting, with a cricket bat. The little boy, stunned and furious, as it is the first time anybody has raised a hand on him, protests strongly and rather unnaturally for his age by saying: "'No one is allowed to touch my body without my permission'" (51). A view which is shared by his parents, who call the police, and, subsequently, file a lawsuit against Harry – especially since the child Harry hit was not his own.

After this incident the party breaks up and, naturally, the guests side either with or against this unexpected incident of physical assault. The latter results in disturbing not only the climate but also the whole nexus of interpersonal relationships of those guests who eye-witnessed the incident, as well as the axis of their viewpoint around which their shallow and unexamined life has revolved so far.

This is supposed to be the thematic nucleus of the novel. I'm using the term "suppose" because, in essence, it is not. Specifically, it seems that the writer's main concern is not to explore the nature and causes of the above physical assault and decide whether it was right or wrong and all the consequential reasoning (e.g. whether it was acceptable, just, moral, lawful, etc.) Simply put, driven by this unfortunate and allegedly superficial but controversial incident, the writer takes advantage, and intelligently so, of this opportunity, in order to create a panoramic mosaic of almost epic proportions and examine multi-prismatically the whole spectrum of family life in modern multiethnic and multicultural Australia. This is achieved through the recounting of the protagonists' stories, who consist of four men and four women representing the corresponding eight chapters: "Hector", "Anouk", "Harry", "Connie", "Rosie", "Manolis", "Aisha" and "Richie."

Through the epiphenomena of the "slap" incident (which essentially functions as a solder and connecting link among the above chapters) and through the dissimilarity (in age, race, financial status, sex, experience, etc) of each one of the characters, there unfold the narration, not only of their personal perceptions and philosophies about the controversial incident but, mainly, their innermost lives and the way they view this as well as the lives of others.

This is what the writer is primarily interested in, that is, to illuminate and highlight these perceptions and inner lives and to a much lesser degree in the whole ado about the "slap" incident as such, which he only uses as a pretext, in order to give an in-depth polyphonic dimension to his novel. Evidence of this is the fact that, often, the characters are carried away and are absorbed so much in their personal stories (past or present experiences, problems, stalemate relationships, adventures, etc) that the initial controversial "slap" incident, if not entirely forgotten, seems to return rather incidentally to the fore as something marginal. And even this happens for the sake of not derailing completely the flow of the "central" story. Thus, the main interest of the "central" story or of the multiple other stories focuses on the various and autonomous happenings and incidents of the heterogeneous protagonists, which are irrelevant to Hugo's slap, and the way the writer handles this dissimilarity which is, nevertheless, the subject-matter *par excellence* of this fictional work. Thus the point in question, regarding the "slap" incident, constitutes the "umbilical chord" of the story without which there would be perhaps less coherence and relevance to the various chapters in the novel.

If we assume that each of the eight chapters of *The Slap* could constitute an autonomous story, then the most interesting and perhaps significant of these chapters is the one entitled "Manolis", as it contains, in a condensed form, the most controversial aspects of the novel. That is why it is worthwhile, I think, to deal with it at some length.

Although on the face of it is difficult for the reader to make out who, out of such a plethora of characters, is exactly the real hero in *The Slap* (due to the way the novel has been structured – eight chapters where each one is represented by one man or one woman – equally divided into four males and four females), a more careful look reveals that the one who is closest to the writer's philosophical universe is the character of Manolis. This character, more than anybody else, reflects the main concerns and issues Tsiolkas wants to highlight in this novel. After all this is natural, as both the gender of this hero (male), his ethnic identity (first generation Greek migrant) and his age (elderly pensioner) as well as his capacity, as Hector's father and Aisha's father in law – in whose house the "slap" incident occurred – allow the writer the greatest possible flexibility in the fictional treatment of his story. That is, Manolis, as a fictional persona, can – for the aforementioned reasons – personify all the converging (centrifugal) and also diverging (centripetal) elements in himself so that any divergences and/or antitheses can be accommodated more easily and can also be understood and justified by the reader more effectively. But let us see specifically and more thoroughly how these capacities of the hero actually function in the novel.

"Greekness"

The fact that Manolis is Greek is not at all coincidental. Nor is it coincidental that another two heroes in the novel (Hector and his cousin Harry – not to mention a few other secondary characters such as Koula, for example) are of Greek heritage. The writer himself is of Greek background. Although Australian-born, he is the son of first generation Greek migrant parents. His first language was Greek. The experiences as well as the family culture and tradition which formed the first decisive years of his life were Greek. This means that the writer knows quite well the roots of his Greek tradition and culture, as well as the Greek mentality – especially that of Greek-Australians – and it is natural for him to make good fictional use of such a goldmine at his disposal.

But this is not the only reason that the writer utilises the "Greekness" of his heroes. That is, Manolis is not only Greek but also a first generation migrant, with whatever that entails: uprooting, problems of settlement, adjustment and assimilation in a new country, learning a new language, finding a job, racism, humiliation, compromises, etc. In other words Manolis is the product of a callous and inhuman post-war government policy in his motherland which had no alternative but to boot its citizens out, by sending them to be "adopted" by another country which, subsequently, received them as a cheap labour-force. Finally, Manolis is a product of a policy that, for better or worse, formed his life (like millions of other migrants) but at the same time his new country (Australia) was also formed by it – more so by a large and dynamic ethnic group such as the Greek Community. Therefore it is reasonable that this phenomenon of "being migrant" and its consequences – which in our days has taken almost epidemic dimensions worldwide – constitute an essential part of Tsiolkas' writing interests and problematization both in this as well as his previous novels.

Age

At least on the face of it, Manolis is also in an advantageous position, as far as his age is concerned (he is sixty nine years old and belongs to the third age), which allows him to be withdrawn and somewhat distanced from life, having an objective overview of humanity and the world. This is an impression that the reader and possibly some of the characters form of him at the beginning – that is of a likeable elderly guy who has nothint to gain by not being objective in his judgement and the stance he adopts. Hence it is not by accident that he assumes the role of the mediator, in order to reconcile his children whose relationships are strained due to the "slap" incident. Although this is an illusion, as Manolis is neither distanced from this incident nor is he or has ever been a consistent and upright character in his life, yet these contradictions of his and mainly his honest self-critical stance make him a spontaneous, genuine and respected human being whose word is often timely and reliable.

Sex

The fact that the Manolis character is a male is not accidental as a narrative choice. The fact that three out of the four male heroes of the novel are Greek and only young Richie is Australian and gay also has its self-evident meaning. That is, Tsiolkas' focus on the importance of being a man both within the traditional patriarchal Greek family (especially in the Greek-Australian context, which remains more traditional and conservative than its counterpart in Greece) as well as in the wider society. By virtue of these characteristics then (excluding the fact that he is a close relative of the story's protagonists, he acts in his triple capacity: that of husband, father and grandfather, that is of the respected paterfamilias) Manolis plays, so to speak, a patriarchal role in the overall story of *The Slap*, even though this role is not a substantial one but rather informal and, occasionally, it is parodied by the various situations and life itself. That is why he feels so humiliated, useless and unhappy (when he fails in his role as a mediator in the family dispute) that he would like to have died ("how much longer must I wait till death comes for me?", 402), as he eventually realises, belatedly, that he had lived under illusions ("Old, old fool, to believe they cared for him, respected him, would listen to him", ibid.), like a foreign body, not only within society ("the village had come with him", 403) but within his family too, since he clashed with his wife, his daughter in law and his daughter ("He could not bear to be with the women", 402). Hence his imperative need to get away, to escape, even for a little while from the suffocating, repressive circle of the "sacred Greek family" and breathe freely, so that he may not go mad.

Furthermore, as a man, Manolis reflects and represents ideally the eternal war between the two sexes. Examining it at depth, one realises that the conflict about the slap-incident is essentially a war between a man (Harry) and a woman (Rosie) or, even better, between men and women at large. That is, this otherwise insignificant incident gets out of control and goes to extremes (ending up in court) because Rosie reacts so superficially and irrationally (by not accepting Harry's apologetic "sorry") and decides impulsively (against her husband's advice) to have an open war with Harry in order to take revenge on him. Possibly not so much for Harry's slapping of Hugo but, most likely, because Harry was much more fortunate (financially and socially) than her and her alcoholic, almost unemployed and hopeless husband. Although she had no previous scores to settle with him, the unexpected "slap" incident becomes the cause for Rosie to express her instincts against a successful "wog", giving thus some meaning to her boring and graceless existence. That does not mean that there are no disagreements among women or among men, regarding the "slap" and its consequences. The real big tensions, however, are seen between the two sexes, as we will see further down.

These conflicts, of course, invisible or visible, pre-existed in the relationships of the two sexes. The unexpected incident of Hugo's slapping simply came to confirm, highlight and exacerbate them, demonstrating thus the perpetual war between the two sexes and, by extension, the hypocrisy and shallowness of family relationships. The most eloquent example is of course that of Manolis. The latter and his wife may brag about the stability of their family life, in comparison to other broken Greek-Australian families, but this is far from the truth, as Manolis' thought reveals so tellingly: "Manolis doubted that there had been a day in his forties and most of his fifties that did not pass without him regretting ever marrying, without him cursing the terrible burden of having a wife and family" (349). But even today, in the twilight of their life, even though the situation may seem calmer and more settled than before, it is not ideal. There are often frictions and arguments in the couple's life (350, 352, 355) to the point where Manolis feels jealous of his divorced old mate Thanassis who, free from restrictive family conventions, leads a liberated love-life with his Filipina girl-friend (374), something which the rest of the Greek males covet (375).

Finally, Manolis' war with the opposite sex (namely with his wife, with Rosie at the court, with his daughter and daughter in law) culminates when he fails to come to an understanding with his daughter in law Aisha and convince her to change her mind and go to Harry's house, especially when he believed that she was the only woman who esteemed and respected him: "So it all meant nothing, all those years of shared jokes, of affection, of defending her, of caring for her children, of assisting her and Hector with money and with time? Love and family meant nothing to her" (401). The harsh and bitter reality of this illusion makes him loathe women as a whole and that is why he chooses not to return to his daughter in law's house (where his wife Koula has gone) but to wander in the streets: "He could not bear to be with the women. He could not bear his wife's scorn once she realised he had not succeeded. [...] He thought she loved him, respected him. [...] He was just a silly old man" (402).

"The characteristic of being migrant" and Mateship

Just as the "slap" incident becomes the starting point where, consciously or subconsciously, the characters of the novel are forced to untangle the skein of their life up to the present, attempting at the same time a review and re-examination of it, the same applies, one would claim, to the "Manolis" chapter. That is, both the latter as well as the other characters are looking retrospectively to the bygones, summing up their lives and reflecting on their forthcoming death. Most importantly, the major themes discussed in this chapter radiate more or less into the other chapters of the novel, as they are favourite subjects of the writer.

The most authentic and effective way in which the theme of "being migrant" is manifested and expressed in this case is that of "mateship". A concept which, although it does not carry the same weight and meaning in the Greek language and culture as the equivalent Australian term, the writer nevertheless manages to equate it in an original and convincing way, highlighting it through that last and most dramatic act of life – death. Hence the eloquent quote below:

> The conversation moved from politics back to their own lives, but this time with a frankness that had not been there before. The wine and the spirits had loosened tongues, but so had something else, a stepping back into the past: they were reminded of a camaraderie that was so exquisite, so cherished, that only drawn together in grief over their friend's death could they admit how much they had missed it, how intense their longing for it had been. Conversation returned to the children and the grandchildren, as it always does, conceded Manolis, among people as old as us, but this time the men admitted to disappointment, to failure. Tales of divorce emerged, as did curses over a child's laziness or his selfishness or her stupidity. Wrong choices in partners, jobs, in life. Disrespect was a consistent theme, as were drugs, alcohol. (368)

That is, we see the following paradox: that a death was needed for these friends to revitalise such strong but half-forgotten old friendships and memories, through which they relive, even temporarily, the good old times of their youth. First of all, the news of Manolis' old friend (Thimios Karamantzis) awakens him, dragging him out of the mental and physical stagnation of his present state as a veteran of life, making him aware of his own forthcoming death. Thus, he begins to meditate about what could be a normal age for someone to die, about God's logic and justice (when he takes away young peoples' lives, 345), about the existence of an after-life ("Paradise-Hell", ibid.) and generally to reflect, philosophise and ponder. But Manolis is getting physically active too, following his decision to meet again with his forgotten friend, after forty years, even by being present at his funeral.

In this chapter the author explores the significant issue of "being migrant" which has been rather overlooked in Australian literature: the loosening of the strong bonds among first generation migrants and the extent to which they are cut off from each other, as a result of the passage of time, something which exacerbates the feeling of loneliness and alienation in the present difficult phase of the third age they are going through. The writer's persistence in emphasizing time and again the strong bonds among the first generation Greek migrants, through his exuberant characters and their remarks, underlines, I think, sometimes directly and sometimes indirectly, the following remarkable aspects of "being migrant".

(i) The bond among the first generation migrants, in most cases, surpassed the limits of friendship and mateship and went much deeper since, the various associations and gatherings formed and forged their future lives, because in the workplaces, the houses of friends and acquaintances and in numerous events, they got to meet each other, to fall in love or to organise arranged marriages, etc. The case of Manolis, for example, is indicative of the above (347, 354).

(ii) The strong bonds which characterised the first migrant generation were not so much a choice as an inevitable necessity, a prerequisite of biological and psychological survival in an unknown, distant, difficult and at times inhospitable country.

Without this interpersonal and community solidarity it would be difficult for them to stand on their feet, let alone prosper in their new country. This bonding and solidarity may not have effaced the pain of the traumatic experience of uprooting and the painful adventure in the foreign land, but it surely alleviated it. Hence the numerous parties organised in those years, usually in the migrants' houses (347-348).

(iii) Time and distance change the dynamics in the migrant's psychology, by deepening the psychological gap between Greek-Australians and Greeks of Greece as, for example, happens in Koula's case, who feels alienated from and resentful of her relatives in Greece ("I've been in this godforsaken country for over forty years and not one of those bastards has bothered to come to see me", 350).

(iv) This means that, with the passage of time, the Greek migrant in Australia ceases to be exactly the Greek of Greece, without having necessarily become Australian either. He is rather a little bit of both, he stands somewhere in the middle, that is, he is half, incomplete. This makes him feel doubly displaced, as he feels, firstly, uprooted (essentially booted out) from his motherland and, secondly, displaced in the wider Australian community, as he can never assimilate fully. A proof of this is that "the village had come to him" (403) and generally he feels like a foreign body in this society: "Manoli shook his head and walked away. They spoke to him with the language of evil. It was not their fault. This was not a time of good men. The smaller girl watched him walk away and he just caught her hiss" (ibid.).

(v) Hence the oxymoron – though understandable and justified – of a euphoria being created during the funeral ceremony (357-358) which continues and culminates after the funeral service outside the church (358-359), reaching a crescendo afterwards at the house of the deceased (368).

Thus, the coincidental meeting of the old friends after so many years and, indeed, at a funeral (where death here comes not so much to part but to unite) is triply revitalizing, exhilarating and necessary: not only because they meet again in person, but also because they remember, contemplate and relive with nostalgia their years of their lusty youth, their erotic adventures and indeed at the most crucial turning-point – now that they are at the twilight of their life. That is why this reunion may be emotionally charged, exhilarating and liberating (having come out of their isolation imposed by old age) but, at the same time, it is also painful. This can be detected in the bitter self-reprimand which Thanassis' words express and which apparently reflect the views of the other members of the group:

> Thanassis seemed suddenly sober. 'How long has it been since I've been with you, you damn cocksuckers, you fucking pair of demons? How long? Why? Why did we drift apart?
> 'Life is like that.'
> 'Why is life like that, Sotiri?'
> 'It just is.'
> 'That's no answer.'
> 'We just got lazy. We just got too comfortable and too lazy. That's what happened.' (375-376)

I think that the word "comfortable" reflects the overall philosophy of the writer who considers "laziness" responsible for the loosening and wearing out of human relationships in modern middle-class society.

The importance of mateship, however, in this chapter does not end here, with the funeral of Manolis' friend, as one would expect. It continues – even in an unconventional and unexpected manner, due to its autonomy in the course of the story – as a complement to the first gathering (in the funeral), since there is talk about the inhumane murder of Dimitri's son Yianni. The mateship phenomenon reaches its peak in dramatic splendour and is completed with Manolis' coincidental visit to his other dying friend Dimitri. And here the following contradistinctions are observed:

Whereas Manolis is informed of Thimios' death through the newspaper and goes to his funeral out of a sense of obligation, as "His initial thought was that they'd made a mistake in attending the funeral" (355), Manolis' visit to his other friend Dimitris seems coincidental (as he passed by his house) but urged by an impulsive need to escape from his house, following the disagreement and quarrel he had with his daughter in law Aisha, in order to let some steam off ("He had no plan; all he knew was that he did not wish to be at home", 404) but also from a sense of guilt for having being cut off from his old friends. Therefore his passing by his friend's house might not have been so coincidental after all – that is, subconsciously he might wanted to visit him, judging from the dialogue between Manolis and Dimitris (" 'I saw so many people from the past, and it made me ashamed of how long it had been since we had seen each other. Forgive me, forgive me, Dimitri' ", says Manolis to his friend, 408). Especially if we take into account that he feels twice as guilty for having learnt about the tragic death of Dimitris' son at Thimios' funeral (" 'I'm so sorry about Yianni, I only heard about him at the funeral,' " 408). That is, it was the first gathering (at the funeral) that had ignited, as an afterthought, the importance of the solidarity of old friendships and his rift with Aisha had definitely contributed to those thoughts. In other words, Manolis could see now the need for friendship as a vital support in the difficult moments of life, more important perhaps than family (as friends have common experiences, memories and can identify better with each other, more so than their off-spring. Hence his transient aversion for his children (" 'But for one night I want to act as if I never had children. For one night I want to forget them' " (413), the family which had lately created bitterness and impasses. Consequently his thought about the wrong course he and his friends had followed all those years, by giving priority to the "rituals of being Greek" and not to the substance: "Let's just talk, let's just spend time together, let's make up for losing ourselves in the petty distractions and foolish pride that occupied so many decades of our lives. The rituals of being Greek; sometimes he hated it. Sometimes he wished he could be an Aussie" (411). This is a fact that Manolis realises painfully, the same as the whole of Dimitris' family tragedy is summed up with an equivalent distress in his phrase " 'Life went too fast and fucking death goes too slow' " (408). Allegorically speaking, this of course concerns all characters – even the young ones – since they are conducting a meaningless, dull and unsatisfied life.

Finally, what is absurdly ironic here is that, as Thimios' death makes the elderly migrants come alive again (with the jokes and memories from their love life of their youth, etc) almost the same happens in the case of dying Dimitris where he attempts desperately to give a happy note to the depressing atmosphere in his house, by saying with self-depreciation and in playful tone to Manolis: " 'Come on,' his eyes were twinkling, 'stop with that fucking long miserable face. I'm not dead yet' " (407). What is most shocking and absurd in the meeting of these two old friends is, when dying, Dimitris concludes categorically: " 'We've done all right ...' " (410). As far as Manoli's laconic reply is concerned, apart from the embarrassment and ambiguity it hides, it is extremely contradictory since the " 'We did it. We survived' " (410) though it seems to agree with Dimitris' realization, does not in fact complement the affirmative 'We've done all right', but essentially it mocks it in a subversive way, given that the 'We survived' does not at all mean " 'We've done all right.' " Indeed, in what way?

Consumerism

We wrote a play with Spiro Economopoulos, the Non Parlo di Salo [...] The play refers to Pier Paolo Pasolini and his last film Salò (Salò or the 120 days of Sodom) which has been banned in Australia. One of the play's heroes asks himself if there is "... a country, a person, a mind that has not been colonised" by consumerism. [...] The homeless are not decadent. The society that causes homelessness is decadent. Because there is what is called a lot of money, a lot of comfort, a lot of wealth, too much food

and drink. This excess, visible in Australia, the USA, Western Europe, is really disgusting, a true sickness. It is carcinogenic.
(Christos Tsiolkas, excerpt from an interview to "Mirandolina", locandiera.blogspot.com, 10.04.2006, my translation)

Eudemonism (that is a good, comfortable life, materialism) is another theme which characterises Tsiolkas' overall fiction, including of course *The Slap*. The writer has always been critical of this issue because he considers it responsible for much suffering in the modern, especially the western world, part of which is Australia too. According to the writer, a materialistic eudemonism in itself is not necessarily a bad thing. But as long as it presupposes the uncontrollable acquisition of wealth by any legitimate or illegitimate means, it contains the carcinomas suffered by humanity, namely: wars, social inequality, discrimination, injustice, etc. The latter spreads the virus of cruelty to people and makes them lose their bearings, the meaning of their life, their humanity and sometimes their life too. A classic example of this is the case of Yianni (the only child of Dimitri and Georgia Portokaliou) who was murdered ten years before the events of the novel due to his involvement with drugs (377). As the unfortunate father explains to his friend Manoli, " 'He was a fool. He wanted the big house, the villa, the swimming pool, the new Merecedes Benz, the best televisions and the best furniture. He wanted his kids in private schools, he wanted his wife in jewels, he wanted it all. He got it all and it killed him' " (409). Thus, the irrepressible craze of becoming a *nouveau-riche* quickly, which characterises a large part of the Australian and the world community, is like a gangrene which saps and eats up slowly and insidiously but surely the cells of humanity.

Although the crucial *nouveau-riche* issue and its consequences are focused on and are amplified in its rather extreme forms in the chapter under examination, this theme is evident throughout the novel. With few exceptions, some of the characters are successful and well-off middle-class individuals, with fine houses, good jobs and comforts, some of whom are *nouveau-riche* such as Harry, for example. Yet, they feel unsatisfied and that is why they resort to extra-marital relationships, to alcohol and drugs in order to fill in this emotional emptiness inside them. Thus, the superficial incident of Hugo's slapping may seem facetious, compared to the double tragic fate of Dimitris who lost his son and is now dying of cancer, but it is not. Because, just like unfortunate Yianni had been spoilt – without any discipline and self-control, succumbing slavishly to the temptations of uncontrollable consumerism – the same can be said of spoilt Hugo who has been brought up to have his way and behave uncontrollably, without any restrictions from his parents, which results in the bitter incident. By extension and relatively speaking, the same can be said of the other children in the story too (judging from the abundance of toys and gifts they are spoilt by the adults) as well as with the adults who are incapable of restraining their passions and addictions, such as Hugo's father Gary, for example, who cannot do without consuming alcohol, or greedy Harry who cannot resist his avarice.

The writer's ironic aversion of the *nouveau-riche* attitude of Greek-Australians is reflected in contrasting their swanky houses today with the modest houses of first generation new migrants, as was the case of Manolis' house which he describes as follows: "The interior was like dozens of Greek homes that Manolis had been in, but nothing about the house reminded him of Thimios, the friend from long ago. The house was full of plush, oversized, intricately upholstered furniture; all the photographs were in heavy, ornate gilded frames. Thimios' tastes had always been simple, sparse. What did you expect, he scolded himself, the unadorned apartment of a bachelor? This is a grandfather's home" (363-364).

Finally, the uncontrollable craze of consumerism and the more overall materialistic culture which characterises our wider society and Greek migrants also causes a sort of an allergy for Manolis who feels as if he is besieged by this plague and tries desperately to escape from it:

> In the end he avoided the plaza, the shops in high Street. He was
> in no mood for gazing at things; his stomach turned in disgust at

the thought of the senseless temptation of so many objects. He also wanted to avoid the faces of his neighbours, the groups of old Greek men and women who congregated at the mall as they once did around the village square as youths. He had left his damn village a lifetime ago, sailed across the globe to escape it, but the village had come with him. (403-403)

Family relationships and the generation gap, mixed marriages and racism

The family is the nucleus around which all the key issues which are of interest to the writer revolve. So the themes and subthemes stated in the above subtitle constitute integral pebbles of the whole fictional mosaic, which are condensed as miniatures in the chapter under discussion.

The writer, by using as a model the allegedly solid and decent family of Manolis, shows in the most effective manner the hypocrisy, the illusions and the impasses of the family as an institution, especially in a multicultural country like Australia, by pointing out that no family in our days can be invulnerable, nor multiculturalism so harmonious as the politicians persist on trumpeting.

(i) Family relationships and the generation gap

In this novel and especially in the chapter we are discussing, Tsiolkas attempts an honest and in depth examination of the crucial, intricate and multidimensional family relationships, especially those of the Greek-Australian family, which highlight and determine other critical aspects such as, for example, those of the generation gap, interpersonal relationships, etc.

For most of post-war migrant groups in Australia the bond of marriage was and, to a degree, still is almost sacred. As for the creation of a family, it was the ultimate and most important purpose in life from which all the other relative objectives derive: successful career, financial independence, happy life, etc. That is why, for the first generation migrants, a basic prerequisite for an auspicious life in the new country was contracting a good marriage which would form the foundation for their further progress. Which means that, for most migrants, marriage was not so much a matter of "romance" – something which was considered a luxury in those days – as much as a joint-venture, a mutual partnership agreement. In many cases the couple were primarily business and secondarily love partners. Evidence of this is the fact that Manolis in *The Slap* had not fallen in love with Koula; "he had not taken much notice of her at first" at Thimios' house (347), he simply got impressed by her singing, but even then he had reservations because she was "a little too short perhaps" (ibid.). As to what an unaccepted luxury it was for such thoughts to cross his mind and what actual qualifications really counted in a wife, is reflected in Thimios' reaction: " 'What the fuck are you looking for, Manoli, a German? Koula's pretty, and a real homemaker. Paraskevi knew her family back in Greece. She's good stock' " (348). But Manolis needs to be convinced more (348-349) and when the couple to be meets again, we observe what Manolis pays greater attention to her: "She was fine looking, no Sophia Loren, but she was delightful when she smiled. She also had spirit, courage: it was obvious in her singing, as it was in the way she dared to contradict and argue with men" (348).

After a life-time of married life, Manolis comes now to the conclusion that "It was clear to him now that Koula was a good spouse. She was steadfast. How many men could say that of their wives?" (349) notwithstanding that a little while ago he had admitted with honesty that "Manolis doubted that there had been a day in his forties and most of his fifties that did not pass without him regretting ever marrying, without him cursing the terrible burden of having a wife and family" (349). There is an ambiguity then on Manolis' part as to whether marriage had been a positive or a negative thing, but obviously he wants to believe the former. In any case, he is more honest and objective when reacting to Thanassis' argument as to why the latter was forced to divorce his seriously sick wife who was suffering from a nervous breakdown (" 'A woman who cannot look after her own house is not good for anything' "), Manolis responds unequivocally (" 'We've become spoilt, Thanassis, we don't know how good we have it' ", 360). Marriage then is a way to accommodate both spouses – something which Koula neither understands nor is she willing to admit. Thus, sanctimoniously she pretends she understands the reasons for which Thanassis got a divorce, but notwithstanding all this, in principle, she is against divorce, due to the harmful consequences it has for the children (" 'Of course, you did what you needed to do. But you can't deny it, the children always suffer when it comes to divorce' ", 362). This enrages Manolis who cannot put up with her hypocrisy or her illusions, thinking with sincere self-criticism: "Her lips were pursed, she had straightened her back: a vision of propriety, of piety and moral rectitude. Manolis asked himself yet again how he could break her unrelenting sense of conviction. Had she forgotten the long, poisonous years in between youth and age, the years of argument and spite and disillusion and despair?" (362).

He equally despises Koula's double standards and her engaging so light-heartedly in gossiping and maliciously judging other people for their misdeeds while, at the same time, turning a blind eye to herself and her own family's faults, which are summarised in the portrait he paints of her:

> His wife was still talking, her lips moved, he heard the rush of sounds, but he blocked her out. He read her face instead. There it was: self-righteousness, the flash of mockery, the pleasure in another's misfortune. Had she forgotten the day he had found her banging her fist against the kitchen floor like a madwoman, flecks of blood spattered over the linoleum, her grief and fury at her daughter's divorce impossible to stem? How she had not been able to face going to the factory, to the shops, to leaving the very house, when Hector told them he and Aisha were not going to marry in a church? Had she forgotten her grief, had she so excised

it from her mind that she could now gloat over another woman's equal misfortunate? Women gave birth to men and hence gave birth to greed. (385)

But neither are their children's marriages unclouded; far from it. For a start, as mentioned previously, although their daughter Elisavet was married to a Greek – according to habits, customs and her parents' wishes – her marriage was unlucky and ended in divorce leaving her with two children in her custody.

For this failure Koula holds her son-in-law responsible (" '... our daughter worked hard in her marriage. It was not her fault that she married an animal' ", 384) and although the divorced couple are still on good terms (apparently for the children's sake) Koula cannot help expressing her indignation in a vulgar manner which is unusual for her age: " 'How's that *ilithio*, that worthless piece of shit? Still screwing around?' " 'Mum!' Elisavet motioned towards the other room. 'They can hear you.' 'Good. They should know what an animal their father is' " (390).

Hector's and Aisha's marriage, even though it seems healthy, is also in trouble. The former has a secret love affair with teenager Connie, whereas the latter, although she seems to be a devoted wife and mother, is also tempted to have a once off sexual relationship with a colleague from Canada, during an overseas professional trip where she is attending a conference. What is bizarre is that, to the end, none of the two spouses learns the full truth about these infidelities – which, once more, confirm the hypocrisy which exists in married couples and the illusion there is of family harmony and happiness.

The Slap also touches emphatically upon the notorious relationship between Greek parents and their children which the writer dares to demythologise in this novel. Specifically, he demolishes the myth about the indestructibility of the Greek-Australian migrant family. For many Greek parents their life is meaningful only through the life, progress and happiness of their children, for the sake of whom they have sacrificed everything and have invested all their dreams. However, although this is true to a large extent (we see, for example, how some parents brag on about their children's successes, as in Thanasssis' case, 359-360) or even about their grandchildren (Dimitris' case, 410), in times of sincere self-criticism they are forced to admit their own bad luck and failures as well as those of their children (368) by pointing out, at the same time, with rare courage a big truth which is expressed in the form of a question (" 'I just mean what do we really know about our children's lives? What they tell us. But how much do they tell us?' ", 371). For example, what did the tragic father of the murdered Yianni know about his son's life and his dealings with drugs? Or what does Manolis – who thinks that his son Hector and daughter in law Aisha " 'They're both fortunate' " (352) – know about their secret love-lives?

Another relative sensitive issue regarding the relationship of Greek parents and their children – which has rarely been explored in literature – is the financial one or that which relates to the matter of inheriting assets.

Although Thanassis' case is an exception to the rule and does not reflect the majority of first generation Greek migrants, it is nevertheless of extreme interest. Thanassis, who has always been promiscuous since his youth, is divorced, as already mentioned, with two adult sons who have made successful careers. To a question posed to him by one of the male group, how is bachelor life, he answers that it is lonely (" 'But I've got myself a Filipina girl' ", 374). Even though they have a ten-year relationship (he also thinks she is a "good woman" and respects her and her children a lot) they do not live together, apparently out of fear that his partner will be entitled to inheriting his assets which, rightfully, belong to his biological children. Thus, notwithstanding that Thanassis is the most daring and radical in the group, and although he does not believe that his children, unlike his partner, are worthy of inheriting his estate, yet he is incapable of going against the tide by violating the common law. Thus, divided, he finds the golden mean by compromising in an unconventional way: " 'I've opened up an account for Antoinetta, I put money in there from time to time. My kids don't know. No reason to find out when I go. Anyway, they'll have my savings, they'll have my house. They're fine. Like all our kids, they'll be fine' " (375).

Here the obvious generation gap issue between parents and children ensues where, in Thanassis' case, the shallow relationship with his children is highlighted and also the hypocrisy of this relationship, as he admits that: (i) Greek children are spoilt and unworthy of their parent's estates (" 'They're good kids. Normal people, not fucking doctors or lawyers or cocksuckers like our spoilt children. Just normal, hard-working, good people. To tell you the truth, they're the ones who deserve my money' ", 375) and (ii) his children have no knowledge that he has opened an account in the name of his Filipina girl-friend and deposits money for her secretly; (iii) in this way he believes he does his duty to both – his children and his girl-friend.

In the case of Manolis and his daughter Elisavet too, things are not any better either. Before we examine this relationship, it should be said that from the beginning of the novel the impression is given that Hector's parents keep a distant, sober and neutral stance regarding Hugo's "slap" incident. But along the way one realises that Manolis does take a stand – regarding the righteousness of this slapping – not only theoretically but practically too, given that he decides to testify as a witness in favour of the culprit Harry, who happens to be a relative of his, something which causes a rift not only between him and Rosie but with Aisha too.

Contrary to custom, Manolis' relationship with his daughter Elisavet, despite the narrator's assurance that Manoli "did love his daughter. He was sure of her love for him" (387) it is more typical and less substantial and strong, as is usually the case between father and daughter and does not correspond to the above statement, as we realise from their meeting:

Wearily, Elisavet leaned over and kissed her father on the check. Manolis returned the kiss. They were both stiff in their greeting. It had been this way ever since she had ceased to be a child. She was reserved around him and he was the same. Defensiveness had become a habit between them. Neither wanted to be the first to start an argument. Once they started arguing it would always escalate. (387)

And this is natural as the girl's character was different to that of Manolis, "Her temper was like her mother's" (387) and the two were incompatible. But the antitheses and disagreements between Elisavet and her parents do not arise out of their different characters (for example she may have her mother's character but that does not prevent them from arguing) and their age gap but also from their educational gap which characterises the majority of older migrants. Indicative of her parents' illiteracy is the fact that they do not understand what exactly a "conference" is (388) or what their daughter means when, referring to it, she says that " 'It's about literacy' " (ibid.). This ignorance of her parents annoys Elisavet, even when she keeps silent about it (the same as her parents are annoyed, without expressing it, as they do not want to upset her, about her slovenly appearance, ibid.) who feels compelled to explain and educate them as if addressing little school children. That is, this is similar to what the teachers in the conference do with the school children who have problems with reading and writing. Here we have the following ironic parallelism: the school children have fallen behind and have problems because of their socio-economic situation, whereas her parents have fallen behind because of their lack of education. It is natural, therefore, that the tension between Elisavet and her parents comes to a climax, as a result of their different stance, regarding Hugo's slapping and Aisha's stubborn refusal to attend Harry's party. Their disagreement and the gap which divides them comes to a climax when, after her departure from their house, her mother, in resignation and with raised arms seals this deadlock with the words: " 'They're mad husband, they're all mad' " (394).

The elderly couple attributes this generation gap and its consequences (misunderstandings, disagreements, lack of respect, etc) to the school children's laziness (" 'If they work hard, then they learn' ", 388) and their poor upbringing ("They were mad, his children's generation. Was it that they had so much money they didn't know what to do with it? Was it his generation's fault for spoiling them? Had they spoiled them?", 391) as Manolis reflects on the consequences of the slapping and Aishas' narrow-mindedness (391) and their egotism (in relation to Aisha and following his failure to convince her, Manolis thinks as follows: "Love and family meant nothing to her at this moment but her pride. Did she think she was being brave in disobeying him? She, Hector, the whole mad lot of them, they knew nothing of courage. Everything had been given to them, everything had been assumed as rightfully theirs" (401). What is ironic in this case is that Manolis is unable to realise that his almost absurdly childish persistence and demand to try to convince her to go to Harry's party (" 'You are going to the party next week?' 'No.' 'Yes, you are.' 'No.' 'Yes' ", 401), essentially is nothing more than emotional blackmail, seeking a favour in return for what he and his wife had done all these years for her and her family ("So it all meant nothing, all those years of shared jokes, of affection, of defending her, of caring for her children, of assisting her and Hector with money and with time? Love and family meant nothing to her", 401). The irony lies in the fact that Manolis cannot or does not want to understand that this "love" he invokes is not so altruistic, selfless and unreserved as he thinks it is, but selfish since, according to Manolis, "Love and family" cannot be one sided but presuppose rights and obligations, it is a give and take business. Hence his bitter conclusion about the young generation: "Monsters, they had bred monsters" (401).

(ii) Mixed marriages and racism

Racism is manifested bluntly and openly in a traditional solid family like the one of Manolis. For a start, his wife Koula has never hidden her dislike for her Anglo-Indian daughter in law Aisha, not for any other reason then that she is not Greek, (since she is pretty, educated, a successful professional and a good mother and wife) which is translated as the unique criticism and complaint against her son: " 'Why couldn't he have married a Greek girl?' " (352). She disdains to call her by her name and prefers to refer to her as "Indian" (" 'He's bringing the kids over tonight for a meal. The Indian has to work late again.' His son had been married to Aisha for nearly fifteen years and still Koula could rarely bring herself to utter her daughter-in-law's name", 351). Responding to her husband (" 'Marrying a Greek did nothing for our daughter, did it? Marrying a Greek messed up our daughter's life' " (352), Koula confronts his argument by simply sending him to hell...

Koula's racist remarks, however, are not only directed at Aisha but are extended to Sandra's marital situation and the problems she faces with her children:

Koula [...] continued her excited chatter.

'Of course, one can't blame Sandra and Stavros for their child being diseased in the brain.' Koula touched wood and her lips drooped. Then she immediately cheered up again. 'But their son sounds like he's hopeless, has no idea of what he wants to do. I'd be tearing my hair out if I was Sandra. But maybe she doesn't care. She is Australian.' (383)

There are of course other racist and funny comments by other secondary characters (such as those of Katina, the widow Paraskevi's sister) about Vietnam, the Vietnamese people, their food (e.g. that they are eating dogs, 366) which are not just interspersed throughout the novel but also emphasise what dimensions the racist phenomenon in Australia has taken, especially among the migrant population. It underlines the fact that racists are not only white Australians but also the migrants themselves. This means that racism is a more widespread, universal phenomenon and is not restricted to specific individuals, countries or ethnicities. The best example, of course, is personified by the hero Manolis himself. Although he constantly resents his wife Koula about her irrational prejudice and animosity towards Aisha and her racist comments in general ("He tried to drown out his wife's chatter.

He wanted a few more minutes in a world where hierarchy and snobbery and vindictiveness did not hold sway", 383), yet he disagrees with and comes to a rift with Aisha, as his strong feelings predominate over his mental composure, understanding and logic: "He wished he could slap her. [...] The idiotic mad Muslims were right. Throw a bloody bomb in this café and disintegrate the whole lot of them. [...] He turned his back to her and walked away. [...] Australians used the word like a chant. Sorry sorry sorry. She was not sorry. [...] *Sorry*. He spat out the word as if it were poison" (402).

The erotic element

Eroticism is one of the most talked about but also misunderstood elements in the novels of Christos Tsiolkas. It is so perhaps because eroticism – especially in its extreme forms, such as raw depictions of naturalistic sex – is so prevalent and dominant in his work, that this frequency creates the impression that this is an end in itself or that it is done deliberately in order to sensationalise, to provoke, etc. Although the frequency, repetitiveness and extreme nature of this phenomenon – especially in books such as *Loaded* – may justify such impressions, this interpretation is short-sighted, rash and risky and, as will be shown in this examination, it is far from the truth.

For a start, the careful reader will notice that the element of extreme eroticism in Tsiolkas' work is not a perverse obsession or an eccentric meretricious caprice of the writer but a useful tool to serve the narrative and fictional needs of his work. The young hero in *Loaded*, for example, as we have seen earlier, resorts to the cocktail of drugs and sex as a reaction but also an antidote to his graceless and aimless existence. It is a substitute for his psychological emptiness, a result of which is his colourless and boring life which he attempts to fill in by resorting to the above practices. On the other hand, these practices he imitates are consistent with the spirit, the trends and culture of the particular social milieu he moves in.

But if we accept that the young hero's obsessive eroticism in *Loaded* is understandable and justified, for the reasons mentioned previously, then what could one say about its use and abuse in *The Slap*? This novel seems populated with normal, middle-class people, most of whom are well off, with a comfortable life, free of financial headaches. Notwithstanding this, however, the characters in this novel still engage in rampant sex and drug use – however occasional and recreational that may be in order to offer even an illusion of relaxation and pleasure to their otherwise dull, unsatisfied and imperfect life. Again, even if we were to accept that the (lawful or unlawful) eroticism which the young, not so young or middle aged characters of *The Slap* are engaged in is acceptable as a means of relaxing and alleviating their personal anxieties and deadlocks, then how does one explain and justify the diffused eroticism of those characters who belong to the third age, such as the elderly Greek migrant Manolis?

Before we examine this issue, it would be useful to keep at the back of our minds a saying by the narrator in one of Michel Houelleberg's works – a controversial French writer who, like Tsiolkas, is also obsessively preoccupied with the depiction of sex. In the novel *The possibility of an island* (2005) Daniel (the narrator) believes that "sexual love is the only genuine love available to humankind", by observing: " 'It was in truth the sole pleasure, the sole objective of human existence, and all other pleasures – whether associated with rich food, tobacco, alcohol or drugs – were only derisory and desperate compensation, mini-suicides that did not have the courage to speak their name.' " (Ben Naparstek, "Michel Houellebecq", *In Conversation*, 43). It is a view that Tsiolkas also adopts in his books even though, as we suggested above, he does not use sex as an end in itself but rather to highlight throughout it other themes he is interested in. Thus focusing on the "Manolis" chapter in *The Slap*, we see that through the sixty nine year-old Manolis, the writer attempts to challenge the general notion that age "kills" human eroticism. Age may slow down biological urges and reduce sexual performance but not sexual desire. Indeed, the biological handicap may even arouse and intensify the desire. The scene in the Iranian coffee shop where Manolis and Koula have gone after Thimios' funeral at the invitation of their friend Thanassis is characteristic. We follow Manolis' eyes staring at the young Iranian waitress, and the desire and erotic dimension of such a staring: "They were interrupted by the young waitress who silently wiped the table clean. She was petite, dark, oh God, oh God, she was luscious, thought Manolis. If only he were still a young man. [...] The waitress brought Koula another coffee and Manolis thanked her. The girl smiled, a smile sweet and indulgent. I'm just a grandfather to you, aren't I? Just an old *papouli*. Age, bitter, invincible age. What a monster it was" (360-361).

Manolis stares at the young woman with the erotic disposition and voraciousness of a young man. If he is expressing self-pity, it is not because of his old age (as we will see further down, even at his age he still has titillating erotic dreams and erections, 381) but because of the way the young waitress is supposed to see him and what exactly he represents in her eyes ("... a grandfather [...] an old *papouli*", ibid.). That is, the self-pity is not based on a real fact (as e.g. physical helplessness or disability) but on a hypothetical view that this girl might have of him, that is, that old age might be equated with physical disability. Hence Manolis experiences the duality of an almost adolescent quickening of desire for the opposite sex and a realization of his physical age, and the duality finally leads to intimations of his mortality. In Manolis' character, Tsiolkas hints at the co-existence of the two most fundamental manifestations of existence (love and death) and that this mysterious co-existence is not an event of cosmic proportions but a common every day one.

Even memories of sexual incidents from the past function as a means of attempting to mount a final resistance in the trenches of the battle against approaching death. Manolis and his friends reminisce about the sexual exploits of their youth in an attempt to feel that they have cheated death, albeit temporarily, and to feel – fleetingly – flashes of youthfulness. But the narrator reminds us that "Death was tightening its grip on them all. One by one, they were like rabbits trying to evade the hunter's rifle.

There was no dignity in being human. Not at the end" (377). Hence in this unequal and doomed showdown, they mobilise spontaneously the seemingly ridiculous weapon of the sex act that they invoke in their memory, which is reminiscent of little children threatening adults with plastic water pistols ... It is a silent acceptance of fate and, at the same time, a last effort to fall with dignity in this unequal battle. The narrator's sober remark is characteristic: " 'There is no dignity in being human. Not at the end' " (ibid). Equally telling is also the funny snapshot of the "brothel" incident that Manolis has immortalised in his memory, which is reminiscent of a childhood scene, as an antidote to this cruel "death's grip":

> Manolis looked at the two old men smoking silently on the verandah. Was it possible that the last time they had been together was at that filthy brothel in Victoria Street, so damn drunk that he could not get it up? He had ended up sucking on the whore's tits, pulling his shameful half-erect cock to a pathetic small splatter of a climax. There had undoubtedly been dances, weddings, baptisms afterwards when they had met up, but it was only that night that claimed any stake in his memory. He smiled to himself. They had been studs then, confident, virile, strong. They had been lads, *palikaria*. Now they were all dying. Maybe not ill yet, but death had begun, had started tightening its inexorable grip. (373-374)

This selective recollection of carnal love is not only comforting but also temporarily liberating in its attempt at exorcising death.

The interjection of the "erotic" element into the sober reality which is diffused in Manolis' life and which encircles his peers as well (especially after Thimios' death, Yiannis' murder and Dimitris' accursed disease and the forthcoming death of all) continues, intensifies and culminates with Manolis' erotic dream which is strongly reminiscent of teenage wet-dreams ("Koula had been young again, as they all had been. Her skin velvety, her body and breasts firm, as she had been when he first met her, when she had caused his eyes and his heart and his loins to tremble. Manolis stripped the sheet off himself. He was wearing flannel pyjamas, and he had been sweating. [...] His cock was hard, upright, was poking through the slot in his pyjama bottoms", 381) until the last and only compensation of the cruel prospect of death ("Now they were all dying. [...] Thimios had died; he too would soon be dead, God willing, as would Koula, as would Paraskevi, as would all of them", 374. See also 382). Except that this time the quickening of desire is not just a mental retrospection to the past, as before, but a real physical event: "His cock was hard, upright, was poking through the slot in his pyjamas bottoms. You old bastard, Thimio, are you reminding me of youth for the last time?" (381).

It is not surprising that this erection he experiences is similar and identical to that he had lived, many years ago, as a child in his family home at the village: "But in being reminded of [...] the inexorable finality of life, he found a renewal of his pleasure in the raw, coarse reality of being alive. Maybe that was why his cock had fought for one last stand. This vulgarity, this blood and flesh was life" (382).

Finally, subsequently, in the same chapter, the writer touches upon an important issue which has hardly been explored in literature – namely that of intimate relationships between elderly couples. Even though it is not discussed thoroughly by Tsiolkas, the fact that he raises it suffices to make the reader think about such a sensitive matter – given the ever increasing life expectancy – which concerns not a negligible percentage of the population. Because the elderly, as veterans of life and non productive units of society, form a divergent and therefore marginalised social class, a subculture, which, for a lot of people is equated with that of invalids and physically disabled and unwanted, that is, social outcasts who are not entitled to participate in the pleasure of love, given that age is often identified as a kind of infirmity or disability, as mentioned before. In this respect, age is seen as an intimation of death, as the narrator concludes: "Manolis ordered his cock into a retreat. Damn you, you're no use to me now. [...] Age was cruel, age was an invincible enemy" (386).

For the hero Manolis, any emotional or intimate relationship with his wife Koula is long dead, a thing of the past. What is left is a formal relationship, a cohabitation of convenience which suits both of them, especially now in their late years. They are (psychologically) estranged from each other, as they are unmatched characters, and Manolis cannot stand her erratic behaviour as we have seen before (385). But sexually too they have been strangers since long ago: "He looked over to his wife and tried but failed to resurrect the girl from the dream. It was years since they had been intimate" (386). Worse of all, however – much worse, perhaps, than the absence of carnal pleasure itself – is that it would be unthinkable of Manolis to speak about this sensitive issue, apparently out of fear of being ridiculed by his wife: "What would Koula do if he stood and asked her to go to bed with him? What possible words were left between them to describe his desire? I want to fuck you wife. She would laugh" (386).

Consequently, Manolis' affliction in this case is fourfold because: (i) even though "He was still hard" (385) he knows too well that (ii) he is unable to respond sexually ("His body failed him when needed [when he had visited a brothel in Collingwood years ago] and now it was taunting him without mercy", 386); (iii) he runs the risk of being ridiculed by his wife had he dared talk to her about it ("She would laugh. She would laugh, she would be cruel...", ibid.) and realises finally with immense sadness that as a couple they have been dead ages ago ("He and Koula would never be husband and wife, not in that sense, not in that way, ever again", ibid.).

Hence he confronts this present and humiliating dead-end situation of his arousal with a sense of an inferiority complex ("He blushed", 385) identifying it with the incident recalled from childhood of his mother finding him in bed with a morning erection and mocking him about the size of his cock (386).

These incidents elicit a variety of emotional states and responses in Manolis: embarrassment, guilt, shame, impotence, the realization that both childhood and old age are painful stages of existence, where a person feels impotent and dependent on others. For Manolis here the feeling is that it is not so much his body that is betraying him but the women in his life: the mother, the whore, the wife. Inevitably then, Manolis identifies his indomitable enemy (old age) with the opposite sex: "Age was cruel, age was an invincible enemy. Age was cruel, like a woman. Like a mother" (386).

Even a brief analysis, thus, suffices to hint at the complexity of the role of the erotic element in the work of Christos Tsiolkas. It is not an element used for titillation, provocation or any other such cheap thrill, but is almost always woven in the course of the narrative with other larger, indeed universal and timeless themes. In the words of the narrator, in this very chapter, "May be that was why his cock had fought for one last stand. This vulgarity, this blood and flesh was life" (382).

Conclusion

In all of Tsiolkas' novels, the family, whether directly or indirectly, plays a pivotal role, as it is the canvass upon which everything else is interwoven. Hence the writer sees it as a blessing but also a curse, that is, a necessary evil for modern man. In *The Slap*, however, the writer – for the first time in his fiction writing, through the thoughts, the actions, the dreams, the relationships, the behaviours and generally the life of his characters – is submerged into a tour-de-force, exploring and questioning the role, the need, the function, the usefulness and, finally, the *raison d'être* of the family in our day and age. He is inclined to view it as an institution on the wane, because it has been eroded by hypocrisy, as it has been moulded by other troublesome institutions (such as church-religion, ethnic and cultural traditions), social beliefs, taboos, etc. The seemingly superficial "slap" incident is an undeniable testimony, confirming in the most obvious manner that the foundations of the pharisaic, priggish modern family in multicultural Australia are rather unstable, when the latter can be so easily shaken by a silly childish incident which tests people's tolerances, putting their interpersonal relationships at breaking point; thus the family institution seems to be almost bankrupt today. In spite of all the above, however, with this novel, Tsiolkas does not seek to do away with it altogether, but he seems to challenge our ideas about the "family" as it is today, in the hope that we might review our perceptions and beliefs of it. Above all – I think – he, indirectly, asks for a "reformed family" built on more genuine, healthy and authentic foundations.

Tsiolkas is a writer of strange and unusual makings and it is probably here that the secret and fascination of his writing lies: that is, in the fact that there is nothing of the *haute culture* element of the European fictional tradition – which he loathes anyway – that characterises his writing. Nor of the cheap, easily digested romance kind of literature, or of the American best seller thrillers that are avidly consumed by the reading masses, even though occasionally he adopts some of their elements. We would say, very schematically, that as a writer he belongs somewhere in-between these two modes, but he cultivates an entirely personal, original and experiential kind of writing which touches the borderlines of "physicality" – something equivalent, that is, to what the acclaimed Greek novelist Costas Taktsis does, as I assert in my biography *Costas Taktsis: The dark side of the moon* (Electra Publishing, Athens 2009).

In short, Tsiolkas is not interested in producing a cerebral, intellectual kind of literature, but he is more into exploring and highlighting the "bodily expressions of feelings," as Constantinos Matsoulas so tellingly points out, by adding: "In an interview [Tsiolkas] reveals that while writing, he often gets up and impersonates physically the characters he describes [...] The use of representative sensory details which help the reader enter into a scene – what is called anchoring – is a technique that, together with the writer's psychological insight lends great immediacy to his writing: *"No! No no no no no!'* It was as if the child had become lost in the very word, as if all the world was contained in the screaming of this one negative syllable" (*Vivliothiki Eleftherotipias*, 12.3.2011).

Perhaps the most important manifestation and expression of "physicality" in Tsiolkas' fiction is located in the strong odours the human body emits (sweat, urine, excrement, sexual secretions, blood, etc) with which the writer is almost obsessively preoccupied. (For example, Hector thinks of his wife: "... she just seemed to barely tolerate the smells [...] of the male body", 1. And elsewhere: "... he was drying himself with the damp towel that smelt of soap, of himself and his wife", 11). This focus on bodily smells and functions, aspects Tsiolkas also dwells on in detail in his other works – in combination with a wide use of authentic dialogues and, to a lesser degree, of narrative monologue and a harmonious balance of the two – lend the story authenticity, by securing the reader's spontaneous involvement. Because *The Slap* is not just well written, but its overall linguistic and narrative structure, in combination with its interesting and controversial theme, excites and mesmerises the reader.

Finally, the most fascinating and moving of the eight chapters is – as I hopefully have indicated in my discussion – that of "Manolis", where the current decline of the first generation Greek is presented in a masterful and throbbingly authentic way. The writer's tender and sharp glance dissects the life and death of the older Greek migrants in Melbourne with admirable mastery, knowledge and surgical precision. This chapter in particular is a sensational and a truly honest "document" of how the Greek Community lives its decline and how it is seen and treated by people of other ethnic groups, through the eyes of a second generation Greek-Australian writer who knows how to utilise the rich mining deposits of his cultural heritage.

EPILOGUE

Loaded: Márquez claims that "In general, I think a writer writes only one book, although that same book may appear in several volumes under different titles" (Plinio Apuleyo Mendoza, *The Fragrance of Guava – Conversations with Gabriel García Márquez*, Faber and Faber 1982). If that is true, then this is ideally reflected in the case of Christos Tsiolkas. From his debut novel *Loaded*, the writer gives the mark of his future direction – that is, the outline of his thematic realm, the framework of his interests and his overall Weltanschauung.

The writing universe and permanent backdrop in which the stories of his novels take place is Melbourne and its working class suburbs, whereas basic axes around which these stories revolve are *grosso modo* the following: (i) "The identity crisis" of the individual (ethnic, cultural, sexual, existential). (ii) "The Greek family as a blessing and curse or 'Greekness' as a centrifugal and centripetal element." (iii) "The escape-flight" (from the unbearable heaviness of being, daily routine, loneliness and boredom) through (iv) "Drugs-sex-music" and (v) "Nihilism as a philosophy and attitude in life." Tsiolkas does not only retain these thematic cores in his subsequent three novels but also extends, probes and elaborates them, enriching them with some new motifs such as, for example, those of the "curse", "suicide", etc.

This tactic by the writer not to depart markedly from his standard themes can be easily taken for an authorial weakness – sterility, lack of imagination, timidity in terms of innovation, etc. But this is far from the case as, one way or the other, it is possible to innovate with the old worn-out materials. Then, generally speaking, Tsiolkas' fictional work is not so simple or one-dimensional as it seems on the face of it. On the contrary, often, it is deceptive and requires persistent circumspection and sometimes several readings, if one is to avoid misreadings and false conclusions.

The fascination of this first novel by Tsiolkas lies in the primitivism and unfeigned naivity, in the spontaneous as well as disarming outburst of a maladjusted and problematic pseudo-rebel teenager, who, unable to find any other way out in his repressed, thankless existence, deems that the (verbal) attack is the best defense for survival. By this strategy Ari not only lets steam off but, behind this façade of being up in arms, also hides his real timid, weak and hopeless character. That is, the fascination of the novel stems from the reversal of some conventional stereotypes since, firstly, a seemingly unlikeable hero gradually becomes likeable, due to his fathomless audacity in going against everybody and everything, by overturning momentarily the order of the world. And, secondly, since a loose and stray narrative, without beginning, middle and end, without any plot and with almost rudimentary action – characteristic of an *anti-literary* or unconventional novel – manages to shake the reader either positively (charmingly) or negatively (repulsively) offering him unprecedented experiences. This becomes possible, as we remarked in our examination of the book via "the irrepressible and irresistible *energy* radiated by a primal heart-rending howl of pain, through the anguished hedonistic spasm of writing."

The Jesus Man: In his second novel, Tsiolkas does not simply carry forward the same patterns-motifs which have also preoccupied him in his previous book for fetihistic reasons or lack of imagination. He does so because these patterns-motifs constitute an experiential material of pivotal importance for him, of which he nevertheless only manages to touch the tip of the iceberg in his first fictional venture. Hence he now attempts a much more ambitious, complex and demanding fictional form than that of *Loaded*, which is not, strictly speaking, a conventional novel but rather a self-confessional narrative.

Thus, in the fixed "identity crisis" of the individual, the ethnic-cultural parameter not only remains intact but is expanded and complicated even further, as the Stefano family is of a three-dimensional character – Greek-Italin-Australian. (Hence the problems of the three brothers – to understand their identity, to find out who and what they are and how they can fit into the Australian society – are aggravated).

As far as the "sexual crisis" parameter is concerned, this also remains the same, except that it is differentiated by changing character. Thus, although the major hero of the novel (Tommy) is neither homosexual nor bisexual but straight, some unexpected events in life (especially the sacking from his job, as well as some past and present family issues) lead him to some deviations which ultimately become addictions (obsessions with his body, voyeurism, pornography, masturbation, frequenting brothels). But although these deviations lead Tommy to murder and suicide, on the other hand – paradoxically – his younger brother Louie, not only has no problem with his homosexuality (he even wants to marry Tommy's girl-frind Soo-Ling, after his death) but is determined to pursue happiness through debauchery – sex, alcohol and drugs.

However, the third and most significant parameter of the "identity crisis" is undoubtedly the "existential" one. This element, which is highlighted strongly in *Loaded*, is elaborated more thoroughly by the writer in *The Jesus Man*, with the parallel introduction of two new elements – the "religious" and "superstitious" ones (in the form of the "family curse", symbolised by the presence of the "crows"). Although these elements are conflicting, or perhaps because of this, the writer presents an ambiguous stance about the positive or negative role of religion in people's lives, and ends up adopting the same utopic and nihilistic attitude as in *Loaded*, that is "-No, there is no curse [...] Or if there is, it is simply the curse of life. That's all" (338). These two new elements ("religious" and "superstitious-curse") which are introduced into his fictional universe, are duly utilised by the writer, demonstrating the decisive role they play. Not only in life and death (as, for example, religion does in Tommy's case) but also in the art of fiction. That is, issues and fixed disputed perceptions-obessions, such as the *myth* and *reality* of the "curse" (as in the case of the Stefano family) through its parody – make for an extremely interesting narrative game.

In this novel, the preoccupation of the writer with the "Greek family" as a blessing and, mainly, a curse, and indeed a kind of an ancestral "original sin" is not absent either. Except that, because of this particular family's gradual degeneration – due to the three-dimensional ethnic hybridity we mentioned, the element of "Greekness" is presented, naturally, more changed and not so unadulterated as in *Loaded*.

Finally, regarding the thematic pattern-motif of "the escape-flight" (from loneliness, boredom and the existential hell of daily routine) here the writer – apart from his hero Tommy escaping through addictive activities, such as, the obsessive preoccupation with the body, sex, pornography and frequenting brothels – innovates by introducing some new elements: the addiction to television and television violence, but in particular the "suicide" element as a last resort to his impasses and absolute stalemate. The act of suicide, as a choice and stance in life does not surprise us. On the contrary it is a natural and rather expected reaction from this particular hero of Tsiolkas. Already, from his very first novel, Ari's overall attitude and behaviour would justify suicide, which however never occurs. Eventually, despite his pessimism and nihilistic attitude, paradoxically, he chooses the affirmation of life over death. Perhaps because Ari is too timid to resort to such a desperate but brave deed. But what Ari does not attempt, Tommy dares to undertake and complete, as if he were somehow a literary incarnation of Ari. This, however, does not necessarily mean that the writer condones suicide as a wise solution to life's problems. He simply finds it sufficent to present it as an absurd, but sometimes inevitable and inextricable part of the human fate. Besides, of all his fictional works, only once – in *The Jesus Man* – does he deal with such a controversial issue.

Tsiolkas also innovates in the aforementioned novel by introducing a "burning" subject that seems to concern him since *Loaded*, but for the first time it is expressed here bluntly – that of the nightmare of unemployment and its consequences. The latter, apart from being an interesting subject in itself is also important, as it is quite a political one – namely the treatment of the Australian working class by the political Establishment – especially with the reference to the ousting of the Whitlam Government, the raise to the political scene of extreme-right elements such as Pauline Hanson, etc.

However, the most paradoxical innovation in *The Jesus Man* is some of its post-modernist practices. Specifically, its self-referentiality, with the use of the "Preface" as well as the role of Louie as a thesis writer at the end of the novel. Being conscious of the shortcomings of this specific experimental novel, the writer adopts these metafictional narrative practices in order to, firstly, predispose the reader about these "defects" in the "Preface" ("I'll try and be honest, tell you what I know [...] But it is an interpretation; and I have to go back to beginnings and in the beginning I wasn't there. So it may be that some of what I say is bullshit, is speculation, lies and fabrications passed on. Myth. But in wishing to describe a family it would be ludicrous to deny it its myths", 7). Secondly, perhaps, to justify – with the alibi that *literariness* (or the flaunting of literary sophistication) is not what counts in a novel, but the pleasure of experimentation and the self-parody of fiction ("There is only one thing I know that I can do, and I don't even know if I can do it well. I can write. Somehow, I've got to trust it, somehow writing has to give me direction. [...] I don't like anything being settled too comfortable", 312).

Dead Europe: The third is the most ambitious and elaborate novel by Tsiolkas and surely marks a radical change in his overall fictional progress. But although this is strongly felt in the narrative technique employed in the novel, the writer's obsessions with his favourite thematic patterns-motifs remain. Indicative of this are for example the following patterns-motifs:

(i) The "importance of place" and its function. Whereas in the two previous novels a permanent backdrop for the unfolding of his stories is Melbourne and its suburbs, here we have a change-over in scenery – even though there are occasional scenes in Melbourne. Specifically, the capital cities of Europe, which the teenage hero of *Loaded* (Ari) was dreaming of visiting one day (especially Greece), escaping from the wretchedness of joyless Melbourne, something which materialises now for the adult hero Isaac. The exception being that the latter is not exactly on a pleasure trip but a trip of self-discovery. Consequently, he does not photograph the well-trodden tourist sights of Europe but the dark side of its capital cities. Thus, the places here function differently and more multiprismatically than in the two previous novels by Tsiolkas.

(ii) The "obsessions with sex" which began in a bulimic frenzy in *Loaded*, in order to culminate and become a fetish in *The Jesus Man* and to reach uncontrolled limits of perversity in *Dead Europe*, to a point where they transform the hero into a kind of vampire. But if there was previously excessive use of sex, in this novel it is narratively justified, in the sense that it is identified with the wider degradation and decomposition of Europe and what the hero experiences there.

(iii) The "identity crisis" (homosexual, artistic, Jewish, minority, marginal, etc.), which is enlarged multiprismatically and more intensely than in the previous novels, as the live contact of the Greek-Australian hero Isaac with Greek reality not only aggravates his pre-existing "burning" questions (as to who and what he is and where he really belongs) but, occasionally, it contradicts them resoundingly.

(iv) The thematic pattern-motif of the "curse" which fascinates and preoccupies the writer constantly in *The Jesus Man* is also transferred now to *Dead Europe*. The difference being that, whereas in the previous novel (*The Jesus Man*) the concept and legend of the "family curse" of the Stefano family remain vague, confused and ambiguous and is used more as an object of parody rather than an ontological question, in the case of *Dead Europe* it is specified. Firstly, on a family and personal level (as it is reflected in the case of Isaac's mother and her family, as well as her son Isaac) and, secondly, on a collective, national level (as it is reflected in the case of the Holocaust of the Jews – that haunts the guilty conscience of

Europe). So that here, the inherited "curse" (of innocent Isaac) becomes tangibly substantiated.

(v) The political pattern-motif here, of course, which was launched in *The Jesus Man*, acquires now a more universal dimension in Tsiolkas' fictional universe, since the whole novel is nothing but a political commentary about a decadent Europe that is slowly dying of the deadly sinful diseases of the capitalist plague. Except that whereas in *The Jesus Man* the political stance of the writer is simple and clear, this is not the case in *Dead Europe*. Thus, a series of ideological-political and other matters (social, philosophical, religious) remain incomplete, without a satisfactorily clarified stance on the writer's part. This is due, firstly, to the multifaceted nature of the novel itself and, secondly, to the fact that the hero functions more as a sexual and, to a lesser degree, as a political subject. A result of this is that, despite the writer's admirable dive into a frenzied *tour de force*, the latter ends up again in a nihilistic outcome, equivalent to that of the two previous novels ("-Religion's fucked. –And capitalism? –Fucked. –Communism. –Fucked. –Australia? –Very fucked. –Europe? –Doubly fucked. –America? – Arse-bleedingly fucked" (349).

The most important innovative elements that Tsiolkas brings in *Dead Europe* are mannenistic and could be summarised as the following: Firstly, the coexistence of two parallel, separate stories-narratives – housed under one book – which alternate, not only for diversification but for feeding and complementing each other. Thus, for example, the (real) journey of the hero to Greece and Europe manages to be extended and complemented by the (mythic) journey into time, history and the legend of Isaac's mother Rebecca, as well as that of Greece itself. Secondly, the ingenious device of the "photographic art", not only as a starting point and justification of the plot (the hero's journey to Greece, for the photographic exhibition and, subsequently, to Europe) but – mainly – as a depictive narration. In the sense, that is, that the "photographs" take on a self-referential role in the novel, as they comment upon both the story and its narration too. Thirdly, the seemingly innocent journey of the hero, which nevertheless develops into a nightmarish personal odyssey, mainly of an internal quest and adventure, which leads him to reform and self-knowledge.

Some models of the above techniques were seen in a rudimentary form in *The Jesus Man* – mainly with the appearance of the "Preface" and Louie's role as a thesis writer – which, even though somewhat awkward, contained the seeds of their future development. In *Dead Europe*, however, these manneristic elements are organised more systematically, are worked out more elaborately and methodically and are more fully fledged and developed effectively.

The Slap: The fourth novel in Tsiolkas' fictional output so far marks a departure from his previous familiar practices and a new beginning in his fictional orientation and quest. It is not at all accidental that this radical switch is also marked by an unprecedented popularity for the writer and this specific novel, as the latter became a world best seller as well as a very successful television series – something which confirms and crowns this radical change (that of a popular, social novel that offers a relaxed reading experience) in Tsiolkas' new writing direction.

However, what is striking in this radical writing is the fact that the latter came about with minor changes to the writer's familiar and favourite thematic repertoire, which essentially remain the same: That is (i) the "family phenomenon" in modern multicultural Australia, with its related subthemes (mixed marriages, family relationships, the generation gap, racism), (ii) the "interpersonal and intercultural relationships" in pluralistic Australia and (iii) the phenomenon of "Greekness" in the context of Australian reality. These are themes which had preoccupied the writer in his previous books too, but which he expands and explores them more elaborately in depth and breadth here.

The legitimate question which arises here too is the following: How is it possible for anybody to process and use the same old recipes and, without renewing them, to be able to retain undiminished an interest in and fascination for their stories? Much more so, how is it possible to innovate effectively in books such as *Dead Europe* and *The Slap*?

For a start, we need to be reminded that any writing renewal does not necessarily presuppose a corresponding thematic renewal. It can be done with thematic variations, with changes to perspective, with manneristic changes – structural, narrative, stylistic, etc. Besides, to reinforce Gabriel García Márquez's saying, quoted at the beginning of this chapter, his Latin American colleague Jorge Luis Borges had found that in the whole of world literature there are overall only seventeen themes which writers throughout history draw on.

The most fundamental novelty in *The Slap* could be detected – generally speaking – in the fact that the writer, without diverging much from his fixed practices, turns to the writing of a purely popular novel with social parameters. Reading this novel is a relaxed, easy exercise. That is, whereas the reader enjoys himself without ceasing to be puzzled, nevertheless nowhere does he feel the anxiety or anxieties that Tsiolkas' previous novels exhibited. Conversely, the reader feels that this novel is read comfortably and pleasantly, that it flows effortlessly, and that its "breathing" rhythms are quite normal – which makes him feel content too – something unusual for a Tsiolkas' book. Thus, apart from the apparent controversial subject matter of the work (and the righteousness or not of Hugo's slap) – which is more a "ploy" rather than an object to be explored as such – the novel's fascination lies in the seeming simplicity and ease that it emits, in other words, in its *non-literariness*. Something, of course, which the writer dares to point out theoretically in *The Jesus Man*, but which he materialises here practically too with the "bodily expression of feelings" and the "physicality" of his writing – a technique that lends great immediacy to his book.

A first remarkable innovation in *The Slap* is that, for the first time the writer attempts to construct a polyphonic, multiracial, multigender novel of eight heros and heroines, not only equal in numbers (four males and four females) but also equal in gravity and importance. The interlinked structure of the novel is such that it creates something like an optical illusion. That is, occasionally you have the impression that one of the heroes/heroines is redundant and sometimes that his or her absence would have a severe impact on the overall balance of the fictional structure.

A second significant innovative parameter is that, through the dynamic as well as colourful and exuberant personality of Manolis, the writer manages to highlight skilfully, firstly, the subject of (a) "Greekness" in a foreign distant land, like Australia, and whatever positive and/or negative aspects that entails and (b) "the characteristic of being migrant-mateship" and how the former is manifested ideally through the latter. Also, how the latter ("mateship") – with the intervention of an imminent death – becomes comparable in gravity to the corresponding Australian one, with the masterful treatment of the depressing but dignified decline of the first generation Greeks of Melbourne.

A third and most important innovative parameter is how the "erotic element in the third age" is manifested and confronted by the elderly themselves and also by the rest of society.

Finally, it is not at all accidental that Christos Tsiolkas caused a stir – and not only in literary circles – with his very first novel (*Loaded*), whereas with his latest fourth one (*The Slap*) he gained world-wide recognition, commercial success and became one of the most talked about contemporary Australian writers. It is apparent that his first three novels form a kind of a loosely interlinked trilogy – not only because of their thematic but also their narratively experimental elements – whereas the fourth one, even though it retains many of the familiar thematic characteristics of his previous works, marks a radical change in the writer's overall direction.

It remains now to be seen what kind of evolution the quite exciting writing career of an exceptionally talented and, at the same time, controversial novelist will have, a writer who has, in any case, already left an indelible mark on the history of Australian literature and perhaps not just that.

ACKNOWLEDGEMENTS

I am duly indebted to Christos Tsiolkas for his patience and friendly collaboration. Without it this book could not have been materialized. Especially I thank him for providing us with his valuable photographs. Many thanks also to Zoe Ali for her cover photo of Christos Tsiolkas. I would also like to express my gratitude to my wife Mary for her valuable critical comments and observations throughout the writing of this book and also for her painstaking editorial work. Finally my heartfelt thanks to my publisher Dr Anthony Cappello for his trust in me and my work.

JV

www.ingramcontent.com/pod-product-compliance
Lightning Source LLC
Chambersburg PA
CBHW052057300426
44117CB00013B/2167